The subject of Britain, 1603–25

Manchester University Press

The subject of Britain, 1603–25

Christopher Ivic

Manchester University Press

Copyright © Christopher Ivic 2020

The right of Christopher Ivic to be identified as the author of this work has been asserted by him in accordance with the Copyright, Designs and Patents Act 1988.

Published by Manchester University Press
Oxford Road, Manchester M13 9PL

www.manchesteruniversitypress.co.uk

British Library Cataloguing-in-Publication Data
A catalogue record for this book is available from the British Library

ISBN   978 0 7190 8870 4   hardback
ISBN   978 1 5261 9113 7   paperback

First published 2020
Paperback published 2025

The publisher has no responsibility for the persistence or accuracy of URLs for any external or third-party internet websites referred to in this book, and does not guarantee that any content on such websites is, or will remain, accurate or appropriate.

EU authorised representative for GPSR:
Easy Access System Europe – Mustamäe tee 50, 10621 Tallinn, Estonia
gpsr.requests@easproject.com

Typeset by
Servis Filmsetting Ltd, Stockport, Cheshire

I dedicate this book to my wife, Amanda.

Contents

List of figures	viii
Notes on the text	ix
Acknowledgements	x
Introduction: accession, union, nationhood	1
1 'Englands King is comming to be Croun'd': English responses to the accession of King James VI and I	11
2 'This mighty worke of vnion': imagining union in early Jacobean panegyric	52
3 'But when this island shall be made Britain': Hume, Bacon, Britain and Britishness	112
4 'Our downfall Birthdome': reimagining nationhood in *Macbeth*	149
Conclusion: the Jacobean writing of Britain	203
Bibliography	215
Index	235

Figures

1 'The trwe picture of one Picte', from Thomas Hariot, *A briefe and true report of the new found land of Virginia* (London, 1590). By permission of The Folger Shakespeare Library.   183

2 John Speed, title page, *Theatrum imperii Magnæ Britanniæ* [*The Theatre of the Empire of Great Britaine*] (London, 1616). By permission of The Folger Shakespeare Library.   210

Notes on the text

When citing material from early printed texts original spellings and punctuation have been retained, except in the case of long 's' and 'vv', which have been modernised. Omitted letters in early printed texts are supplied in italics: e.g., 'fro*m*'. My transcription of early modern manuscript material seeks to capture as closely as possible the appearance of the handwritten text.

Where confusion could arise because of the existence of multiple copies of early printed texts Short Title Catalogue numbers are supplied.

Unless otherwise noted, quotations from Shakespeare's plays are from Charlton Hinman's Norton facsimile of the First Folio and are given parenthetically, citing Through Line Numbers (TLN). When abbreviated titles of works by (or partly by) Shakespeare are supplied, I follow the Arden Shakespeare conventions: e.g. *KL* for *King Lear*.

Acknowledgements

I owe much to those wonderful scholars – supervisors, fellow researchers, colleagues – who have been not only helpful but also exemplary to me over the years. Many thanks to Sandra Clark, Ian Gadd, Elizabeth Harvey, John Jowett, James Knowles, Steve May, Andrew McRae, Andrew Murphy, John Pitcher, Philip Schwyzer, Richard Stamp, Paul Stevens, Margaret Tudeau-Clayton, Paul Werstine and Grant Williams. A special thanks to Jim Doelman, Tracey Hill and Willy Maley for reading and commenting on sections of this book. Thank you also to the MUP's anonymous readers for the invaluable feedback they provided. And thank you, Matthew Frost, for taking on this book and being very patient.

I would like to record my gratitude to the following funding bodies, whose generosity made possible the archival research for this book: The Bibliographical Society, The British Academy, The Folger Shakespeare Library, The Huntington Library, The Centre for the History of the Book/The Institute for Advanced Studies in the Humanities (The University of Edinburgh), The National Endowment for the Humanities, The Newberry Library and the Social Sciences and Humanities Research Council of Canada.

Introduction: accession, union, nationhood

The 'subject' of this book's title refers to a geographical entity as well as its inhabitants: namely, Britain (geopolitically, Britain and Ireland) and Britons (or the English, Scottish and Welsh; geopolitically incorporating Ireland's increasingly culturally and religiously diverse subjects). *The Subject of Britain*, therefore, explores one island's, at times two islands', geography, history (indeed antiquity), people and real and imagined polities, and it does so through the eyes of those who surveyed the island's geography, wrote the island's history, staged its intra- and inter-island warfare and formed its multinational writing communities. Centred chronologically by the years 1603–25, this book explores Britain and its writing subjects within the context of the unprecedented triple monarchy of the Scottish King James VI and I, whose accession to the English throne in 1603 and desire for Anglo-Scottish or British union prompted his subjects to reflect on questions of cultural memory, intermingling, nationhood, national sovereignty, neighbourliness and political subjectivity/citizenship in new and exciting ways.

Richard Helgerson opens his groundbreaking *Forms of Nationhood: The Elizabethan Writing of England* with a list of seminal texts, including William Camden's *Britannia*, Michael Drayton's *Poly-Olbion*, William Shakespeare's English history plays and John Speed's *Theatre of the Empire of Great Britaine*; of these texts he has this to say: '[n]ever before or since have so many works of such magnitude and such long-lasting effect been devoted to England by the members of a single generation'.[1] Camden's Latin *Britannia* was republished in 1607, and in 1610 an English-language edition appeared. Drayton and Speed published their major works in 1612. As a member of the King's Men, Shakespeare's acting company produced plays set in medieval Scotland and ancient

Britain, and the publication of his collected plays was, of course, a Jacobean event. Never before or since, to paraphrase Helgerson, have so many works of such magnitude and such long-lasting effect been devoted to Britain by the members of a single generation. Thanks to Helgerson's magisterial work, the idea that a sense of nationhood emerged in the early modern period is one with which we are familiar. *Pace* Benedict Anderson's belief that nations and nationalism arose in the eighteenth century, historians and literary historians point to the sixteenth-century, Tudor England in particular as a crucial site for the birth of modern national consciousness.[2] 'The original modern idea of the nation', Liah Greenfeld argues, 'emerged in sixteenth-century England, which was the first nation in the world', adding 'by 1600, the existence in England of a national consciousness and identity, and as a result, of a new geo-political entity, a nation, was a fact'.[3] English nationhood was by no means forged in opposition to monarchy but rather within an increasingly centralised realm ruled by charismatic and powerful monarchs with supranational interests, not to mention Welsh blood. Under King Henry VIII, England became an 'empire', meaning '[a] country that is not subject to any foreign authority; an independent nation' (*OED, n.* 3). Under Henry VIII, moreover, the kingdom of England shifted from a one-nation to a two-nation realm with the political incorporation of Wales. And it was under Henry, who claimed suzerainty over Scotland, that the title of England's monarch changed from Lord to King of Ireland. The 'new geo-political entity' that emerged under the Tudors (and, more fully, under the Scottish Stewarts)[4] was not just 'a nation' but also a dual (come 1603 triple) monarchy.

The same year in which Greenfeld's book appeared, Helgerson's *Forms of Nationhood* marked a seminal moment in the study of the relation between literary texts and national identity, as well as nationalism. Rightly, Helgerson's work has been criticised by literary historians informed by the New British History for its too-narrow focus on England.[5] Helgerson's readers, for instance, are never really directed to the nation where Spenser wrote the bulk of *The Faerie Queene* or to the Irish, Welsh, Scottish presence in Shakespeare's so-called English histories. In response to England-centred literary historians, David Baker, Kate Chedgzoy, Andrew Hadfield, John Kerrigan, Willy Maley and Philip Schwyzer have pushed early modernists to explore this period's literature within a wider British, archipelagic, indeed transatlantic framework. Philip Schwyzer's *Literature, Nationalism, and Memory in Early Modern England and Wales*, for example, examines the production of a British national consciousness in the sixteenth century. However, his study of predominantly Tudor texts, the very Jacobean *King Lear* being an exception, concludes a narrative on Britain and Britishness at a point in time when British subjects were responding – imaginatively, ambivalently, critically – to the accession of a self-styled King of Great Britain who sought to form a unified British state and a united British nation.

Such a state never materialised in the Jacobean period, nor did such a nation; the 1707 Act of Union, the story goes, produced the island's modern Britain and Britons.[6] James's accession, Brian Levack reminds us, produced 'a strictly dynastic, regal, and personal union, not an incorporating union of the two kingdoms'; it did not, he adds, 'create a united kingdom, a united British state, or a single British nation'.[7] Acknowledging that the word 'British' in this period is 'hard to avoid', John Kerrigan's monumental *Archipelagic English* warns of uncritical uses of this term. 'It tends to imply,' he writes, 'if not the existence then the inevitability of a state that was only just, unevenly, forming, in the seventeenth century, and it suggests that there was more cultural Britishness around the islands than can be found.' 'Overall', Kerrigan adds, 'there are few signs of a newly synthesized identity'.[8] Still, as John Morrill notes, 'men and women both developed a new or transformed sense of themselves as Irish, Scots, Welsh, English, and came to recognise themselves as subjects of a British king, while also developing – in some but not all cases – new and varied senses of themselves as Britons'.[9] Whilst the Jacobean period may or may not have witnessed the invention of a British national consciousness and a British identity, neglecting the wider British (and Irish) geopolitical framework within which a nascent sense of Englishness emerged risks obscuring the ways in which a burgeoning internal British Empire conditioned such an identity. Rather than positing a teleological narrative of the 'forging' of Britishness, *The Subject of Britain* investigates the complex and often contradictory ways in which the heterogeneous writing of Britain put in place new ideologies and new ways of thinking about collective and individual identities within the context of the island's increasingly intersecting and intermingling peoples and cultures.

The Subject of Britain contributes to a flourishing field of study in three significant ways. First, my focus on identity formation seeks to advance knowledge by foregrounding instances of fruitful cultural production in this period. Critics tend to highlight ways in which the early modern period anticipates modernity's fears and anxieties. My research has led me to reflect on the ways in which the early seventeenth century gave voice to ideas of peoples and nations joining together, however tenuously. To read, for instance, Francis Bacon's and David Hume of Godscroft's pronouncements on the common ancestry, the cultural proximity of Britain's inhabitants against Richard Verstegan's proclamation of England's Saxon roots in his *Restitvtion of Decayed Intelligence* (1605) is to acknowledge the complex and often contradictory ways in which writing on Britain and Britishness unleashed a rethinking of group identities, although not a rethinking radical enough to include the Gaelic communities of Scotland and Ireland. Second, by attending to texts printed in not just London but also Edinburgh, as well as manuscript material that circulated within and across Britain and Ireland, my work contributes to a field of study that is paving the way for literary historians to glean valuable new perspectives on literary and extra-literary texts in light of the wider British and Irish context that informed, indeed enabled, their production. An expanding canon of anglophone writing is fostering not only a deeper understanding of early modern texts and writing subjects but also innovative ways of reading and interpreting early modern texts and subjectivities. Third, by combining the historical study of literary and non-literary texts with the history of political thought and the history of the book broadly defined, my research offers fresh approaches to early modern literature and culture.

Exploring writing on political and cultural union spawned by the 'union of the crowns of England and Scotland',[10] a topic that remains unexplored in book-length form, *The Subject of Britain* is organised into four chapters, and it takes as its centrepiece responses to King James's English accession and his call for Anglo-Scottish union. 'I desire a perfect Vnion', James stated in 1607, 'of Lawes and Persons, and such a Naturalizing as may make one body of both Kingdomes vnder mee your King'.[11] My work is distinguished by the fact that it expands our understanding of 'union literature', for I examine Jacobean union tracts and treatises alongside other modes of cultural production in the period: for instance, illustrations, maps, masques, plays, poems, proclamations and various forms of prose. By defining union literature much more broadly than political historians hitherto have, my work aims to advance our understanding of a signal moment in Britain's (and Ireland's) history.

Many historians (and literary historians) dismiss English engagement with the question of Britain. In reference not to James's reign *per se* but to the sixteenth and seventeenth centuries in general, John Morrill, a leading proponent of the new British history, writes

> while the early modern period does represent a fairly inexorable advance of lowland *English* social, political, religious and cultural institutions throughout the archipelago, it can be argued that the *English* are the least interested parties in thinking through, articulating, above all redefining the relationship of the component parts of what had become the multiple or composite kingdom of the house of Stewart.[12]

Perhaps because Morrill's work has very little to say about Jacobean union tracts and treatises he can make such an assertion, one that seems to foreclose investigation into English engagement with Anglo-Scottish union. The presence of extant anti-union manuscript tracts as well as evidence of oppositional readers of pro-union printed tracts – I have in mind a handwritten response to John Hayward's *A Treatise of Vnion of the two Realmes of England and Scotland* and marginalia in a copy of John Thornborough's *A Discovrse Plainely Proving the euident vtilitie and vrgent necessitie of the desired happie Vnion of the two famous Kingdomes of England and Scotland*[13] – could, of course, be cited to support Morrill's claim that the English were resistant to redefining their relationship to their non-English neighbours. Alternatively, do these material traces of early modern readers not document Jacobeans' intellectual engagement with union? Other manuscript tracts and marginalia in other printed union tracts, however, bear witness to authors and readers seriously rethinking their place within a multination polity. Surely Shakespeare's shift from writing English history plays before 1603 to British tragedies and romances (not to mention co-authoring a very different kind of history) after 1603 was conditioned if not determined by a recognition of 'the relationship of the component parts of what had become the multiple or composite kingdom of the house of Stewart'. Take, for example,

King Lear, which was performed at court in December 1606 and has often been read as toeing a pro-union line. As Schwyzer suggests, 'the convergence of theme ['British antiquity'], occasion ['unionist campaign'], and artist ['nationalist playwright'] would have seemed to promise a masterpiece of British nationalism'; however, he labels *King Lear* a play 'deeply troubled [in] relation to British nationalism'. The context for this court performance, Schwyzer reminds us, was 'the unionist campaign, when writers of all stripes and talents, from bishops to hacks, were bubbling over with prince-pleasing effusions in favour of a reunited Britain'.[14] Schwyzer offers Samuel Daniel's *Panegyrike Congratvlatorie to The Kings Maiestie* (1603) as an example of such prince-pleasing, but in doing so he obscures the poem's moments of profound ideological and political negotiation and contestation. Jacobean texts like Daniel's *Panegyrike*, not to mention *King Lear*, point to the need for a critical vocabulary that goes beyond a pro- and anti-union opposition. Moreover, the strain of English nationalism forged during Elizabeth's reign, especially after 1588, that English history plays of the 1590s at once incorporate and interrogate was never matched by an equivalent 'British nationalism' on Jacobean London's stages.[15]

The first chapter attends to English responses to King James VI's accession to England's throne as registered in the rich and various texts that constitute 1603 succession literature. Bruce Galloway's description of the encomia that greeted James early in his reign as 'commentaries on the union of the crowns, rather than examinations of the further union that James might wish to achieve' is not inaccurate.[16] Voicing relief as well as anxiety, these early Jacobean texts are remarkable precisely because they evince a struggle to make sense of the novelty of what one union tract terms 'this triangle monarchie' as well as the place of its heterogeneous subjects.[17] In this, these printed texts adumbrate much of the union debate and dialogue that emerged in full in the spring of 1604, as James sought to effect more than a dynastic union of the crowns; moreover, they anticipate topics explored in more detail in subsequent chapters.

Building on the first chapter, the second chapter examines panegyrics written in the wake of James's arrival in London by three major authors: Michael Drayton, Samuel Daniel and Ben Jonson. These so-called occasional texts are situated within the wider context of these three authors' literary works and careers in order to shed light on how each author responds to James's accession, handles the transition from Tudor to Stewart and (re)imagines Britain. This chapter firmly establishes this book's attention to the material contexts of Jacobean literature: namely, forms of textual production (print and manuscript cultures); the various cultural sites from which literature emerged and within which it circulated (country houses, civic functions, social/literary networks/coteries); and the role that textual culture played in shaping knowledge communities and individual and collective identities. This chapter also supplies material evidence against the argument that ideas on Britain and Britishness faded away with the conclusion of formal Parliamentary debate on Anglo-Scottish union in the first decade of the century. Andrew McRae and John West note that James's 'union policy became one of the most unpopular of his reign'; the King's union policy, they add, was 'shelved within a few years of his accession'.[18] There is, I argue, more to this story, especially if we shift our critical attention from formal Parliamentary union debate to writing on and about Britain and Britishness. Jonson's epigram 'On the Vnion' emerges as a key text in this chapter, for although union debate died down in Parliament after 1608, this poem's textual transmission via commonplace books and verse miscellanies reveals a sustained dialogue on Britain well into the seventeenth century. To the charge that union ideas faded with the failure of Anglo-Scottish union, this chapter concludes by turning to the vibrant handwritten worlds of the early seventeenth century in order to supply material evidence of reading and writing subjects thinking through questions of not only dynastic but also cultural and national union.

The third chapter focuses on print and manuscript union tracts and treatises, the writings of Bacon and Hume in particular. Morrill's claim that the English showed little or no interest in matters of British state formation will once again be put to the test. Anglo-Scottish union tracts and treatises, I argue, offer fertile evidence of English as well as Scottish subjects thinking through, articulating and redefining a British, indeed British-Irish, polity. This chapter breaks new ground by exploring connections between Bacon's political, philosophical and scientific writings within the context of a proposed union; in doing so it captures the boldness and vibrancy of early seventeenth-century responses to the dominant political topic. The intersection of Bacon's statements on joining bodies under a new form in his *Briefe Discovrse, Touching the Happie Vnion of the Kingdoms of England and Scotland* (1603) and on 'commixture' in the defamiliarised utopian space of *The New Atlantis* (1627) reveals Bacon to be a subject seriously engaging with questions of cultural union. Bacon's political writings on union, so often dismissed by scholars as the product of a sycophant, emerge from this chapter as a laboratory for thought about early modern notions of collective identities and cultural hybridity. What distinguishes Bacon from his fellow common-lawyer MPs is his willingness and ability to think through union matters relatively free of the insularity of English legal jurisdiction and, crucially, sustained by an intellect grounded in philosophical and scientific innovation. By concluding this chapter with Bacon's writing on the Ulster Plantation – with a cursory glance at Jonson's *Irish Masque* – I warn against a too-optimistic recovery of his and others' seemingly progressive political ideas. Like many of his fellow Jacobeans, including Hume and Robert Pont, Bacon's views on the native Irish (as well as non-Lowland Scots) are underpinned by deep ethnic and racial prejudices.

The fourth chapter explores Shakespeare's *The Tragedie of Macbeth*, which was composed and performed at the height of Anglo-Scottish union debate and just as the plethora of union tracts and treatises were circulating. Rather than simply reading 'the Scottish play' in relation to union debate and dialogue, this chapter treats the play as a profound reflection by an English subject of a Scottish monarch, who was, of course, also that playwright's patron. *Macbeth* may not be a British play in the manner of *The Tragedie of King Lear* and *The Tragedie of Cymbeline*, but it does revisit and rewrite Shakespeare's earlier inscriptions of nationhood as voiced in the Elizabethan history plays by situating them within a larger British-Irish geopolitical framework. Rather than abandoning the patriotic and nationalistic voices that punctuate Shakespeare's earlier histories, this King's Men's play seriously scrutinises such voices. The result, I argue, is not a pro- or anti-union play but instead a play that invites its early modern viewers and readers to reassess Britain's intra- and Britain and Ireland's inter-island relations under the rule of a multisceptred monarch.

The Subject of Britain concludes with a brief examination of select but significant publications in 1612, the year of the Prince of Wales's death: Daniel's *The First Part of the Historie of England*, Drayton's *Poly-Olbion* and John Speed's *Theatre of the Empire of Great Britaine*, the first two works having been touched on in the

Accession, union, nationhood 9

second chapter. Although I do not delve deep into these rich texts, I turn to them as further examples of the ways in which the heterogeneous writing on Britain by subjects of a self-styled British monarch of Scottish descent continued well into, indeed beyond, James's reign.[19] All three of these texts, which bear witness to the Jacobean writing of, even against, Britain, would be revised and republished in various forms before and even after James's death in 1625. The shaping and reshaping of these texts reflects the heterogeneity of early seventeenth-century writing on Britain and Britishness.

Notes

1 Richard Helgerson, *Forms of Nationhood: the Elizabethan writing of England* (Chicago: University of Chicago Press, 1992), 1.
2 For a focus on Scottish national consciousness in the period, see Arthur H. Williamson, *Scottish National Consciousness in the Age of James VI: The Apocalypse, the union and the shaping of Scotland's public culture* (Edinburgh: John Donald, 2003).
3 Liah Greenfeld, *Nationalism: five roads to modernity* (Cambridge: Cambridge University Press, 1992), 14, 30.
4 Throughout this book I follow the spelling of surnames as they appear in the *Oxford Dictionary of National Biography* (*ODNB*).
5 Although Helgerson examines a number of Jacobean texts – Michael Drayton's *Poly-Olbion*, John Speed's *Theatre of the Empire of Great Britaine* – he does not situate these texts within the wider framework of James's composite monarchy. In short, Helgerson views James VI and I as James I. For a critique of Helgerson, see David J. Baker, *Between Nations: Shakespeare, Spenser, Marvell, and the question of Britain* (Stanford, CA: Stanford University Press, 1997), 15–16.
6 See Linda Colley, *Britons: Forging the nation 1707–1837* (New Haven, CT: Yale University Press, 1992).
7 Brian P. Levack, *The Formation of the British State: England, Scotland, and the union 1603–1707* (Oxford: Oxford University Press, 1987), 1.
8 John Kerrigan, *Archipelagic English: literature, history, and politics 1603–1707* (Oxford: Oxford University Press, 2008), 23–4.
9 John Morrill, 'The British problem, c. 1534–1707', in Brendan Bradshaw and John Morrill (eds), *The British Problem, c. 1534–1707: state formation in the Atlantic archipelago* (Basingstoke: Palgrave Macmillan, 1996), 2.
10 Thomas Craig, *De Unione Regnorum Britanniæ Tractatus*, C. S. Terry (ed.) (Edinburgh: T. and A. Constable, 1909), 207.

11 [James VI and I], *His Maiesties Speech to both the Houses of Parliament, in his Highnesse great Chamber at Whitehall, the day of the Adiournement of the last Session, which was the last day of March 1607* (London, 1607), B3^v.
12 John Morrill, 'The fashioning of Britain', in Steven G. Ellis and Sarah Barber (eds), *Conquest & Union: fashioning a British state, 1485–1725* (London and New York: Longman, 1995), 13.
13 See 'Notes on Doctor Haywards Book of the Union. Imperfect', British Library, Harleian MS 292, fol. 128^v and one of the Folger Shakespeare Library's copies (copy 2 Bd.w.) of John Thornborough, *A Discovrse Plainely Proving the euident vtilitie and vrgent necessitie of the desired happie Vnion of the two famous Kingdomes of England and Scotland: by way of answer to certaine obiections against the same* (London, 1604).
14 Philip Schwyzer, *Literature, Nationalism, and Memory in Early Modern England and Wales* (Cambridge: Cambridge University Press, 2004), 159, 158.
15 For a critical survey of Britishness on the Jacobean stage, see Tristan Marshall, *Theatre and Empire: Great Britain on the London stages under James VI and I* (Manchester: Manchester University Press, 2005).
16 Bruce Galloway, *The Union of England and Scotland, 1603–1608* (Edinburgh, John Donald, 1986), 30.
17 [Anon.], 'The Diuine Providence in the misticall and reall union of England and Scotland both by nature and other coherences with motives for reconcilinge such differences as may now seeme to hinder the same', British Library, Additional MS 38139, fol. 42.
18 Andrew McRae and John West, 'General introduction', in Andrew McRae and John West (eds), *Literature of the Stuart Successions: an anthology* (Manchester: Manchester University Press, 2017), 15.
19 John Thornborough's pro-union writing reappeared in 1641 under the title of *A Discourse Shewing the Great Hapinesse that hath, and may still accrue to His Majesties Kingdomes of England and Scotland, by Re-vniting them into one Great Britain. In two parts: by John Bristol*. For a reading of Anne Bradstreet's *The Tenth Muse* (1650) within the context of a transatlantic 'Britishness', see Christopher Ivic, '"Our British Land": Anne Bradstreet's Atlantic perspective', in Simon Mealor and Philip Schwyzer (eds), *Archipelagic Identities: Literature and Identity in the Atlantic Archipelago, 1550–1800* (Farnham: Ashgate, 2004), 195–204.

1

'Englands King is comming to be Croun'd': English responses to the accession of King James VI and I

How did English subjects receive the Scottish monarch who succeeded Queen Elizabeth I upon his entrance to their country? According to that Scottish king, unforgettably:

> shall it euer bee blotted out of my minde, how at my first entrie into this Kingdome, the people of all sorts rid and ran, nay rather flew to meet mee? their eyes flaming nothing but sparckles of affection, their mouthes and tongues vttering nothing but sounds of ioy, their hands, feete, and all the rest of their members in their gestures discouering a passionate longing, and earnestnesse to meete and embrace their new Soueraigne.[1]

Like many memories, this one of a rapturous meeting between a new monarch and his subjects may owe more to hyperbolic rhetoric than actual historical events. Although proclaimed Elizabeth's successor on 24 March 1603, King James VI and I initially saw little of his English subjects, or, more importantly, James's English subjects initially saw very little of him. James departed the capital and royal seat of his Scottish kingdom on 4 April 1603, slowly making his way 400 miles south to the capital of his English kingdom. Purposely avoiding Queen Elizabeth's funeral (28 April), James finally arrived at Whitehall on 7 May. England's new king, as James Doelman notes, 'did not enter London until the middle of May, and soon after, the plague forced James to retreat from the city'. 'For this reason,' Doelman adds, 'public access to the King was sharply curtailed, and through the first spring and summer of his reign James became known to his subjects largely through his book, *Basilikon Doron*', which was entered into the Stationers' Register on 28 March 1603.[2] *Basilikon Doron*, Francis Bacon would later remark, fell 'into every man's hand [and] filled the whole realm as with a good perfume or incense before the King's coming in'.[3] Whereas the accession of England's Tudor monarchs was a home-grown affair – even the Welsh-born, Brittany-based King Henry VII, crowned on 30 October 1485, had been in England (via Wales) since August 1485 – James's journey to his royal seat involved a border crossing. The liminal period between James's Edinburgh departure and London arrival afforded his English subjects the opportunity to publish texts in praise of their new monarch, an opportunity, judging by the plethora of extant texts that constitutes the succession literature of 1603, they seized.[4] These texts, the product of early modern England's burgeoning print culture, appeared in many shapes and sizes: ballads, epistles, genealogies, maps, narrations, panegyrics, royal proclamations, sermons, songs, speeches and welcomes.[5] This diverse material, moreover, was produced by a socially heterogeneous group of writers: civic authorities, clergymen, lawyers, MPs, pamphleteers, playwrights, poets, satirists and soldiers. Befitting its authorial and formal diversity, 1603 succession literature registers a range of responses to England's new monarch, which is why these texts are a prime repository for gauging the English reception of James.

With the exception of a few poems, the various texts that constitute Jacobean succession literature have only recently solicited critical interest as valuable historical documents rather than mere occasional texts, necessarily devoid of insight and reflection.[6] Published in the first few months of James's English reign, many of these texts have traditionally been treated as the work of obscure, unimportant writers. Only a handful of poets who have come to occupy a central place in English literary history contributed poems in praise of James in 1603: notably, Samuel Daniel and Michael Drayton (to whom I turn in chapter 2, section headed 'This Brittaine hope, Iames our vndoubted king').[7] William Shakespeare, to our knowledge, produced no non-dramatic verse in praise of England's new king, under whose protection Shakespeare's acting company was placed.[8] Some but by no means all of the printed texts on James's accession were published anonymously, which, no doubt, has contributed to the assumption that Jacobean succession literature was produced in the main by writers of little or no significance, or, as more than one historian describes them, '[a]nonymous hack poets'.[9] Furthermore, these texts are hastily dismissed as the work of writers caught up in the euphoria sparked by the accession of a male, Protestant monarch with a wife and three children, two of whom were male and therefore potential future kings.[10] The sense of relief, not to mention anticipation and expectancy, produced by James's accession is palpable in these texts. Hailing James as Caesar, Samuel Rowlands announces 'Sound *Triton* through the Seas vast kingdame, sound/That *Englands King* is comming to be Croun'd'.[11] James's imminent arrival in London and the dynastic and religious continuity that his and his family's arrival secured unleashed expressions of joy, particularly because for the general public the succession question was shrouded in mystery – with Queen Elizabeth never publicly announcing her successor – as a subject not to be broached in print.[12] Although these texts clearly capture popular consent, they are by no means merely given over to celebration. Many of the authors of 1603 succession literature seize upon the moment of regnal transition to examine the relation between the new monarch and his collective subjects, resulting in profound reflections on monarchic authority, the state, national sovereignty and, in particular, the fate of their nation under a Scottish king.

The succession literature of 1603 is distinguished not simply by the fact that Queen Elizabeth died without an heir but also by the fact that the Queen's closest royal relative resided beyond England's borders in a northern kingdom that had long been allied with France and often at war with its southern neighbour. Before 1560, England and Scotland 'were two of the most hostile nations in Christendom'.[13] Not surprisingly, English responses to James's accession blend praise for England's new monarch with anxieties about England's national sovereignty. 'Oh what an Earthquake is the alteration of a State!', Thomas Dekker writes in his pamphlet *1603. The Wonderfull yeare*, which narrates London's plague, eulogises Elizabeth and welcomes James.[14] As evident in Dekker's choice of words – earthquake, alteration – a blend of contrasting, conflicting fears and desires attend the anticipation and/or reception of James and mark English assumptions and attitudes at the time of James's accession. Claire McEachern has argued that 'James I of England sought to mute the novelty of his arrival in the familiar metaphors of Elizabethan national integrity'.[15] Such cultural and ideological work, however, was not solely in James's hands, for representations of James began to circulate in print well before his arrival in London. 'Manifold written works greeted the new reign', Doelman notes, 'indeed, through the spring of 1603 the majority of works registered by the Stationers' Company concerned James's accession'.[16] James, of course, had never set foot in England before April 1603. First-hand English knowledge of Scotland's king was restricted to an elite, mostly courtly, group. 'For all that they had prepared for his accession', it has been suggested, 'James's new English subjects had only a limited understanding of their king'.[17] If 1603 succession literature bears witness to this 'limited understanding', then it also illustrates the extent to which London's burgeoning print culture played a pivotal role in presenting 'James' to his new English subjects. This chapter examines 1603 succession literature in order to gauge early English responses to the accession of the Scottish King James VI to the English throne as King James I. How did James's English subjects welcome a Scottish monarch to his (or was it their?) kingdom? How did they respond to a form of rule that had no precedents in British history? How did James's English subjects construct, appropriate and disseminate their new Scottish king?

'Our Lion comes as meekely as a Doue'

Writing a couple of years after the event, David Hume of Godscroft captures 'the divergent feelings of the English and Scottish people' occasioned by his king's 'setting out for England': '[o]n one side you would see exuberance, high spirits, joy, everything happy and festive; on the other, sighs mixed with happiness for the king's good fortune'.[18] English reports of their northern neighbours at the time of James's departure also foreground the collective lamentation expressed by the people of Scotland. The anonymous author of *Englands Wedding Garment. Or A preparation to King Iames his Royall Coronation* states '[t]he Scottish Ile doth streame with teares,/ Shed forth for absence of her King' – returning to Edinburgh only once, in 1617, James became something of an absentee monarch to his native kingdom.[19] A contemporary and so-called 'true' English account describes the moment of James's departure as follows:

> as ioyfull as [his Scottish subjects] were of his Maiesties great aduauncement and enlarging of his Empire, so were they ... for their priuate want of him no lesse filled with grief, as aboue all other times was most apparantly expressed at his departure from *Edenburgh* towards *England*: the cries of poore people being so lamentable and confused, that it moued his Maiestie to much compassion: yet seeing

their clamors was only of affection, and not grounded on reason, with many gracious and louing words he left them, and proceeded on his Progresse.[20]

If James's departure from Edinburgh drew tears from his fellow countrymen and countrywomen, his long progress south to London occasioned an altogether different response from the English subjects over whom he now ruled: '[t]he bankes of English Ile for ioy', writes the author of *Englands Wedding Garment*, 'With Ecchoes sounding loud shall ring'.[21] As these lines attest, the texts printed in England in 1603 hailing England's new monarch record the jubilant mood at the time of the royal succession. These same texts also manifest the fears and anxieties brought about by dynastic change. Dominating the bulk of Jacobean succession literature, and therefore distinguishing it from Elizabethan succession literature of 1558, is James's unparalleled status as England's first Scottish monarch, a king, moreover, of both England and Scotland, not to mention Ireland and France.[22] Consider, again, *Englands Wedding Garment*:

> In Spring of Infant age, Prince *Iames*
> Of Scots was croun'd their King,
> In Spring of yeare he comes to vs,
> When birds their merrie carrols sing.[23]

The author's use of 'vs' and 'their' reveals an awkward reception of a king who comes to England's throne not as the child of the previous monarch but rather as a foreigner, as another nation's king. Associating James's Scottish rule with the past and his English rule with the present and future is one way to come to terms with the dual nature of James's monarchy, even though it obscures the political reality of that duality. The enjambed 'Prince *Iames*/Of Scots' raises questions. Is James '[o]f Scots', or is he 'Prince ... [o]f Scots', or both? What would have been certain to the English is the fact that a king '[o]f Scots' now sat on England's throne. A similar awkwardness is reflected in *The True Narration*'s reference to 'his Maiesties great aduauncement and enlarging of his Empire'. The primary meaning of 'Empire' here (*OED n.*5a) concerns James's rule of multiple kingdoms: he has 'enlarg[ed] his Empire' by adding England and Ireland to his Scottish rule. King Henry VIII's break from Catholic Rome, arguably the foundational moment of English national self-determination, was underpinned by the belief that '[t]his realme of England is an Impire';[24] 'Impire' in this instance signifying the nation's independence. A heightened sense of English nationhood and an attendant nationalism at once dominates and complicates the English reception of James in 1603. Reconciling James's foreignness and England's national sovereignty was one of the many tasks facing authors of succession literature. After over a century of Tudor rule, and a half-century of female rule, what impact would a Stewart king have on his new English subjects and, crucially, their 'English Ile'?

The texts examined in this chapter do not betray any kind of radical resistance to James's reign in the manner of Elizabethan succession tracts such as the Jesuit Robert Persons's *A Conference abovt the Next Svccession to the Crowne of Ingland* (1595), which favoured the Infanta Isabella, King Philip II's daughter, as Elizabeth's successor, and which, paradoxically, did James's cause in Protestant England more good than harm.[25] Moreover, one is hard pressed to locate any overt anti-monarchical strains in these texts, which would have been out of place and impolitic given the occasion and the medium. The succession literature of 1603 does, however, mask the rather rocky road that led James, who had ruled Scotland since 1567, to the English throne. 'Many late Elizabethans', we must remember, 'did not see the Scottish King as the incontrovertible heir or rally to his cause'.[26] Succession literature of 1603 also reveals the ways in which English writers anxiously received a Scottish monarch and struggled to make sense of the novelty and nuances of a form of monarchic rule utterly unfamiliar to them. Is it any wonder, then, that political works on the topic of multiple kingdoms, unions and the Spanish *monarchía*, such as Gerolamo Franchi di Conestaggio's *Historie of the Vniting of the Kingdom of Portvgall to the Crowne of Castill* (1600), were attracting keen readers in the early years of James's English reign? In a letter dated 3 November 1604 from Alexander Seton to Robert Cecil, the Scottish Seton writes of reading 'the history of that union written by Conestaggio Genevois in Italian'; '[w]hen your leisure may serve', he adds, 'I will be glad of some conference with you anent the propositions to be confered on at our next meeting in the treaty of Union'.[27]

English attitudes toward James were conditioned, on one hand, by deeply engrained cultural attitudes to their northern neighbours and, on the other, by a profound attachment to their own land and nation. As much as James is greeted as '*our most potent soueraigne*', English authors' anxieties manifest themselves in those moments when the new monarch's political power is symbolically divested. Henry Chettle's ideologically charged account of James's arrival supplies a prime example of such a divestment of power:

> The Saxon, & the Dane, scourgd with sharp steele,
> (So did the Norman Duke) this beauteous Land,
> Inuading Lords raigne with an yron hand:
> A gentler ruling in this Change we feele,
> Our Lion comes as meekely as a Doue,
> Not conq'ring vs by hurt, but harty loue.[28]

Chettle dissociates the Scottish monarch from the host of historical predators who have laid waste to England. He does so by initially invoking the Lion Rampant of Scotland's Royal Standard only to replace that symbol of Scotland's martial prowess with James's representation of himself as *Rex Pacifici*.[29] Although no mere 'Duke' or 'Lord', dove-like James is rendered peaceful, gentle and, significantly, meek. These lines are undoubtedly offered as praise, but they are underpinned by a political fantasy of monarchic disempowerment, grounded less in, say, republican political ideology or xenophobia than the uncertainty that surrounded the arrival of a foreign monarch in 'this beauteous Land'.[30] When Chettle writes 'for neuer English ground,/Bore such a Soueraigne as this royall Lord', the intended compliment contains within it another truth: the unsettling novelty of a Scot ruling the English.[31] Malcolm Smuts writes of 'late Elizabethan anxieties about England's future under a foreign-born king';[32] such anxieties, I want to argue, continued well beyond Elizabeth's death. In its attempt to manage political anxieties brought about by the accession of a Scottish king to the English throne, Chettle's text bears witness to the ideological pressures underpinning Jacobean succession literature.

'[L]ineally and lawfully descended from the body of Margaret'

Succession literature is by nature bittersweet, a paradoxical combination of mourning one monarch and hailing the accession of another. Daniel captures the Janus-like nature of 1603 succession literature when he writes to James, 'giue vs leaue, if wee/Reioyce

& morne'.³³ Many, but not all, of the texts printed in 1603 that welcomed England's new king were preceded (or followed) by verse on the death of Queen Elizabeth.³⁴ Consider, for example, the following titles: *Aue Cæsar. God saue the King. The ioyfull Ecchoes of loyall English hartes, entertayning his Maiesties late ariuall in England. With an Epitaph vpon the death of her Maiestie our late Queene; Elizaes Memoriall. King Iames his arriuall. And Romes downefall; King Iames his welcome to London With Elizaes tombe and epitaph, and our Kings triumph and epitimie. Lamenting the ones decease, and reioycing at the others accesse; Queene El'zabeths losse, and King Iames his welcome; Sorrowes Ioy. Or a Lamentation for our late deceased Sovereigne Elizabeth, with a triumph for the prosperous succession of our gracious King, Iames; Weepe with ioy a lamentation for the losse of our late soueraigne lady Queene Elizabeth, with ioy and exultation for our high and mightie Prince, King Iames, her lineall and lawful successor.* As these titles suggest, the Queen's death cast a shadow over James's reign, one that intensified over the years as a result of disgruntlement with the new monarch – especially among members of Parliament – as well as a burgeoning nostalgia for an imagined Elizabethan golden age. In their ample devotion to the deceased queen who had ruled for forty-five years, for many English men and women the only English monarch they had known, some of these texts have very little to say about England's new king.

Take, for example, *Sorrowes Ioy*, a collection of elegies printed in Cambridge. The second entry by the Cambridge antiquary Richard Parker, titled 'Englands farewell', names James only in the final line of a seventy-six-line poem.³⁵ With most of Parker's poem dedicated to the late queen, the final couplet – '[t]hou sentst from North past all our hopes,/king Iames his glorious sunshine' – comes across as an afterthought.³⁶ By no means is Parker's the sole text to present James in such a manner. Of the forty-four pages that constitute the text of Chettle's *Englands Mourning Garment* only in the final four is James addressed, in a poem titled 'The Shepheards Spring Song, in gratulation to the royall, happy, and flourishing Entrance, to the Maiestie of *England*, by the most potent and prudent Soueraigne, *Iames* king of *England*, *France*, and *Ireland*'.³⁷ In his haste to compose a poem congratulating England's new monarch, Chettle, it appears, forgot that his king was also, and was to remain until his death in 1625, Scotland's king. Perhaps James's full title was pointed out to Chettle shortly after the publication of *Englands Mourning Garment*; the second edition addresses James as 'king of England, Scotland, France, and Ireland'.[38] As the aforementioned titles suggest, the texts mourning Elizabeth's death and celebrating James's accession are hybrid not just in content but also in form, for they contain contrasting discursive modes: elegy and panegyric, lamentation and congratulation. One result of this hybrid form is the presence of a solemnity that works to curb unreflective euphoric pronouncements. In other words, lavish praise for England's newly enthroned monarch is tempered by the memory of Elizabeth's recent death. One would be hard pressed to detect nostalgia for the late queen in 1603, but Elizabeth's legacy (or an Elizabethan legacy) certainly conditioned, perhaps clouded, the English reception of James. Dekker's reflections on Elizabeth's funeral in *1603. The Wonderfull yeare* exemplify the way in which the late queen remained deeply embedded in English national consciousness: '[n]euer did the English Nation behold so much black worne as there was at her Funerall'.[39] Public mourning of the former queen inscribes a cultural memory that serves to consolidate a community of English men and women: 'the English Nation'. When Dekker describes England as 'a nation that was almost begotten and borne vnder her', he acknowledges the Virgin Queen's reign as the crucible out of which English nationhood emerged.[40]

Elegies in honour of the deceased queen are permeated with anti-Catholic sentiments. Many of the texts that mourn the late queen triumphantly revisit England's defeat of the Spanish Armada. 'In peace thou ruld vs foure and fourtie yeare', writes the clergyman Thomas Rogers, figuring Elizabeth as 'Spight of proude *Rome*, and ambitious *Spaine*'.[41] These details may seem irrelevant when discussing the arrival of a Protestant male monarch, but it is important not to overlook the full complexities of the regnal transition, including the Catholicism of James's mother, Mary Stewart, as well as his wife, Anne of Denmark.[42] What I am suggesting, and what Rogers's text reveals, is that a Scottish king succeeded to the English throne amidst a public reassertion of England's militant Protestant national identity, an identity that was forged under Elizabeth in opposition to predominantly Catholic enemies on the Continent but also neighbouring nations, including, of course, 'the weazel Scot'.[43] Such a reassertion of English nationalism did not bode well for a Scottish monarch who, in the second year of his reign and as self-proclaimed 'King of Great Britain', promoted not only a united British polity but also a unified British cultural and national identity. The succession literature of 1603 hails the peace and concord that the union of the crowns has brought about, but as a body of literature it registers little to no commitment to a cultural union of English and Scots.

If, as Kevin Sharpe has suggested, James's arrival in England 'presented a shock both to the monarch and his subjects', then one transitional strategy was to associate James with his female predecessor.[44] In fact, a dominant succession image is that of James as phoenix: '[a] *Phoenix* from her ashes doth arise,/A King at whose faire Crowne all glory amyes'.[45] For some critics, Elizabeth's legacy was integral to the favourable reception that James received in England. 'James's panegyrists', according to John Watkins, 'familiarize[d] him to his new subjects in Elizabeth's mythic role as the defender of embattled Protestantism against Catholic insurgency'. Pursuing this line of thought, Watkins argues that '[b]y treating James's succession as an event that miraculously averted a crisis threatening the realm's religious and constitutional foundations, the panegyrists were free to honor James himself as an Englishman, a Tudor descendant of Henry VII, and the deceased queen's masculine counterpart in the struggle against false religion'.[46] Ample textual evidence for Watkins's argument exists. The earliest royal proclamation published after Elizabeth's death – drafted by Robert Cecil and approved by James in Scotland (before Elizabeth's death) – grants the crown 'absolutely, wholly, and solely' to 'the High and Mightie Prince, *Iames* the sixt King of Scotland … our Onely, Lawfull, Lineall and Rightfull Leige Lord'.[47] Given the fact that foreigners were barred from inheriting England's throne, and given the fact that Henry VIII's will 'by its silence on the matter excluded the Stewart descendants of his elder sister, Margaret',[48] this proclamation necessarily represents James not as an alien, even though he was born outside the realm of England, and not as the son of Mary, whose execution Elizabeth had reluctantly warranted in 1587. Instead, James is presented as

> lineally and lawfully descended from the body of Margaret, daughter to the High and Renowned Prince Henrie the seuenth King of England, France, and Ireland, his great Grandfather, the said Lady

Margaret being lawfully begotten of the body of Elizabeth, daughter to King Edward the fourth (by which happy coniunction both the houses of Yorke and Lancaster were vnited, to the ioy vnspeakable of the Kingdome, formerly rent & torne by the long dissention of bloody and Ciuil Warres) the same Lady Margaret being also the eldest sister of Henry the eight, of famous memorie King of England.[49]

If this official proclamation fashions a royal lineage that legitimates (note the repetition of 'lawfully') James's claim to the English throne, then it also makes a non-native monarch familiar to his English subjects by rendering him more Tudor than Stewart, even though Margaret Tudor – daughter to King Henry VII, sister to King Henry VIII – through marriage to King James IV of Scotland, who receives no mention, and who was killed by English forces at the battle of Flodden in 1513, had become Scotland's queen and, briefly after her husband's death, its regent. The use of such familial terms as 'daughter', 'Grandfather' and 'sister' secures for the decidedly Stewart James a place within his Tudor family.

Although less official and more popular in nature, many of the printed texts of 1603 also obscure James's Scottishness, figuring the Northern monarch, who was also the eldest of King Henry VII's living descendants, not simply as king of England but as an English king to boot. *Englands Wedding Garment*, for instance, refers to James as an 'English Lion'.[50] 'See here his worthy princely *Ancestors*', writes the pamphleteer Anthony Nixon, 'His lineall discent and rightfull claime:/Of English blood were his progenitors'.[51] Although the Englishness of James's ancestors is acknowledged, whether James is also '[o]f English blood' is less certain. Robert Fletcher, however, supplies a fuller Anglicisation of James:

> O Lorde we do giue thy deuine Maiesty most humble and harty thankes, in that it hath pleased thee to send vs a Prince of our English Tribe extracted from loines of our most famous Kings and Queenes, not deuided from vs by seas, not alienated from vs by nature, nor much by the very *Elimologi* of our vulgar speache, but principally and before all things, O gratious God: not differing from vs in religion and the trueth of thy blessed word.[52]

As manifested in Fletcher's language – 'not alienated by vs by nature' – England's new king is a natural Englishman, if not through ethnicity than certainly through ancestry. As 'a Prince of our English Tribe', James, through common descent and, crucially, a common confessional identity, is made a member of the English community – the only exception being his speech, which Francis Bacon described as 'swift and cursory, and in the full dialect of his country', and which, in 1603, Fletcher may or, more likely, may not have encountered.[53] Rather than acknowledging and/or accommodating James's Scottishness, the majority of the texts that constitute 1603 succession literature downplay the king's nationality and, by association, his Scottish rule. As the passages cited above reveal, many of these texts are committed to a possessive, interpellative Anglicisation of 'Englands king'.

'King *Iames* is Englands, Scotlands, Fraunce, Irelands king'

As the previously cited royal proclamation attests, James's accession assuaged fears over the question of Elizabeth's successor as well as the concomitant threats of foreign invasion and 'ciuil tumults'.[54] 'Our neighbours', the Scottish lawyer and jurist Thomas Craig writes, 'anxiously watched the closing of the reign of the most august Queen Elizabeth, anticipating commotions in our island'. The proclamation of James as England's king, according to Craig, worked 'to protect our cherished island from the spite of the foreigner'.[55] According to Catherine Loomis, 'the failure to accept James as Elizabeth's successor would have had dire consequences for the English people, civil war chief among them'.[56] Writing just over a year after James's accession, an anonymous Scottish author asks

> [a]nd if after the death of their late sovereigne they had not so willingly acknowledged his Majestie's undowted right and so peaceably embraced the same, having recourse thereto as to the only phisike of their diseassed commonwealth, how calamitous and miserable should their condition have been? Should not the homeborne pretenders have rent asunder the body of their estate by devided factions and civill warres?[57]

That such a power struggle was averted is a key factor in why the printed texts of 1603 celebrate King James I in the manner that they do. Just as the royal proclamation does, Jacobean succession literature often invokes the traumatic fifteenth-century Wars of the Roses to remind readers of past troubles and to rejoice in England's smooth regnal transition. Chettle, for example, proclaims

Now from the *Orchades* to the *Cornish* Iles,
From thence to *Cambria*, and the Hybernian shore,
The sound of Ciuill warre is heard no more,
Each Countenance is garnished with smiles.⁵⁸

In these lines relief mingles with joy as well as expectancy. Accompanying Chettle's sense of relief, moreover, is an imagining, however formulaic, of James's kingdoms on an archipelagic scale, as the reference to England's and Scotland's outlying 'Iles' as well as Ireland's 'shore' attests. Peace has come not only to England but also to the entire island of Great Britain and, for some writers, not just Britain but also Ireland, with whom England had been at war since 1593. Sir John Davies, poet and lawyer of Welsh descent, who attended Prince Henry's baptism in 1594, who accompanied James's train from Edinburgh to London and to whom James would grant the offices of solicitor-general (1603) and then attorney-general (1606) in Ireland, proclaims

On, for the birds will helpe to fill thie songe,
Whereto all English hart-stringes doe agree;
And th'Irish harpe stringes that did jarre soe longe,
To make the musicke full, nowe tuned be.⁵⁹

Dekker offers perhaps the most wildly revisionist historiography: 'in an houre' of James being proclaimed king 'two mightie Nations were made one: wilde *Ireland* became tame on the sudden'.⁶⁰ It was in fact Hugh O'Neill, second earl of Tyrone's surrender to Charles Blount, Baron Mountjoy on 30 March 1603 that facilitated the heralding of James as 'great Monarch of these Isles'.⁶¹ John Savile's representation of James as monarch of 'these Isles' reveals an astute awareness of the geopolitical reality of James's multiple kingdoms:

Irefull cold *Ireland*, cease from thy rage at last,
To yeeld subiection to thy King make hast,
Sound out Saint *Patricke*, Scotland Saint *Andrew* sing
King *Iames* is Englands, Scotlands, Fraunce, Irelands king.⁶²

Savile was by no means alone in his recognition of James's composite monarchy. 'God saue King *Iames*, glad English crie', one text reads, adding '[l]et Scots the like and Irish say'.⁶³ Henry Petowe, poet and freeman of the Company of Clothworkers, welcomes his new monarch as '*Iames* the first of that name of these three vnited Kingdoms, *England, France* & *Ireland*, and of *Scotland* the sixt'.⁶⁴

'Fower Kingdomes now are knowne', writes the author of an anonymous ballad printed in Edinburgh by Robert Waldegrave, the King's printer, but aimed at an English readership, '[t]o be *King Iames* his owne'.[65] Samuel Rowlands, moreover, describes the king as '*IAMES* the first of *England*, and of *Scotland* sixt'.[66] And the author of *The True Narration* presents James as 'an English & Scottish king, both included in one person'.[67] Petowe, Rowlands and the author of *The True Narration* echo the 24 March 1603 royal proclamation's presentation of '*Iames* the sixt King of Scotland' as '*Iames* the first, King of England, France and Ireland'.[68]

But not all authors of succession literature, the evidence suggests, grasped the reality of James's composite monarchy. Whilst James's (ventriloquised) Scottish subjects may have viewed the succession of their king to the English throne as a 'great aduancement' and an 'enlarging of his Empire', many of his new English subjects were less accommodating. In his *King Iames His Welcome to London*, John Fenton concludes his poem with '[h]aile Kingly *Iames*, foes terror, *Englands* pride'. We, Fenton continues, 'may tryumph thou tookest in hand,/The government of this our English land'.[69] What is remarkable about Fenton's representation of the new monarch's assumption of power is the qualifying reference to 'this *our* English land': James's regal authority is counterbalanced by the hold that his English subjects have over their land, a sentiment reinforced by the presence of both the bold deictic and the possessive pronoun. The very texts that honour James's accession are valuable historical documents precisely because they inaugurate public dialogue on the cultural and political issues that took centre stage in the early years of his reign.

The printed texts of 1603 that welcomed James to his new capital and celebrated the royal coronation at Westminster Abbey (25 July, St James's Day) draw attention to a key consequence of the accession of a Scottish monarch to England's throne: what contemporaries referred to as 'the union of the crowns of England and Scotland'.[70] The 'Union of the Crowns', as Jenny Wormald notes, 'was not simply the bringing together of two kingdoms, although that was how it was described, but the addition of another kingdom to the multiple kingdoms of England and Ireland, with the dependency of Wales thrown in'.[71] Richard Martin, friend of Ben Jonson and a Member of Parliament who would later oppose James's Anglo-Scottish union plans, conceives of 'the addition of another kingdom' in an altogether different way: 'what great cause haue we to welcome to the territories of our Cittie your most excellent Maiestie, who (to make vs the glorious and happie head of this Iland) haue by your fyrst entrance brought vs th'addition of another kingdome'.[72] Printed in both England's and Scotland's capital, Martin's speech was readily available to English and Scottish readers; his use of 'we' and 'vs', however, hints at, if not an English incorporation of Scotland, a decentring of Edinburgh and its Scottish Parliament and a recentring of London ('our Cittie') as capital city of 'this Iland'.

For all the relief brought about by a smooth regnal transition and for all the awareness of James's title(s), many of the authors of English succession literature struggled to make sense of the accession of a foreign monarch to the English throne, a king who still was, and would continue to be, the ruler of England's northern neighbours. The following passage from Dekker, who, along with Ben Jonson, made signal contributions to the 1604 royal entry, has little to say about James's Scottish kingship:

> *S. George* and *S. Andrew* that many hundred yeares had defied one another, were now sworne brothers: *England* and *Scotland* (being parted only with a narrow Riuer, and the people of both Empires speaking a language lesse differing than english within it selfe, as the prouidence had enacted, that one day those two Nations should marry one another) are now made sure together, and king *Iames* his Coronation, is the solemne wedding day. Happiest of all thy Ancestors (thou mirror of all Princes that euer were or are) that at seauen of the clock wert a king but ouer a péece of a little Iland, and before eleuen the greatest Monarch in Christendome.[73]

In his refiguring of past Anglo-Scottish hostilities, Dekker supplies a wonderful instance of what Benedict Anderson terms 'reassuringly fratricidal wars'. For Anderson, the need to at once remember and forget the past plays an integral part in the formation of a collective national consciousness, or, as Anderson puts it, a 'family history'.[74] Consider, for example, the invocation of reassuring fratricide in Richmond's unifying speech at the close of *The Tragedy of Richard the Third*: 'England hath long beene mad, and scarr'd her selfe;/ The Brother blindely shed the Brothers blood' (TLN 3869–70). But for all its emphasis on Anglo-Scottish fraternity and sameness (although not exactly a British band of brothers), Dekker's text posits an awkward neighbourliness. The reference to Scotland as 'a péece of a little Iland' is ultimately, perhaps unintentionally, a compliment of sorts; it certainly contradicts his earlier description of England and Scotland as 'two mightie Nations'. Like many of his fellow English subjects, Dekker acknowledges James's dual monarchy, but James's English rule is paramount. In *1603. The Wonderfull yeare* he includes just one reference to 'Scotland', whilst there are eleven occurrences of 'English', six of 'England' and one of 'Englishmen'. Dekker struggles to find a language that accommodates 'both Empires'. For the soldier-poet Robert Pricket, the intra- and inter-island peace and concord brought about by James's accession puts in place the prospect of unity. In his earliest contribution to succession literature, *A Souldiers Wish vnto His Soveraigne Lord King Iames* – entered in the Stationer's Register on 3 April 1603 – Pricket, poet, former soldier and supporter of Robert Devereux, second earl of Essex, presents himself as a defender of England: '[i]n dust and blood my life Ile sacrifice,/To serue my king gainst Englands enemies'.[75] In a work published a few months later, Pricket, counselling against Anglo-Scottish warfare, reimagines himself as a member of a larger polity:

> those that would arightly be, true valiant minded men: ought thus to vse the exercise of martiall discipline, not thereby within your Maiesties vnited kingdoms, to infringe the happines of a long continued peace, but that by their experience in the vse of warre, they may become the most commended is to maintaine the dignitie thereof, against all occasions and powers, that shall seeke to disturbe or ouer throw the same.[76]

Exactly how Pricket conceives of James's 'vnited kingdoms' is unclear, but what is clear is the fact that England and Scotland are separate 'kingdoms'. In *A Souldiers Wish* Pricket writes '[v]nite two lands that but by name stands parted,/Their people blesse, and make them single harted'. But (perhaps remembering a performance of Shakespeare's *The life and death of King Richard the Second* or one of a number of history plays produced during Elizabeth's reign) he then goes on to describe 'England' as 'that Ile with seaes inclosde'.[77] The succession literature of 1603 reveals glimpses of emergent, newer imaginings of community; however, residual, older imaginings dominate these texts, most evident in the numerous inscriptions of England as an island-nation: recall *Englands Wedding Garment*'s

'English Ile'. When Chettle writes '[o]ne King, one people, blessed vnitie,/That ties such mightie Nations to agree' the shift from singular '[o]ne King, one people' to the plural and distinct 'mightie Nations' is not insignificant.[78] Not even the harmonising space of a rhyming couplet can meld the novelty of James's dual monarchy and the force that is early modern English nationalism.

'[O]lde Brutaines hope'

In their struggle to come to terms with the accession of a Scottish king, many English authors of succession texts presented James as a (re)unifier of a British polity. Accompanying this discourse of (re)unification is less an Anglicisation of James than a Briticisation (even Bruticisation) of the Scottish monarch. For example, an anonymously published ballad in *textura*, or black letter, figures 'Iames our king' as 'olde Brutaines hope', but to whom, or to what, does 'olde Brutaines' refer? 'Brutaines' here could mean 'old Britons' hope' as well as 'old Britain's hope', the fomer a reference to an ancient people, the latter a reference to an ancient place or concept, the 'olde' reinforcing the antiquity.[79] Given that the ballad names James's mother as 'the Scottish Marie' – his father, 'Lord Darlie', is not assigned a nationality – the reference to James as 'olde Brutaines hope' at once divests him of Scottishness and appropriates him within a British genealogical myth used by England's Tudor monarchs to mystify and legitimate their rule. Representations of James as a British monarch or as Britain's monarch at the beginning of his English reign are riddled with historical and ideological complexities and contradictions. Invocations of a real or imagined ancient Britain and of real or imagined ancient Britons in 1603 are informed by various discourses – antiquarian, geographical, historical, poetical, political – that were, on one hand, acknowledged and accepted and, on the other, scrutinised and ridiculed. A wide and diverse range of myths, narratives and texts underpinned early modern understandings of ancient Britain and Britons: from the much-maligned Galfridian tradition to Spenser's *Faerie Queene* to William Camden's *Britannia* to William Harrison's *Description of Britaine*. Early modern writing on ancient Britain and Britons afforded a variety of perspectives: Britons could be ancient or savage, noble or ignoble; Britain could designate the entire island of Great Britain or England and Wales only or England only.

'I am not ignorant', Camden declared in what emerged as the key text on ancient Britain and Britons, 'that the first originalls of nations are obscure by reason of their profound antiquitie'.[80] Not surprisingly, regarding 'the most ancient and the very first Inhabitants of this Ile' and 'whence this word *Britaine* had the originall derivation', Camden responds '[n]either can we hope to atteine unto any certaintie heerein'.[81] In one extant manuscript of Spenser's *A View of the Present State of Ireland*, one of the dialogue's speakers scorns the stories told by 'our vayne Englyshemen' about 'the tale of Brutus, whome they devise to haue firste conquered and inhabited this lande'.[82] The myth of Britain's Trojan origins was not altogether abandoned at the beginning of the seventeenth century, however; it surfaces again and again in the succession literature of 1603. Savile, for example, posits James's reign as marking a reunification of a Britain that has been divided since the days of Brutus, the legendary Roman of Trojan descent and first king of Britain after whom the island was supposedly renamed:

> Besides your sacred selfe, doth bring with you,
> A Kingdome neuer knit to these till now,
> As *Camdens Brittaine* tells, since *Brutus* daies,
> Than let vs thank our God, sing Roundelaies,
> England reioyce, Saint *George* for England shout,
> For ioy Saint *Denis* crie, all Fraunce throughout.
> Double thy ioys o *Albion*, harke *Cambrian* banks,
> God hath enrich'd thee with a Prince, giue hartie thanks.[83]

Savile is not alone in positing James as the first 'Prince' to unite or 'knit' Britain's separate and independent kingdoms since Brutus. But what is remarkable about Savile's 'salutatorie Poeme' is its refusal to name the island Britain; the reference to '*Brittaine*', the only use of this word in the text, is not a geographical reference but rather a textual one to Camden's chorographical work on early Britain, first published in 1586 in Latin and translated into English in 1610. *Englands Wedding Garment* also avoids naming the island Britain by using the awkward '[i]n English, Scottish Ile', perhaps out of a fear of obscuring the name England.[84] 'Name', as Bacon would write later in 1603, 'though it seeme but a superficiall and outward matter; yet it carrieth much impression and inchantment'.[85] Writing shortly after James's accession – the poem was entered into the Stationers' Register on 12 April 1603 – Anthony

Nixon hails his new monarch (who travelled south by land, not by sea!) as follows: '[t]hrice welcome then vnto our English shore,/ Thrice worthy *Monarch* of faire *Albion*'.[86] Like Savile, Nixon invokes '*Albion*', but what did 'Albion' mean to early modern readers? Is 'Albion' a reference to Scotland, as it appears to be in Savile's poem?[87] Or is 'Albion' a reference to 'our' England – that is, the English nation or the Kingdom of England, which included a politically incorporated Wales? Or, based on pre-Brutan mythology, does it signify the entire island of Great Britain, a term that John Mair's (or Major's) *Historia majoris Britanniae tam Angliae quam Scotiae* (1521) put into public circulation?[88] William Warner's *Albions England* (1586) notes that 'our whole Iland [was] aunchiantly called Brutaine, but more anchiantly Albion'.[89] In his *A briefe description of the whole worlde* (1599), George Abbot uses Albion to refer to the island of Britain: '[t]he most renowned Iland in the worlde is Albion, or Britannia; which hath heretofore contained in it many seuerall kingdomes; but especially in the time of the Saxons. It hath now in it the two kingdoms of England and Scotland.'[90] And Richard Verstegan refers to 'the Ile of *Albion* otherwise called *Britaine*, conteyning *England*, *Scotland*, and *Walles*'.[91] However, when the word 'Albion' surfaces in succession literature, as in Shakespeare's plays, the reference is not always self-evident.[92] At issue here is a profound uncertainty about how to address not simply a monarch of two kingdoms housed within Great Britain but also a Scottish king of an English nation.[93]

Like 'Albion', use of the concept of 'Britain' is not without complications and complexities. In the lines below, Fletcher, given that the context is the death of Elizabeth and the arrival of James, designates the land of '[t]rue English harts' as '*Britaine* soile':

SVch mirth from moane, such ioy from care,
In *Britaine* soile was neuer seene:
True English harts did all prepare,
To mourne the losse of their good Queene.
But now reioyce with harts content,
For this good King which God hath sent.[94]

Fletcher appears to be using Britain as a synonym for England. From a less Anglocentric perspective, one author willing to invoke 'Britain' is Joseph Hall – clergyman, author of religious works as well as satire, and chaplain to Prince Henry (1607–12) – who, perhaps referring to Merlin's prophecies in Geoffrey of Monmouth's *Historia regum Britanniae*, writes

> False starres, and falser wisards that foresaine
> By their aspects the state of earthly things:
> How bene your bold predictions proued vaine,
> That here brake off the race of Brittish Kings?
> Which now alone began; when first we see
> Faire *Britaine* formed to a Monarchie.[95]

For the staunchly Calvinist Hall, the accession of a Protestant, Scottish king to the English throne marks at once a British revival but also, it seems, an originary moment of British rule: 'when first we see/Faire *Britaine* formed to a Monarchie'. If this is the case, then it could be argued that Hall, not unlike the Tudors, is appropriating Welsh cultural and political myths to serve English/British purposes. Given Hall's confessional identity, might his '[f]aire *Britaine*' be a reference less to a culturally or politically unified 'Monarchie' than to one unified by the true religion? One is hard pressed to find in Jacobean succession literature a clear and coherent geopolitical discourse in celebration of James's reign. Should James be heralded as a reunifier of Britain? Or does James's composite monarchy constitute a foundational moment in the history of monarchy in Britain or what Camden terms 'the British Ilands, that is to say, Britaine and Ireland'?[96] Sharing Hall's vision of James as the first historical monarch of Great Britain is Francis Bacon, who, in the earliest prose piece on the topic of Anglo-Scottish union, informs his new monarch that it 'dooth not appeare by the recordes and memories, of any true history, nor scarcly by the fiction and pleasure of any fabulous narration, or tradition: that euer, of any antiquity, this Iland of great *Brittaine* was vnited vnder one King, before this day'. For Bacon, then, James is the first monarch 'to vnite these two mighty and warlike nations of *England* and *Scotland*, vnder one Soueraignety and Monarchy'.[97] 'It was neuer seene in any age', writes John Gordon, 'that the nations of the Ilands of *Brittanie*, were vnited in hart and affection vnder one King, as the admirable power of God hath lately brought them vnder your maiesty: whereof the true and onely cause is the purity and truth of Christian religion'.[98] The Anglo-Scot Gordon's use of the plural 'nations' and 'Ilands' makes it clear that he, unlike his English counterparts, is much more alert to James's three-kingdom, four-nation rule. But Chettle complicates matters by offering another option. In a passage on Queen Elizabeth I's genealogy, Chettle says of King Henry VII: '[t]his King, Grandfather to our late Queene, was the first Brittish King, that many a hundred yeares before wore the Emperiall Diademe of *England, France* and *Ireland*: in him began the name of *Tewther*, descended from the ancient Brittish Kings, to florish'.[99] Chettle's two uses of British seem to refer, in the first instance, to the Welsh and, in the second, to the Britons, whom Camden describes as 'the most antient people of this Isle'.[100] It appears that Chettle is excluding England's Scottish king from this British family; however, given James's descent from Henry VII, Chettle, it could be argued, is actually relocating the Scottish James in a long line of British/Welsh monarchs.[101]

If making sense of the accession of a Scottish monarch to England's throne in historical and political terms was not without complication, then another, perhaps less perplexing, subject to enlist in favour of England's new monarch was geographical contiguity.[102] The integrity and singularity of Great Britain's geography lent itself nicely to ideological appropriation. By pointing out to James that 'there be no Mountaines or races of hils, there be no seas, or great riuers, there is no diuersity of toung or language, that hath inuited or prouoked this ancient separation, or diuorce', Bacon enlists geography and language in support of Anglo-Scottish proximity and commonality.[103] Hall figures Britain's island status as the work of providence (as his use of 'fore-set', meaning set or determined beforehand, suggests):

> Well did the wise Creator, when he laid
> Earth's deepe foundations, charge the watery maine,
> This Northerne world should by his waues be made
> Cut fro*m* the rest, and yet not cut in twaine
> Diuided, that it might be blest alone,
> Not sundred, for this fore-set vnion.[104]

But what, for Hall, does 'vnion' entail? Beyond territorial unity, in what manner was this 'Northerne world' united? We might also ask how did James's English subjects understand the concept of 'vnion' at the time of his accession? According to Fletcher, 'vnion' has historical purchase: 'it is not yet much aboue fifty yeres since a coniunct vnion was sought to haue knit both the Realmes of *England* and

Scotland together'.[105] For some Englishmen at the time of James's accession the 'Rough Wooing', to which Fletcher alludes, served as a historical precedent for Anglo-Scottish union. The 'Rough Wooing' refers to an attempt on England's part to unite the crowns of England and Scotland through dynastic marriage. The 'negotiations' were led by Edward Seymour, duke of Somerset, who served briefly as warden of the Scottish marches. In 1545 Somerset was engaged as the broker of a potential marriage between England's then Prince Edward and Scotland's Queen Mary, which Scotland rejected. More martial than diplomatic, the 'Rough Wooing' saw Somerset, now Protector during King Edward VI's minority, leading an English force into Scotland in 1547 in order to force Mary's hand. This military campaign was accompanied by print material, especially in the form of the England-based Scot James Henrisoun's (Harrison) *An exhortacion to the Scottes to conforme them selfes to the honorable, expedie[n]t, and godly vnion, betwene the twoo realmes of Englande and Scotlande*. Henrisoun's text, probably printed in advance of the Somerset-led English army's victory over the Scots at the Battle of Pinkie, opens with a preface addressed to Somerset, wherein Henrisoun calls for a cessation of Anglo-Scottish hostilities:

> CAllyng to mynde (as I do oft) moste excellent Prince, the ciuill discencion and mortal enemitie, betwene the twoo Realmes of Englande and Scotlande, it bryngeth me in muche marueill, how betwene so nere neighbors, dwellyng within one land, compassed within one sea, alied in bloude, and knitte in Christes faithe, suche vnnaturall discorde should so long continue. Vnnaturall, I maie wel call it, or rather a Ciuill warre, where brethren, kynsmen or countreymen be diuided, and seke ye bloud of eche other.[106]

Henrisoun's emphasis on Anglo-Scottish neighbourliness draws upon ideas that dominate Jacobean succession literature: ethnic and geographical proximity and a common (Protestant) religion – complicated, in 1547, by the young Mary's Catholicism. This leads the author to term Anglo-Scottish warfare 'Ciuill warre' – yet another instance of reassuringly fratricidal warfare. The preface concludes with a call for English Edward to 'bee restaured to the whole isle of Britayn, wherunto as he is iustely entitled'; 'graunte to the Kynges Maiestie of England his righteous possession of the whole monarchie of Britayn', Henrisoun adds.[107] Whether he held a fundamental belief in a restoration of a British monarchy or whether an antipathy to Catholic Mary motivates his discourse is unclear; he attributes his writing of this text to 'loue to my countrey on the one side, and desire of concorde and quietnes on the other side'.[108] With 100 references to Britain and Britons, but no instances of British, Henrisoun's call 'to reduce the islande to the firste estate, to one Monarchy, vnder one kyng and gouernor, as it was in the Britons tyme' paves the way for an English monarch to claim much more than suzerainty over Scotland.[109] Premised on English dominance and superiority, allusions to the Rough Wooing, such as Fletcher's, mark an inauspicious start to post-Elizabethan dialogue on Anglo-Scottish relations.

For many authors the meaning of 'vnion' was contained in another historical example: the union of the houses of Lancaster and York. Fletcher, for instance, writes:

Of *Britaine* Ile in briefe to speake,
That now one Monarch must maintaine:
Conioyning harts must malice breake,
Be reconcil'd and friendes againe.
Let euery former foughten field,
Like sonnes vnto their fathers yeelde.
Like *Lancaster* and *Yorke* in loue,
Must *England* now and *Scotland* ioyne:
Such vnity God grant may prooue,
No forraine power dare then purloyne
One foote of ground from *Britaines* peace,
But *Britaines* may their ground increase.[110]

This passage turns to historical precedent as the model for contemporary Anglo-Scottish union. Just as Henry Tudor's victory over King Richard III at the Battle of Bosworth put an end to the Wars of the Roses as well as English national discord, so, too, must the former warring kingdoms of England and Scotland embrace peace, concord and union: '[l]ike *Lancaster* and *Yorke* in loue,/Must *England* and *Scotland* ioyne'. But a signal difference distinguishes the fifteenth-century Wars of the Roses from early seventeenth-century Anglo-Scottish relations: warring Lancastrians and Yorkists were (aristocratic) Englishmen, hence the recurrent representation in the Elizabethan period of the Wars of the Roses as fratricidal broils. Take, for example, the Duchess's account of fratricidal war in *The Tragedy of Richard the Third*:

> And being seated, and Domesticke broyles
> Cleane ouer-blowne, themselues the Conquerors,
> Make warre vpon themselues, Brother to Brother;
> Blood to blood, selfe against selfe. (TLN 1552–5)

The historical animosity between England and Scotland ran deeper and wider. 'One of the main sources of animosity between Englishmen and Scots', Brian Levack points out, 'was the memory of previous armed conflict between them'. 'Less than sixty years before the Union of the Crowns', he adds, 'England and Scotland had been at war with each other'.[111] John Gordon recalls intra- and inter-island violence when he reminds James that '[t]he people (SIRE) of the Ilands of great Brittaine, were not vnited in religion, in peace, in concorde, in like affections and will vnder one King, but they haue beene long banded one agaynst an other, in a Sea of discordes, discentions, and cruell warres'.[112] Writing in 1604, John Russell records 'ane hatrent irreconciliable' between England and Scotland, adding the two nations have 'mair blood spent in thair querrellis than evir be the Romanes in all their conquestis'.[113] One not-too-distant and decisive battle between England and Scotland had been fought at Flodden (1513), which Fletcher's text seems to recollect aurally in the phrase 'foughten field'. That battle between English and Scottish armies saw the death of King James IV, husband of Margaret Tudor. On the Borders, Anglo-Scottish animosity was by no means confined to the past. For Lancastrians and Yorkists to reunite as Englishmen was one thing; for English and Scots to become '*Britaines*' in the face of emergent English and Scottish national consciousnesses underpinned by bitter memories of past Anglo-Scottish broils was quite another.

How do authors of succession literature voice a desire for Anglo-Scottish unity, if not union? The anonymous author of *Englands Wedding Garment* also refers to the union of the red and white rose as a model for Britain's unity:

> The Red Rose and the White doe now,
> And still we hope shall flourish long,
> And rare exploites of *Henries* race,
> For euer grace our Britaine song.
>
> The English, Scots, and Irish true,
> Of three are now combin'd in one,
> Their hartes a true loue knot fast knit,
> All former malice now is gone.

As visage and the phrase of toung,
Twixt Scots and English neere agree,
So guider of all hartes, their hartes
Conioyne, that loyall they may bee.[114]

The question these lines raise is to whom do they refer? To whom does 'our Britaine song' belong? This text addresses the readers as 'King *Brutus* race',[115] but who exactly constitutes such a race? Are the descendants of '*Henries* race' the English, or the Welsh, or the English and the politically incorporated Welsh, or perhaps all of Great Britain's inhabitants – that is, all of James's British subjects? Another question to ask is who precisely are the 'Irish true': all loyal subjects in Ireland (the native Irish, the predominantly Catholic Old English, the Protestant New English) or, more likely, the New English only? Whilst the second stanza envisions Anglo-Irish-Scottish concord, the following stanza's account of Anglo-Scottish proximity fails to include the Irish. According to Morrill, English 'historians and antiquarians spurned the opportunity to invent a past that incorporated [Ireland]'.[116] Even Anglo-Scottish proximity is troublesome: '[a]s visage and the phrase of toung,/ Twixt Scots and English neere agree'. Sameness is gestured to but, as 'neere agree' reveals, difference is hard to overcome. Of particular interest in these lines (indeed, in much of the succession literature) is the omission of Wales and the Welsh. The most likely explanation for this omission is that the author assumes Wales and its inhabitants have been incorporated into an English polity just as '[t]he English, Scots, and Irish true … are now combin'd in one'. Perhaps a similar incorporating union between the kingdoms of England and Scotland is what the anonymous author desires and expects. Indeed, the invocation of Brutus and the British History is very much grounded in English aggrandisement. As Roger Mason notes, the appropriation of the British History by English writers was done 'in such a way as to make quite explicit their belief that the kingdom of the Scots was in the past and remained in the present a mere principality subject ultimately to the kings of England'.[117] Complicating matters, of course, was the fact that in March of 1603 a Scottish king had come to claim the English throne. James's claim was uncontested; unsurprisingly, succession literature of 1603 reveals no signs of resistance to James's accession. What this body of literature does reveal, however, is an appropriation and an interpellation of England's Scottish king. Whilst far from monolithic, underpinning representations of James at the time of the accession are English attitudes and ideas that serve to accommodate the Scottish monarch – culturally, ideologically, politically – to his new English subjects. In order to make James familiar to his southern subjects, those subjects rendered him less Scottish and more English or more British, albeit a concept of Britishness that served English interests.

'For all he did, or meant to haue done'

If 1603 produced an outpouring of print material in celebration of the accession of King James I – perhaps the logical response to the English Parliament's 1571 ban on public debate of the succession – this period also witnessed uncertainty about the novelty of a monarch who ruled over multiple kingdoms. Jacobean succession literature does not, perhaps could not, give voice to political resistance to James. It does register, paradoxically, an intense interest in the cultural and historical roots of Britain and Britishness and an ideological resistance to newer imaginings of Britain and Britishness. Nowhere is this more evident than in the inconsistent invocations of the British History. Consider, again, this quatrain from *Englands Wedding Garment*, cited in the opening paragraph:

> The Scottish Ile doth streame with teares,
>   Shed forth for absence of her King,
> The bankes of English Ile for joy,
>   With Ecchoes sounding loud shall ring.

These lines are remarkable for their figuring of a separate Scottish and English 'Ile' – or, in other words, their a refusal to name a common British isle. If the anonymous author is using 'Ile' to denote 'kingdom', then these lines are prescient, for, despite various efforts, no united British kingdom materialised in the early seventeenth century: England and Scotland remained separate kingdoms, and throughout his English reign King James would remain James VI of Scotland and James I of England. An anonymous and untitled manuscript poem produced after James's death recognises the king's triple monarchy: 'Deaths iron hand hath clos'd those eyes/W:[ch] were att once three kingdomes spyes'. This poem continues:

For two feirce kingdomes ioyn'd in one
For all he did, or meant to haue done
Doe this for him write ore his dust
Iames the peacefull and the iust.[118]

As much as James is heralded for joining 'two feirce kingdomes', his reign is defined both by what he did and what he did not do. If, as has been suggested, 1603 succession literature 'captures a moment in which voices of celebration and hope predominated', then it is fair to say that such voices were matched by collective anxiety and uncertainty.[119] What makes the succession literature of 1603 so valuable, then, is its collective consideration of cultural and political issues in advance of serious and sustained debate that emerged in full in 1604, both inside and outside Parliament. Indeed, the texts studied in this chapter anticipate the dialogue and debate on Anglo-Scottish union as well as kingship, the ancient constitution and parliamentary prerogative that would come to dominate the early years of James's English reign, a period when, many historians argue, James quickly alienated himself from not just his English Parliament but also his English subjects. That James's 'reign aroused conflicting opinions from the early seventeenth century onwards' has long been upon historical record.[120] We need look no further than the succession literature of 1603 to discover the emergence of these 'conflicting opinions'.

'The Isle should yet her ancient Name regaine'

James's English subjects were not alone in hailing his accession to England's throne; James's countrymen, too, produced public pronouncements on the dual monarchy effected in 1603.[121] Whereas the English are anxious about the arrival of a Scottish monarch, the Scottish mourn the departure of not just their king but also the entire royal family. Thomas Craig, who would serve on the Anglo-Scottish Union Commission and who composed a lengthy union tract, published two Latin poems lamenting the departure of not only King James but also Prince Henry, heir to Scotland's throne.[122] Not until 1617, when James made his one and only return to Scotland, which retained its parliament, Kirk and distinct legal system, did his Scottish subjects produce the kind of writing that James's accession to the English throne occasioned. A host of texts appeared in 1617 welcoming the King's return to his 'Natiue Towne' and 'natiue Kingdome', including a welcome poem by Alexander Craig celebrating James's visit to Kinnaird Castle, John Hay's *A Speach, Deliuered to the Kings most excellent Maiestie, At his Entrie into his Good-Towne of Edinbvrgh* and Hume's *Regi suo, post bis septennium in Patriam ex Angliâ redeunti, Scotiae gratulatio*. Some of these 1617 publications were reprinted in John Adamson's hefty composite volume *The Mvses Welcome to the High and Mighty Prince Iames*, which appeared in 1618. Hay, for example, echoes 1603 succession literature in his valorisation of James's 'prudencie, wisedome and constancie in Uniting the disjointed members of this Common-wealth'.[123] Striking a different note, John Leech's *Lachrymæ in Augustissimi monarchæ, Jacobi. I. Magnæ Britanniæ, Franciae, & Hiberniae*, as its title reveals, bewails James's return in August to England and the monarchy's absence from Scotland.

More so than any other piece of 1617 welcome literature, William Drummond of Hawthornden's *Forth Feasting. A Panegyricke to the Kings most excellent Maiestie* captures the conflicting attitudes of James's Scottish subjects upon his homecoming: anxious, desirous to greet their king, yet fully aware that the return to his native city and country is temporary. Noting that 'regret at James's absence looms larger than the occasion requires', Kerrigan argues that Drummond's poem tests the bounds of the genre.[124] Instances of encomium in the poem, particularly those heightened by anaphora and rhyme, are often undercut by an acute awareness of the King's absenteeism: '[b]y Wonder borne, by Wonder first enstall'd,/By Wonder after to new Kingdomes call'd'.[125] Just as Drummond's poem voices an appreciation of James's 'new Kingdomes', it also appears deeply 'ambivalent about the union', Kerrigan notes.[126]

The poem's ambivalence is by no means a product of an oppositional ideology or xenophobia. But from this ambivalence an ideology emerges, one grounded in time and, especially, place. In its attention to history, to land and to country, *Forth Feasting* is very much in dialogue with the *Poly-Olbion* of Michael Drayton, a writer whose work Drummond owned and with whom Drummond corresponded.[127] More so than Drayton's major poem, Drummond's panegyric praises James's benevolent rule: '[i]f *Pict, Dane, Norman*, Thy smooth Yoke had seene,/*Pict, Dane*, and *Norman*, had Thy Subjects beene'.[128] If the poem's historical references establish James as a pan-British monarch, then so do its geographical ones: '*Tweed* which no more our Kingdomes shall diuide'. The plural 'Kingdomes', however, acknowledges the fact that in 1617 England and Scotland, despite sharing a monarch, remained separate realms. One of those realms, moreover, had not seen its king for fourteen years. Like many writers before him, Drummond lauds James as '[t]he Man long promis'd, by whose glorious Raigne,/The Isle should yet her ancient Name regaine'.[129] Interestingly, that 'Name', Britain, never surfaces in the poem: '[t]he Isle should yet her ancient Name regaine' foregrounds an awkward relation between a geopolitical entity and its various nations. What makes Drummond's panegyric unique is its use of the non-national 'Isle', including '[t]hine Isle', to refer to the space over which James rules.[130] That 'Isle' was, of course, Britain, but the culturally and intellectually cosmopolitan Drummond shows little commitment to a British national consciousness. 'Eye of our westerne World ... To which *Thame*, *Liffy*, *Taye* subject their Streames' acknowledges James's triple monarchy. The novelty of James's three-kingdom rule – or, to put it another way, his absenteeism – facilitates Drummond's investment in Scotland's topography, displacing the King as the poem's centrepiece in favour of 'the Land'.[131] The following lines, for instance, ostensibly posit the King, who returned in May, as regenerator of Scotland's desolate landscape:

> As lookes a Garden of its Beautie spoil'd.
> As Wood in Winter by rough *Boreas* foil'd:
> As Pourtraicts raz'd of Colours vse to bee:
> So lookt these abject Bounds depriu'd of Thee.[132]

Although the poem presents a land somewhat forlorn because of the monarch's absence, that absence enables the poem's sustained attention to and evocative representation of the nation's landscape, evinced in the many references to Scotland's lakes, mountains, rivers: 'Grampius Mists', 'the fertile Spay', '[s]trange Loumond', 'lowd-bellowing Clyd', '[t]he Eskes, the Solway'.[133] Reflecting on Scotland's place within a multiple-kingdoms geopolitical framework, *Forth Feasting* offers a prime example of the ways in which subjects of a self-proclaimed British monarch participated in the production of culturally and politically inflected images, memories and vocabularies that shaped and reshaped dominant attitudes towards crown and country throughout the Jacobean period.

Notes

1 [James VI and I], *The Kings Maiesties Speech, as it was deliuered by him in the vpper house of the Parliament to the Lords Spirituall and Temporall, and to the Knights, Citizens and Burgesses there assembled, On Munday the 19. day of March 1603* (London, 1604) (STC 14390), A3^{r-v}.

2 James Doelman, '"A King of Thine Own Heart": the English reception of King James VI and I's *Basilikon Doron*', *The Seventeenth Century*, 9 (1994), 1. The London publication of *The Trve Lawe of Free Monarchies* and *Daemonologie* soon followed (both were entered into the Stationers' Register on 3 April 1603).

3 Francis Bacon, *The Beginning of the History of Great Britain*, in James Spedding, R. L. Ellis and D. D. Heath (eds), *The Works of Francis Bacon*, 14 vols (London, 1857–74), XI, 410.

4 Based on 'items available in Early English Books Online', Paulina Kewes and Andrew McRae identify 128 works on succession published in 1603, which equates to '17 percent of all surviving items': Paulina Kewes and Andrew McRae, 'Introduction', in Paulina Kewes and Andrew McRae (eds), *Stuart Succession Literature: moments and transformations* (Oxford: Oxford University Press, 2019), 1.

5 The first publication listed under 'Regis Jacobi' in the Stationers' Register is '*Basilicon Doron*' (28 March), followed by '*the Pictures of the kinge and Quene, and the Twoo yo[u]nge princes their sonnes*' (29 March) and 'a thing in verse called *Kinges JAMES proclaimed*' (30 March): Edward Arber (ed.), *A Transcript of the Registers of the Company of Stationers of London: 1554–1640 AD*, 5 vols (London, 1876), III, 230. John Speed commemorates James's accession in his untitled map of 1603–04 with elaborate heraldry and a royal genealogy of, to cite the cartouche, '[t]he most Royall Progeny of the Kings of England continved from William Sirnamed Conqveror, to ovr most graciovs Soveraigne Iames the First King of England, Scotland, France and Ireland'. The untitled map is housed in the Bibliothèque nationale de France (GE DD-6056).

6 See, for example, Judith M. Richards, 'The English accession of James VI: "national" identity, gender and the personal monarchy of England', *The English Historical Review*, 117 (2002), 513–35; Richard A. McCabe, 'The poetics of succession, 1587–1605: the Stuart claim', in Susan Doran and Paulina Kewes (eds), *Doubtful and Dangerous: the question of succession in late Elizabethan England* (Manchester: Manchester University Press, 2014), 192–211; and, especially, Kewes and McRae (eds), *Stuart Succession Literature*. See also McRae and West (eds), *Literature of the Stuart Successions*, especially 29–73. Jane

Rickard, *Writing the Monarch in Jacobean England: Jonson, Donne, Shakespeare and the writings of King James* (Cambridge: Cambridge University Press, 2015), 29–37, focuses on the reception of James as 'writer-king'.

7 Chapter 2 will also focus on Ben Jonson, whose 'On the Vnion' is usually dated 1603 by Jonson's editors.

8 The rather elliptical Sonnet 107 is something of an exception. This does not preclude the possibility that Shakespeare wrote or rewrote a play or plays in anticipation of or after the fact of James's accession. *Macbeth*, as I argue in chapter 4, was determined by James's accession to the English throne. For readings of the First Folio's *The Life of Henry the Fift* as a play that anticipates or reflects James's English rule, see Neil Rhodes, 'Wrapped in the strong arms of the union: Shakespeare and King James', in Willy Maley and Andrew Murphy (eds), *Shakespeare and Scotland* (Manchester: Manchester University Press, 2004), 37–52 as well as Christopher Ivic, 'Making and remaking the British kingdoms – *Henry V*, then and now', in Karen Britland and Line Cottegnies (eds), *King Henry V: A Critical Reader* (London: Bloomsbury, 2018), 156–79.

9 D. R. Woolf, 'Two Elizabeths? James I and the late Queen's famous memory', *Canadian Journal of History*, 20 (1985), 175.

10 'The accession and coronation', according to one historian, 'were celebrated by writers and hacks falling over one another to get into print': Keith M. Brown, 'The vanishing emperor: British kingship and its decline, 1603–1707', in Keith M. Brown and Roger A. Mason (eds), *Scots and Britons: Scottish political thought and the union of 1603* (Cambridge: Cambridge University Press, 1987), 65. For an argument against the ephemerality of occasional texts, although one that does not focus on 1603 succession literature, see Malcolm Smuts, 'Occasional events, literary texts and historical interpretation', in Robin Headlam Wells, Glenn Burgess and Rowland Wymer (eds), *Neo-historicism, Studies in Renaissance Literature, History, and Politics* (London: D. S. Brewer, 2000), 179–98.

11 Samuel Rowlands, *Aue Cæsar* (London, 1603), B3^v.

12 See the essays collected in Jean-Christophe Mayer (ed.), *The Struggle for the Succession in Late Elizabethan England: politics, polemics and cultural representations* (Montpellier: Astraea Collection, 2004). 'James VI and his nobility waited in largely paralysed hope to see what would happen when the ageing Queen died, but they committed little to paper and entrusted little to one another that has left traces in the archives': Morrill, 'The British problem', 26.

13 Galloway, *The Union of England and Scotland*, 163.

14 Thomas Dekker, *1603. The Wonderfull yeare* (London, 1603), B2^v.

Writing around 1610, Bacon recalls false rumours that 'after Queen Elizabeth's decease, there must follow in England nothing but confusions, interreigns, and pertubations of estate, likely far to exceed the ancient calamities of Lancaster and York': Bacon, *The Beginning of the History of Great Britain*, 407.

15 Claire McEachern, *The Poetics of English Nationhood, 1590–1612* (Cambridge: Cambridge University Press, 1996), 140.
16 James Doelman, 'The accession of James I and English religious poetry', *Studies in English Literature*, 34 (1994), 23.
17 Glenn Burgess, Rowland Wymer and Jason Lawrence, 'Introduction', in Glenn Burgess, Rowland Wymer and Jason Lawrence (eds), *The Accession of James I: historical and cultural consequences* (Basingstoke: Palgrave, 2006), xiii.
18 Paul J. McGinnis and Arthur H. Williamson (eds and trans.), *The British Union: a critical edition and translation of David Hume of Godscroft's De Unione Insulae Britannicae* (Aldershot: Ashgate, 2002), 121.
19 [Anon.], *Englands Wedding Garment. Or A preparation to King Iames his Royall Coronation* (London, 1603), A4^r. For a rich reading of William Drummond's poetry, especially his *Forth Feasting, A Panegyricke to the Kings Most Excellent Maiestie* (Edinburgh, 1617) within the context of James's 1617 return to Edinburgh, see Kerrigan, *Archipelagic English*, 141–52.
20 T[homas]. M[illington]., *The True Narration of the Entertainment of his Royall Maiestie, from the time of his departure from Edenbrough; till his receiuing at London: with all or the most speciall Occurrences* (London, 1603), B4^{r-v}.
21 [Anon.], *Englands Wedding Garment*, A4^v.
22 At this historical moment, the inclusion of 'France' in the title of England's monarch was nominal; the loss of Calais in 1558 marked the end of England's hold on any Continental territories. James VI and I had, of course, a Scottish as well as an English coronation; he did not have an Irish coronation.
23 [Anon.], *Englands Wedding Garment*, A2^v.
24 The Act in Restraint of Appeals (24 Hen. VIII c. 12).
25 For an early Jacobean response to Persons, see John Hayward's *An Answer to the First Part of a Certain Conference Concerning Succession* (London, 1603); see also Thomas Craig's *De Unione Regnorum Britanniæ Tractatus* (c. 1605), wherein Craig writes of James in response to Persons 'never has a prince been called to and received a kingdom with such general approval, popular applause, and rejoicing': Craig, *De Unione*, 412–13. Writing a few years after Hayward, John Speed mocks Persons (Doleman) when discussing

James's accession to the English throne: '[l]et *Doleman* therefore dote vpon his own dreames, and other like Traitors fashion their barres vpon the Popes forge': John Speed, *The History of Great Britaine under the conquests of ye Romans, Saxons, Danes and Normans* (London, 1611), 884. See also Paulina Kewes, '"The idol of state innovators and republicans": Robert Persons's *A Conference About the Next Succession* (1594/5) in Stuart England', in Kewes and McRae (eds), *Stuart Succession Literature*, 149–85.
26 Susan Doran and Paulina Kewes, 'Introduction: a historical perspective', in Doran and Kewes (eds), *Doubtful and Dangerous*, 4. 'Once a disputed succession had been settled,' Doran and Kewes add, 'people tended to jump on the bandwagon of the successful candidate, or at least to keep quiet about their misgivings, making the outcome seem more inevitable than it actually was'. 'This is evident', they go on to argue, 'in the orchestration of James's proclamation and arrival in England in 1603 and the outpouring of gratulatory addresses and poems': Doran and Kewes, *ibid.*, 12.
27 *Calendar of the Manuscripts of the Most Hon. the Marquess of Salisbury, preserved at Hatfield House, Hertfordshire*, 23 vols. (London, HMSO, 1883–1976), XVI, 345.
28 Henry Chettle, *Englandes Mourning Garment: Worne here by plaine Shepheards; in memorie of their sacred Mistresse, Elizabeth, Queene of Vertue while shee liued, and Theame of Sorrow being dead. To the which is added the true manner of her Emperiall Funerall. After which foloweth the Shepheards Spring-Song, for entertainment of King Iames our most potent Soueraigne* (London, 1603) (STC 5121), F4^v.
29 An image of 'Iacobus Rex' as 'Beati Pacifici' graces the frontispiece in John Adamson's *The Mvses Welcome to the High and Mightie Prince Iames* (Edinburgh, 1618). Speed writes of James, 'for his mott, as is most meet; BEATI PACIFICI': Speed, *The History of Great Britaine*, 161.
30 Not that such xenophobia did not exist: after commenting on those involved in the Bye and Main Plots as well as their punishments, Jenny Wormald adds '[m]ore generally a host of small people – saddlers, weavers, and yeomen – were indicted in the southern counties for speaking against the accession of a king whom they regarded as foreign, and therefore no true king of England': Jenny Wormald, 'James VI and I', *ODNB*, https://doi.org/10.1093/ref:odnb/14592. Accessed 11 December 2015.
31 Chettle, *Englandes Mourning Garment*, F4^v.
32 R. Malcom Smuts, 'States, monarchs and dynastic transitions: the political thought of John Hayward', in Doran and Kewes (eds), *Doubtful and dangerous*, 276.

33 Samuel Daniel, 'A Panegyrick congratulatorie To the Kinges most Sacred Maiestie By Samuel Danyel', British Library, Royal MS 18 A.LXXII, fol. 3^r.
34 For an in-depth analysis of one particular text, see Patricia Phillippy, 'London's mourning garment: maternity, mourning and royal succession', in Naomi J. Miller and Naomi Yavneh (eds), *Maternal Measures: figuring caregiving in the early modern period* (Aldershot: Ashgate, 2000), 319–32.
35 [Anon.], *Sorrowes Ioy. Or, a Lamentation for our late deceased Sovereigne Elizabeth, with a triumph for the prosperous succession of our gracious King, Iames, &c* (Cambridge, 1603), 3–6.
36 Ibid., 6.
37 Chettle, *Englands Mourning Garment*, F4^r–G1^v.
38 Henry Chettle, *Englands Mourning Garment: Worne heere by plaine Shepheards, in memorie of their sacred Mistresse, Elizabeth; Queene of Vertue while she liued, and Theame of Sorrow being dead. To the which is added the true manner of her Emperiall Funerall. With many new additions, being now againe the second time reprinted, which was omitted in the first Impression. After which followeth the Shepheards Spring-Song, for entertainment of King Iames our most potent Soueraigne* (London, 1603) (STC 5122), F2^r. Uncertainty concerning James's title continued beyond 1603. In one manuscript pro-union tract, the author offers the following dedication: '[t]o the Mighty Prince Iames, by the grace of god, king of Great Britaine, ffrance, and Ireland'. 'Great Britaine', however, is a paste-on cancel overwriting 'England and Scotland'; the tail of 'g' in 'England' and, from the verso, the 'S' in 'Scotland' can just be made out. See William Clerk, 'Ancillans Synopsis', Trinity College Library, Dublin, MS 635, fol. F5^r.
39 Dekker, *1603. The Wonderfull yeare*, B2^r. In 1612, Michael Drayton writes of Elizabeth as having '[t]his Iland kept in awe': Michael Drayton, *Poly-Olbion* (London, 1612), 264. Famously, James forbade members of the court from wearing mourning attire for Elizabeth.
40 Dekker, *1603. The Wonderfull yeare*, B2^r. Might Dekker's use of 'almost' be an invocation of Henry's VIII's reign? 'King Henry and his royal servants had made a revolution; their Elizabethan successors were left to make sense of the result': Helgerson, *Forms of Nationhood*, 4. Many of these 'Elizabethan successors', I argue throughout this book, were also Jacobean successors.
41 Thomas Rogers, *Anglorum Lacrimæ: In a sad passion complayning the death of our late Soueraigne Lady Queene Elizabeth: Yet comforted againe by the vertuous hopes of our most Royall and Renowned King Iames* (London, 1603), B2^v.

42 For a review of Queen Anne's Catholicism, see Leeds Barroll, *Anna of Denmark, Queen of England: a cultural biography* (Philadelphia: University of Pennsylvania Press, 2001), 162–72.
43 [William Shakespeare], *The Cronicle History of Henry the fift, with his battell fought at Agin Court in France. Togither with Auntient Pistoll. As it hath bene sundry times playd by the Right honorable the Lord Chamberlaine his seruants* (London, 1600), A3^v.
44 Kevin Sharpe, *Remapping Early Modern England: the culture of seventeenth-century politics* (Cambridge: Cambridge University Press, 2000), 208.
45 Henry Petowe, *Elizabetha quasi viuens Eliza's Funerall. A fewe Aprill drops, showred on the hearse of dead Eliza. Or The Funerall teares af [sic] a true hearted Subiect* (London, 1603), B3^v. Another text terms James '[a] Phœnix from *Elizaes* ashes bred': Anthony Nixon, *Elizaes Memoriall. King Iames his arriuall. And Romes Downefall* (London, 1603), D3^r. The image of Elizabeth as phoenix had staying power: in the final scene of *The Famous History of the Life of King Henry the Eight* Cranmer terms Elizabeth 'the Mayden Phoenix': Charlton Hinman (ed.), *The Norton Facsimile: the first Folio of Shakespeare* (New York: W. W. Norton, 1968), TLN 3411. Subsequent references to Hinman's edition of the First Folio will be given parenthetically, citing Through Line Numbers (TLN).
46 John Watkins, *Representing Elizabeth in Stuart England: literature, history, sovereignty* (Cambridge: Cambridge University Press, 2002), 15. See also Curtis Perry, *The Making of Jacobean Culture: James I and the renegotiation of Elizabethan literary practice* (Cambridge: Cambridge University Press, 1997), 153–87.
47 England and Wales. Privy Council, *Forasmuch as it hath pleased Almighty God to call to his mercy out of this transitory life our soueraigne lady, the high and mighty prince, Elizabeth late Queene of England, France, and Ireland* (London, 1603).
48 Patrick Collinson, 'Elizabeth I (1533–1603)', *ODNB*, https://doi.org/10.1093/ref:odnb/8636. Accessed 19 September 2015.
49 England and Wales. Privy Council, *Forasmuch as it hath pleased Almighty God*.
50 [Anon.], *Englands Wedding Garment*, B1^r.
51 Anthony Nixon, *Elizaes Memoriall*, C3^v.
52 Robert Fletcher, *A Briefe and Familiar Epistle shewing His Maiesties most lawfull, honourable and iust title to all his Kingdomes* (London, 1603), B3^v. I read Fletcher's '*Elimologi*' as a printer's error for '*Etimologi*'.
53 Francis Bacon, 'A letter to the Earl of Northumberland after he had been with the King', in James Spedding (ed.), *The Letters and the Life of Francis Bacon*, 7 vols. (London, 1861–72), III, 77.

54 Joseph Hall, *The Kings Prophecie: or Weeping Ioy. Expressed in a Poeme, to the Honor of Englands too great Solemnities* (London, 1603), A4^v.
55 Craig, *De Unione*, 207, 208.
56 Catherine Loomis, '"Withered Plants Do Bud and Blossome Yeelds": naturalizing James I's succession', in Robert S. Sturges (ed.), *Law and Sovereignty in the Middle Ages and the Renaissance* (Turnhout, Belgium: Brepols, 2011), 136.
57 [Anon.], 'A treatise about the Union of England and Scotland', in Bruce R. Galloway and Brian P. Levack (eds), *The Jacobean Union: six tracts of 1604* (Scottish History Society, fourth series, number 21) (Edinburgh and London: Clark Constable, 1985), 52.
58 Chettle, *Englands Mourning Garment*, G1^r.
59 John Davies, 'The Kinges Welcome', in Robert Krueger and Ruby Nemser (eds), *The Poems of Sir John Davies* (Oxford: Oxford University Press, 1975), 229. Although Davies did not publish this poem in his lifetime, two extant manuscript copies survive: All Souls College, Oxford, MS 155 and, a shorter version, Edinburgh University Library, MS La. III. 444, which includes a sonnet addressed to Queen Anne.
60 Dekker, *1603. The Wonderfull yeare*, C1^r. Writing a year later, Robert Pont points to Anglo-Scottish union as the grounds whereby 'the savadg wildnes of the Irish, and the barbarous fierceness of other ilanders shall easily be tamed': Robert Pont, 'Of the Union of Britayne', in Galloway and Levack (eds), *The Jacobean Union*, 18.
61 Rowlands, *Aue Cæsar*, A2^r.
62 John Savile, *King Iames his entertainment at Theobalds: With his welcome to London, together with a salutatorie Poeme* (London, 1603), C3^v.
63 [Anon.], *Englands Wedding Garment*, A2^r.
64 Petowe, *Elizabetha quasi viuens*, A2^v.
65 [Anon.], *A new song to the great comfort and reioycing of all true English harts, at our most Gracious King Iames his Proclamation, vpon the 24. of March last past in the Cittie of London* (Edinburgh, 1603), ll. 42–3.
66 Rowlands, *Aue Cæsar*, B1^r.
67 T[homas]. M[illington]., *The True Narration*, C1^r.
68 England and Wales. Privy Council, *Forasmuch as it hath pleased*.
69 John Fenton, *King Iames His Welcome to London* (London, 1603), C4^v, B3^v. See also the ballad *A New song to the great comfort and reioycing of all true English*: 'He is our Royall King,/And our Countrey will defend' (ll. 21–2).

70 Craig, *De Unione*, 207.
71 Jenny Wormald, 'The creation of Britain: multiple kingdoms or core and colonies?', *Transactions of the Royal Historical Society*, sixth series, 2 (1992), 184–5.
72 Richard Martin, *A Speach Delivered, to the Kings most excellent Maiestie in the Name of the Sheriffes of London and Middlesex* (London, 1603), B2^v–B3^r.
73 Dekker, *1603. The Wonderfull yeare*, C1^v. See also Dekker's account of St George and St Andrew and their 'leagued Combination, and new sworne Brother-hood': Thomas Dekker, *The Magnificent Entertainment: Giuen to King Iames, Queene Anne his wife, and Henry Frederick the Prince, vppon the day of his Maiesties Tryumphant passage (from the Tower) through his honourable Cittie (and Chamber) of London, being the 15. of March. 1603* (London, 1604), A2^v.
74 Benedict Anderson, *Imagined Communities: reflections on the origin and spread of nationalism*, rev. ed. (London: Verso, 1991), 200, 201.
75 Robert Pricket, *A Souldiers Wish vnto His Soveraigne Lord King Iames* (London, 1603), C1^v.
76 Robert Pricket, *Vnto the Most High and Mightie Prince, his Soueraigne Lord King Iames. A poore Subiect sendeth, a Souldiors Resolution; humbly to waite vpon his Maiestie* (London, 1603), F3^{r-v}.
77 Pricket, *A Souldiers Wish*, C2^r, C3^r.
78 Chettle, *Englands Mourning Garment*, G1^r.
79 [Anon.], *An excellent new Ballad, shewing the Petigree of our Royall King Iames, the first of that name in England* (London, 1603). One definition of 'Brute' offered by the *OED* is 'A Briton, a Welshman' (*n.*^{2} 1).
80 William Camden, *Britain, or a Chorographicall description of the most flourishing Kingdomes, England, Scotland, and Ireland, and the Ilands adioyning* (London, 1610), ¶4^r.
81 *Ibid.*, 4.
82 The manuscript is housed in the National Archives (SP 63/202 Pt 4, fols 127^r–91^r); however, Renwick's edition of the *View* reproduces this variant passage: see W. L. Renwick (ed.), *Edmund Spenser, A View of the Present State of Ireland* (Oxford: Clarendon Press, 1970), 197.
83 Savile, *King Iames his entertainment at Theobalds*, C3^r.
84 [Anon.], *Englands Wedding Garment*, B2^r.
85 [Francis Bacon], *A Briefe Discovrse, Touching the Happie Vnion of the Kingdomes of England, and Scotland Dedicated in priuate to his Maiestie* (London, 1603), B8^v–C1^r. This text was entered into the Stationers' Register on 10 June 1603.
86 Nixon, *Elizaes Memoriall*, C4^v.

87 The full title of John Monipennie's *The abridgement or Summarie of the Scots Chronicles* (London, 1612) includes a reference to 'Albion, now called Scotland'.

88 When William Harrison writes of '[t]he Ile of Albion', he means the island of Great Britain: Harrison, *The Description of Britaine*, in *The first and second volumes of Chronicles, comprising 1 The description and historie of England, 2 The description and historie of Ireland, 3 The description and historie of Scotland: first collected and published by Raphaell Holinshed, William Harrison, and others: now newlie augmented and continued* (London, 1587), 7. Camden writes of 'Britaine or Britannie, which also is Albion': Camden, *Britain*, 1. Speed refers to Great Britain as '*Great Albion* (another name of this famous Iland)': John Speed, *The Theatre of the Empire of Great Britaine* (London, 1612), 1. Roger Mason notes that in the Scottish historiographical tradition (Fordun, Boece and, occasionally, Buchanan) Albion, as opposed to Britain, is the term used to denote the whole island of Britain: Roger Mason, 'Scotching the Brut: politics, history and national myth in sixteenth-century Britain', in Roger A. Mason (ed.), *Scotland and England, 1286–1815* (Edinburgh: Edinburgh University Press, 1987), 63. See also Alan MacColl, 'The meaning of "Britain" in medieval and early modern England', *Journal of British Studies*, 45 (2006), 248–69.

89 William Warner, *Albions England. Or historicall map of the same island* (London, 1586), a.iii[r].

90 George Abbot, *A briefe description of the whole worlde wherein are particularly described all the Monarchies, Empires, and kingdomes of the same, with their seuerall titles and situations thereunto adioyning* (London, 1599), H4[r].

91 Richard Verstegan, *A Restitvtion of Decayed Intellengence: In Antiquities. Concerning the most noble and renowmed English nation* (Antwerp 1605), †††4[r].

92 The First Folio includes five Elizabethan uses of 'Albion' and just one Jacobean one: '[i]n that nooke-shotten Ile of Albion' (*H5*, TLN 1393); '[i]s this the Fashions in the Court of England?/Is this the Gouernment of Britaines Ile?/And this the Royaltie of *Albions* King?' (*2H6*, TLN 429–31); '[f]or loosing ken of *Albions* wished Coast' (*2H6*, TLN 1813); '[f]rom worthy *Edward*, King of Albion' (*3H6*, TLN 1783); 'I was (I must confesse)/Great Albions Queene, in former Golden dayes' (*3H6*, TLN 1730–31); '[t]hen shal the Realme of *Albion*, come to great confusion' (*KL*, TLN 1746). Robert Allott's *Englands Parnassus* (1600) includes a version of John of Gaunt's 'this sceptred Isle' speech (*R2*, TLN 681) under the heading 'Of Albion'. According to Anthony Munday, '*Neptune* put his son *Albion* the Gyant in possession of this

land, who subduing the *Samotheans*, called this Iland *Albion* after his owne name': Anthony Munday, *The Triumphes of re-vnited Britania* (London, 1605), A2ᵛ.
93 'On his accession', according to S. T. Bindoff, 'James was proclaimed, first in Westminster and London, and later throughout the country, "King of the realms of England, France and Ireland" ... The same style was used when, on 25 July 1603, James and Anne were crowned. From the time of his arrival in England, however, the king had adopted his full style of "James, by the grace of God, King of England, Scotland, France and Ireland, Defender of the Faith, &c"': S. T. Bindoff, 'The Stuarts and their style', *The English Historical Review*, 60 (1945), 192.
94 Fletcher, *A Briefe and Familiar Epistle*, B2ʳ.
95 Hall, *The Kings prophecie*, A6ᵛ.
96 Camden, *Britain*, 2.
97 [Bacon,] *A Briefe Discovrse*, A7ʳ.
98 John Gordon, *A Panegyrique of Congratulation for the Concord of the Realmes of Great Britaine in Vnitie of Religion, and vnder one King* (London, 1603), B2ᵛ.
99 Chettle, *Englands Mourning Garment*, A4ᵛ.
100 William Camden, *Remaines of a Greater Worke, Concerning Britaine, the inhabitants thereof, their Languages, Names, Surnames, Empreses, Wise speeches, Poësies, and Epitaphes* (London, 1605), 7. A reference to 'the Britains' in Camden's *Britain* is glossed 'Welchmen': Camden, *Britain*, 15.
101 Writing to and about King James in 1604, the Welshman George Owen Harry lists 'Owen Tudyr' as 'his Maiesties auncestour': see the title page of Harry's *The Genealogy of the High and Mighty Monarch, Iames, by the grace of God, king of Great Brittayne* (London, 1604).
102 'The British Isles existed as a geographical term; but there was no term for, and no *concept* of, a single polity, entity, state incorporating the islands of Britain and Ireland': Morrill, 'The British problem', 5.
103 [Bacon], *A Briefe Discovrse*, A7ᵛ–A8ʳ.
104 Hall, *The Kings Prophecie*, A8ʳ.
105 Fletcher, *A Briefe and Familiar Epistle*, A3ʳ.
106 James Harrison (Henrisoun), *An exhortacion to the Scottes, to conforme them selfes to the honorable, expedie[n]t, and godly vnion, betwene the twoo realmes of Englande and Scotlande* (London, 1547), a.ii.ʳ⁻ᵛ.
107 *Ibid.*, a.a.vi.ᵛ⁻ʳ, a.vii.ᵛ.
108 *Ibid.*, b.i.ʳ.
109 *Ibid.*, b.iiii.ʳ⁻ᵛ.

110 Fletcher, *A Briefe and Familiar Epistle*, B2^v. See also Gordon, *A Panegyrique*, B3^v–B4^r.
111 Levack, *The Formation of the British State*, 193.
112 Gordon, *A Panegyrique*, B2^r.
113 John Russell, 'A Treatise of the Happie and Blissed Unioun', in Galloway and Levack (eds), *The Jacobean Union*, 78.
114 [Anon.], *Englands Wedding Garment*, A3^v.
115 *Ibid.*, A2^r.
116 Morrill, 'The fashioning of Britain', 17.
117 Mason, 'Scotching the Brut', 62. Mason's essay details various sixteenth-century English appropriations of the British History to justify Anglo-Scottish union.
118 Trinity College Library, Dublin, MS 877, fol. 342, fol. 343.
119 McRae and West (eds), *Literature of the Stuart Successions*, 31.
120 Pauline Croft, *King James* (Basingstoke: Palgrave, 2003), 1.
121 On responses to James's English accession in Ireland, see Brendán Ó Buachalla, 'James our true king: the ideology of Irish royalism in the seventeenth century', in D. G. Boyce, Robert Eccleshall and Vincent Geoghegan (eds), *Political Thought in Ireland since the Seventeenth Century* (London: Routledge, 1993), 7–35; see also Richard A. McCabe, 'Panegyric and its discontents: the first Stuart succession', in Kewes and McRae (eds), *Stuart Succession Literature*, 31–4.
122 Thomas Craig, *Serenissimi, & invictissimi Principis, Iacobi Britanniarvm et Galliarvm Regis, Stephanophoria* (Edinburgh, 1603); *Ad Serenissimvm Britanniarum Principem Henricum, è Scotia discendentem propempticon* (Edinburgh, 1603). See also John Echlin, *De regno Angliae, Franciæ, Hiberniæ ad serenissimum et inuictiss. Iacobum 6. Scotorum Regem vltrò delato. Panegyricon* (Edinburgh, 1603).
123 John Hay, *A Speach, Deliuered to the Kings most excellent Maiestie, At his Entrie into his Good-Towne of Edinbvrgh* (Edinburgh, 1617), A2^r, A4^v, A4^r.
124 Kerrigan, *Archipelagic English*, 142.
125 Drummond, *Forth Feasting*, B2^v.
126 Kerrigan, *Archipelagic English*, 141.
127 Included among Drummond's donated books now housed in the Edinburgh University Library are Daniel's *Works* (1602 – De.4.73), Drayton's *Poems* (1608 – De.1/1.21) and *Poemes Lyrick and Pastorall* (1606 – De.1/1.21), and the following union texts: John Gordon's *Enōtikon* (1603 – Dd.7.32, 34), Hume's *De Vnione Insulæ Britannicæ Tractatus 1.* (London, 1605 – De.3.67/3) and the anonymously published pro-union tract *Rapta Tatio* (London, 1604 – De.3.109).
128 Drummond, *Forth Feasting*, B2^v.

129 *Ibid.*, A3ʳ, B3ʳ.
130 *Ibid.*, A4ᵛ.
131 *Ibid.*, B2ᵛ, A2ʳ.
132 *Ibid.*, A3ᵛ.
133 *Ibid.*, A3ʳ.

2

'This mighty worke of vnion': imagining union in early Jacobean panegyric

Among the various texts that hailed the accession of Scotland's King James VI to England's throne, the jewel in the crown was panegyric.[1] By no means was Jacobean succession panegyric restricted to 1603. In the following year, the royal family were the centrepiece of a public event that was by nature panegyrical: namely, the belated royal entry of 15 March 1604 – the original royal entry was postponed owing to the plague that hit London in the spring of 1603 – as well as the king's progress to Westminster Hall and his opening of Parliament on 19 March. Commendatory speeches written by Thomas Dekker, Ben Jonson and Thomas Middleton were among the event's highlights, and two of these playwrights subsequently committed their royal entry texts to print. Poems in praise of James would, of course, continue to be produced until (and even after) his death in 1625.[2] Three of the most prominent encomiasts were Samuel Daniel, Michael Drayton and Ben Jonson. All three poets wrote panegyrics celebrating James's accession and rule at the commencement of his English reign. Moreover, the arrival of the Stewarts had a profound impact on the careers of all three authors, for better or for worse. This chapter attends to the ways in which three of England's major authors – of plays, poems and prose – seized the occasion of regnal transition to renegotiate patronage networks, engage critically with James's composite monarchy as well as the question of Anglo-Scottish union and assert their authorial and communal identities.

This chapter also aims to foster a fuller appreciation of early Jacobean panegyric within the crucial context of James's accession, which, I believe, requires a reassessment of dominant and often dismissive attitudes to panegyric. Such a reassessment involves two critical tasks. The first involves developing a critical vocabulary that

'This mighty worke of vnion' 53

allows for a wider range of political ideologies and meanings than a simple for-or-against binary. Such a vocabulary must be sensitive to the ways in which James's accession to the English throne offered authors such as Daniel, Drayton and Jonson an opportunity to reimagine or reinforce their sense of self, especially as they came into contact with new and enabling patrons. Secondly, any reassessment of early Jacobean panegyric must rethink impoverished models of textual production and transmission that posit panegyric as little more than propaganda produced by poets who tell James what he wants to hear in the hope of securing royal patronage. Crucial, here, is attention to the material contexts of Jacobean panegyric, including forms of textual production (print and manuscript cultures), the various cultural sites from which panegyric emerged and within which it circulated (country houses, civic functions, social/literary networks/coteries) as well as the role textual culture plays in shaping knowledge communities and individual and collective identities. Attending to the material contexts of Jacobean panegyric allows for a fuller appreciation of how these ostensibly occasional texts impacted Jacobean literary and political culture well beyond the occasion for which they were produced.

'[O]ne people, brethren and members of one body'

Many historians and literary historians tend to treat the texts examined in this chapter as evidence of an author's attempt to secure royal patronage by saying things that would please James, especially on the topic of Anglo-Scottish or British unity.[3] In short, panegyric and 'propaganda' go hand in hand. The problem with the inflexible term 'propaganda' is that it assumes that at the outset of James's English reign a concept of Anglo-Scottish or British union was a stable enough political idea or ideological construct to allow a poet to be for or against it. By no means was 'union' as politically and ideologically coherent a concept in 1603 as it would eventually become when serious debate and dialogue on the union of England and Scotland emerged and circulated within and outside Parliament. That John Russell writes 'I will thairfoir declair qhat is meanit be the uord unioun' in a treatise written sometime between May and October of 1604 reveals the term's slipperiness.[4] Daniel and Drayton wrote their panegyrics at a moment when ideas of an Anglo-Scottish union were at an embryonic stage: that is, before the publication of printed tracts and treatises and the circulation of manuscript tracts and treatises.[5] Jacobean panegyric is often misunderstood precisely because it is read, on the one hand, in relation to the formal discussions and debates on a potential union that began in the spring of 1604 and, on the other, in relation to the union tracts and treatises that were produced and disseminated in 1604–05. In other words, later and fuller union ideas have been mapped onto 'union' texts produced in 1603, resulting in a distortion of our understanding of these rich texts. Sandra Bell, for instance, argues that Daniel's 1603 panegyric 'employs the natural, geographical imagery found in James's proclamation on Great Britain'. 'He favours', she adds, 'a union of Scots and English whose differences are dissolved under one king, and thus reiterates James's desire to de-emphasize and even erase the Scottish partner in the union.'[6] The proclamation to which Bell refers, however, was issued on 20 October 1604; Daniel's poem appeared over a year before the publication of the royal proclamation.

By no means am I suggesting that discourse on Anglo-Scottish union was absent from the public sphere in the spring of 1603. Rather, my point is that such discourse was far from coherent. Such ideological incoherence can be traced, for example, in a dialogue published in December 1603: Thomas Powell's *A Welch Bayte to spare Prouender*. The title page of Powell's text promises that the third part of the dialogue will examine 'the Aptnesse of the English and the Scotte to incorporate and become one entire Monarchie: with the meanes of preseruing their vnion euerlastingly'; however, this five-page section, titled 'The Scottish Englishing', offers very little in terms of effecting union beyond comparing the 'Aptnesse in the Scot to incorporate with the English' with 'the Scithian to incorporate with any the most ciuill nation, that is'.[7] Consider, also, the following passage from a royal proclamation published on 19 May 1603, which communicates 'his Maiesties resolution for the vnion of the two Realmes', and which appeared after the composition of Drayton's and Daniel's panegyrics:

> his Maiestie hath found in the hearts of all the best disposed Subiects of both the Realmes of all qualities, a most earnest desire, that the sayd happy Vnion should bee perfected, the memory of all preterite Discontentments abolished, and the Inhabitants of both the Realmes to be the Subiects of one Kingdome: so his Highnes will with all conuenient diligence with the aduice of the Estates and Parliament of both

the Kingdomes make the same to be perfited. And in the meane time till the sayd Vnion be established with the due solemnitie aforesayd, his Maiestie doth hereby repute, hold, and esteeme, and commands all his Highnes Subiects to repute, hold, and esteeme both the two Realmes as presently vnited, and as one Realme and Kingdome, and the Subiects of both the Realmes as one people, brethren and members of one body.[8]

As a statement on 'Vnion', this royal proclamation is far from simple and straightforward. In fact, multiple denotations of 'Vnion' surface in this passage. Underpinning the proclamation's use of 'the sayd happy Vnion' is the historical fact of 'the uniting of the English and Scottish crowns in 1603' (*OED n.*[2] 3.b.): what historians term the union of the crowns or the Jacobean union. But other meanings are at play: for instance, one concept of 'union' invoked in this proclamation is '[g]eneral agreement or concord between different people, nations, institutions, etc.; absence of dissension, discord, or difference in opinion or doctrine' (*OED n.*[2] 2.a.). This notion of union as concord is evident in the title of a panegyric written by the Protestant countryman of the King, John Gordon – *A Panegyrique of Congratulation for the Concord of the Realmes of Great Britaine in Vnitie of Religion, and vnder one King* – as well as in the panegyric's opening lines: 'the concord & vnion of the people, & nations ouer whom God hath made you King, is the accomplishment and perfection of all the precedent benefites which his diuine bountie hath bestowed vppon the people vnder your most happie gouernment'.[9] This particular meaning of union as concord is apt given that, as both the title and the opening lines of the royal proclamation make clear, the immediate context is the historically and contemporaneously troublesome Borders, an area also referred to at the time as 'the Scottish and English pale'.[10] The proclamation's invocation of union as 'general agreement or concord' or 'absence of dissension' is made in the face of 'the slaughters, spoyles, robberies, and other enormities ... so frequent and common vpon the Borders of these Realmes'. Anglo-Scottish Borders violence threatens concord and unity just as it threatens the creation of 'one Realme and Kingdome'; moreover, it serves to remind the proclamation's intended audience of the precise thing that James wishes away: the existence of a border that divides the two nations. One other meaning, a crucial one, is also at play here, although more on the level of desire: '[t]he action or an act of uniting several territories into a single state, kingdom, or political entity, usually with one central legislature; the state or fact of being so united' (*OED n.*² 3.a.). The various meanings of 'union' in the proclamation include the dynastic union of the English and Scottish crowns in the body of one monarch, union as concord as well as an anticipatory rhetoric of political and cultural union. If the proclamation's reference to 'Subjects of both the Realmes' registers the political reality of James's dual monarchy, it also gestures towards a political fantasy: namely, the desire for a political and cultural union between the two kingdoms – 'the Subiects of one Kingdome ... as one people, brethren and members of one body' – in short, British subjects of a united Kingdom of Britain.

Although the royal proclamation of 19 May 1603 is generally regarded as James's 'first public statement' on union, his best-selling *Basilikon Doron* is another seminal text wherein James broaches union.[11] Completed in manuscript form in 1598, and written in Middle Scots, published in Scotland in 1599, now in English (although to a select readership; the king's printer, Robert Waldegrave, printed just seven copies), *Basilikon Doron* was made available to London book buyers by 28 March 1603; it went through eight editions in the spring of 1603 alone (a Welsh translation appeared in 1604). Written as an instruction manual to a very young Prince Henry, *Basilikon Doron* offered English readers access to James's earliest thoughts on union precisely because James envisions that his eldest son and heir will inherit not only Scotland's throne but also England's. In the prefatory 'To the Reader', added to the 1603 publication, James addresses his readership as 'the people of this whole Ile'; 'this whole Ile' is also what Prince Henry stands to inherit 'according to Gods right & [his] lineall discent'.[12] In fact, throughout this work James reiterates his desire that his son will inherit the crowns of Scotland and England (although he is careful to avoid naming 'England'): 'I hope yee shall be King of moe countries than this'; 'if God prouide you with more countries then this'; '[a]nd in case it please God to prouide you to all these three Kingdomes'; '[a]nd since my trust is, that God hath ordayned you for moe Kingdomes then this'.[13] Among the plethora of advice that the Scottish monarch proffers to the young prince is the following, which details how best to effect some kind of union between England and Scotland:

letting it be brought on with time, and at leasure: specially by so mixing through alliance and daily conuersation, the inhabitants of euery Kingdome with other, as may with time make them to growe and weld all in one: Which may easily be done betwixt these two nations, being both but one Ile of *Britaine*, and alreadie ioyned in vnitie of Religion, and language.[14]

The word 'union' is absent from the main text, but a gloss on the passage cited above reads '[t]he fruitfull effects of the vnion'.[15] *Basilikon Doron*, therefore, provided James's English subjects, including his panegyrists, with some of his earliest public pronouncements on union. Jenny Wormald has argued that 'the political issue which concerned him most when he succeeded to the English throne was not divine right monarchy at all, but union'.[16] James's panegyrists, as we shall see, had concerns of their own, concerns that no doubt emerged from their reading of and critical engagement with their new monarch's own writings on monarchical power as well as union.

'This Brittaine hope, *Iames* our vndoubted king'

Issued and reissued as a quarto in the spring of 1603, Michael Drayton's *To the Maiestie of King James: A Gratulatorie Poem* ranks among the earliest English poems printed in response to James's accession.[17] As indicated by its title, Drayton's 'gratulatorie' poem compliments and congratulates Elizabeth's successor, although any reference to the deceased queen is strikingly absent from the poem. Literary historians agree that Drayton, like Daniel, offered his poem of praise in expectation of some form of royal favour or patronage. 'From every indication, Drayton at first hoped for both national and personal advancement under James I. He published his first tribute to the King in the final sonnet of the 1600 *Idea*, hailing James as "Of Kings a Poet and of Poets King".'[18] To dismiss Drayton's 'gratulatorie' poem as an instance of sycophancy, however, risks foreclosing fruitful avenues of study. *To the Maiestie of King James* is a key yet underappreciated text within the *oeuvre* of an author who occupies an important place in literary history and whose interest in the subject of Britain spans a lengthy Elizabethan and Jacobean (indeed Caroline) writing career.

Like the majority of Jacobean succession texts, *To the Maiestie of King James* celebrates a peaceful regnal transition. Relief manifests itself at the outset of Drayton's poem, as does an acknowledgement of the violent power struggles that often attend the death of a monarch, especially a childless one:

> A Counsailes wisdome, and their graue fore-sight,
> Lends me this luster, and resplendent light:
> Whose well-prepared pollicie, and care,
> For theyr indoubted Soueraigne so prepare,
> Other vaine titles strongly to withstand,
> Plac'd in the bosome of a peacefull Land:
> That blacke destruction which now many a day,
> Had fix'd her sterne eye for a violent pray,
> Frustrate by their great prouidence and power,
> Her very nerues is ready to deuoure,
> And euen for griefe downe sincking in a swound
> Beats her snak'd head against the verdant ground.[19]

The smooth regnal transition from Elizabeth to James has thwarted any threat of a competition for England's crown. Elizabethan literature of the 1590s – Shakespeare's history plays, Daniel's epic poem on the Wars of the Roses and, indeed, Drayton's *Mortimeriados* – is at once fascinated and haunted by the civil wars unleashed by competition for the throne, so it comes as no surprise that James's accession is hailed for preserving 'a peacefull Land'. Of particular interest here is the representation of England's Privy Council, the political body whose 'wisdome', 'fore-sight', 'well-prepared pollicie' and 'great prouidence and power' secured a peaceful regnal transition. Drayton, to be sure, represents James as the legitimate successor to Elizabeth: as we shall see, at the poem's centre is an account of James's Tudor/Stewart lineage that legitimates his claim to England's throne. However, the opening lines are remarkable for the emphasis they place on conciliar election: that is, the representation of the Privy Council as kingmakers.[20] In a rather bold move – bold because it foregrounds the political acumen and agency of England's Privy Council – James is figured as an 'indoubted Soueraigne' selected by England's councillors.[21] Whilst committed to praising James, Drayton, like so many authors of succession literature, was not overcome by the euphoria of the occasion. Far from a regnocentric poem, *To the Maiestie of King James* immediately seeks to place limits on a monarch who, in *The Trve Lawe of Free Monarchies*, heralded his absolutist political theories.[22]

The centrepiece of Drayton's gratulatory poem is an account of James's 'true descent'.[23] This account of James's lineage draws upon the conventional *topoi* for invention of *laus*, or praise.[24] A major *topos* of praise is *genus*, or praise through descent. Divided into *gens* (race), *patria* (native land), *maiores* (ancestors), and *patres* (parents), the rhetorical *topos genus* foregrounds the importance lineage played in fashioning the subject of praise. The tracing of a royal lineage clearly performs crucial ideological work. One of the earliest royal proclamations published after Queen Elizabeth's death presents James as 'by Law, by Lineall succession, and vndoubted Right' Elizabeth's successor.[25] Legitimating James's claim to the English throne here is his Tudor lineage: his grandmother, Margaret Tudor, was the daughter of Henry VII and sister of Henry VIII. Perhaps what is most striking in this account of James's genealogy is the fact that his mother, Mary, who had been imprisoned and, eventually, executed in England, is never mentioned; in fact, James's Scottish descent is overlooked. Drayton's account of James's descent differs from the royal proclamation not just in its genealogical fullness but also its emphasis on 'the old Brittons':

> Which now in order let me first dispose,
> And tell the vnion of the blessed Rose,
> That to thy Grandsire *Henry* I may bring thee,
> (From whom I after to thy birth may sing thee.)
> That *Tudors* blood did worthily prefer,
> From the great Queene that beautious Dowager,
> Whose sonne braue *Richmond* from the Brittons set,
> Graft in the stock of Princely *Sommerset*,
> The third faire Sien, the sweet Roseat plant,
> Sprong from the Roote of the Lancastrian *Gant*,
> Which had seauenth *Henry*, that of royall blood
> By his deere Mother, is the Red-rose bud,
> As theyr great *Merlin* propheci'd before
> Should the old Brittons regalty restore,
> Which *Henry* raigning by th'vsurpers death,
> Maried the Princesse faire *Elizabeth*
> Fourth *Edwards* daughter, whose predest'nate bed
> Did thus conioyne the White-rose, and the Red:
> These Roseall branches as I thus entwyne,
> In curious trayles embelishing thy lyne,
> To thy blest Cradell let me bring thee on,
> Rightly deriu'd from thy great Grandsires throne.[26]

Drayton's rehearsal of James's lineage – the reissue of the 1603 quarto includes an engraved genealogy – is significant for two reasons: echoing the royal proclamation, it presents England's new, peace-loving king as the product of the conjoining of the white and red rose, thereby emphasising concord; it also renders England's Scottish monarch as one of their own, for James is '[o]f Henries line by Father, and by Mother'.[27] Like Drayton, Bacon would later comment on the fact that James was 'descended of the same Margaret by both father and mother', adding 'so that by a rare event in the pedigree of Kings, it seemed as if the Divine Providence, to extinguish and take away all note of a stranger, had doubled upon his person, within the circle of one age, the royal blood of England by both parents'.[28] 'The transition from Elizabeth to James was also the transition', Curtis Perry writes, 'from a Tudor to a Stuart'.[29] Although Drayton traces James's Scottish lineage and names Mary ('the Scotch Queene'), he hails James not as a Stewart but rather as a Tudor.[30] By foregrounding James's Tudor roots Drayton heralds England's new king as, if not a king of Britain, a British king. Rather than anglicising James in the manner of the royal proclamation, Drayton renders him British. Whilst the first reference to 'Brittons' in the passage above is likely a reference to the Welsh, the second reference is clearly to the ancient Britons. *To the Maiestie of King James* invokes not only 'old Brittons' but also the word 'Britainne' when it labels James '[t]his Brittaine hope'.[31] What exactly does it mean to herald James as '[t]his Brittaine hope'? Is Drayton heralding James's 'hopefull raigne' as the hope of Britain or as the hope of the British or Britons? In *The Trve Lawe*, James traces his Scottish rule back to a system of hereditary monarchy established by 'our first King *Fergus*', but Drayton's account of James's 'true descent' makes no reference to Scotland's first king.[32] In Drayton's account of James's descent there is no room for Fergus, who is displaced in favour of the myths that were more familiar to and frequently employed by Drayton and his fellow English writers: namely, those of the legendary British king Arthur, who 'came to be seen as a hero of a composite people, uniting Britons, Saxons and Normans' (but also vanquisher of the Picts and Scots), as well as Brutus, the eponymous founder of Britain.[33] For the English, Roger Mason notes, 'it was easier and much more satisfying to identify the new British king with Brutus, Arthur and Constantine than to greet him as the lineal descendant of Fergus Mac Ferchard'.[34] An ancient Trojan, British or Roman lineage was much more palatable than James's actual Gaelic one.

Some authors were more forthcoming about the British regality that James would restore. Writing in 1604, the Welsh George Owen Harry's enthusiastic genealogy of James heralded England's new monarch as

> IAMES the sixt, King of Scots, and the first of that name, King of England after the Conquest, but the second King of Brittayne, (which Iland hauing suffred many diuisions, as first, the whole Ile deuided into England, Scotland, and Wales; then England deuided into seuen Kingdomes; then Wales deuided into three partes, betweene the three sonnes of *Rodri* the great), beganne his raigne ouer this Land the foure and twentyeth day of March, *Anno* 1602, bringing with him Vnity, Peace, and Profite to all these Realmes, by vniting and knitting together all the scattered members of the Brittish Monarchy, vnder the gouernment of him, as one sent of GOD, to fulfill his diuine predestinate will, reuealed to KADWALADER, as our ancient histories doe testify, fifteene hundred yeeres past, that the time should come, that the Heires descended of his loynes, should bee restored agayne to Kingdome of BRITTAYNE, which was partly performed in King HENRY the seuenth; but now wholly fulfilled in his Maiesties owne person.[35]

Drayton is not averse to 'our ancient histories', but his response to James's accession is more pragmatic. The following lines, which echo (or are in turn echoed in) much of the succession literature of 1603, herald the strength of Britain's newly united kingdoms as well as a subjected Ireland:

> From *Cornwall* now past *Calidons* proude strength,
> The Empire beares eight hundred miles in length:
> Halfe which in bredth her bosome forth doth lay
> From the faire *German* to'th *Vergiuian* sea:
> Thy Realme of *Ireland*, a most fertile Land,
> Brought in subiection to thy glorious hand,
> And all the Iles theyr chalkie tops aduance
> To the sunne setting from the coast of Fraunce.[36]

Among the words employed by Drayton to designate the political space over which James rules are nation, kingdom and realm. As the passage above attests, Drayton also invokes '[t]he Empire'. Does 'Empire' signify James's expanding sovereignty within the context of a multinational British empire, one that may or may not include the 'Realme' of Ireland? Or does Drayton's use of '[t]he Empire', as opposed to 'Thy Empire', point to a particular nation as laying claim to this island-empire? Certainly Drayton's inclusive geography marks a stark contrast to that of *King Richard the Second*'s very Elizabethan-sounding John of Gaunt, whose figuring of England as an island 'bound in with the triumphant sea' (TLN 702) obscures Scotland and Wales. Drayton's poem serves as a prime example of the way in which the accession of a Scottish king to the English throne caused many of James's subjects to reimagine their place – culturally, geographically, historically, politically – within a larger British geopolitical framework. We could contrast, for example, the inclusive Jacobean geopolitics of *To the Maiestie of King James* with Drayton's earlier, Elizabethan imaginings of Britain and its inhabitants. In a poem published in 1596, Drayton, Gaunt-like, describes William the Conqueror, who failed to conquer Scotland, as 'Conqueror of this Ile'.[37] In the same poem he lists the troops of Robert, Duke of Normandy as consisting of not fellow Britons but '[t]he Redshanck'd Orcads', '[t]he light-foote Irish', '[t]h'ranck-ryding Scot' and '[t]he English Archer'.[38] In a later, Jacobean reworking of this passage, Drayton tones down his language, offering a much more inclusive British force under Robert:

> To his victorious ensigne comee from farre,
> Th'in Iled Red-shanks toucht with no remorse,
> The light-foote Irish, that with darts do warre,
> The Scot so much delighting in his horse,
> The English Archers of a Lions force,
>   The valiant Norman most his troupes among
>   With the braue Britton wonderfully strong.[39]

In another of his Elizabethan poems, Drayton writes of 'the Gardants of the Brittish pales,/Defending England, and preseruing Wales'.[40] It seems that for Drayton, like many of his contemporaries, Wales was very much the preserve of Britishness. Camden, for instance, says of the ancient Britons 'although the Romanes, Saxons and Normans have subdued them and triumphed over them, yet hitherto have they preserved their old name and originall language'.[41] In Drayton's 'Owen Tudor to Queen Katherine', the Welsh Owen Tudor speaks of '[o]ur Brittaine necks'; and the poet says of Wales 'since great *Brutus* first arriu'd, haue stood/The onely remnant of the Troyan blood'.[42] In his annotations to this poem, Drayton adds '[t]he Welchmen be those ancient Brittaines, which when the Picks, Danes, and Saxons inuaded heere, were first driuen into those parts, where they haue kept theyr language euer since the first, without commixtion with any other language'.[43] If James is '[t]his Brittaine hope', then perhaps he is in the sense that he is the hope of 'Brittaines' – that is, the fulfilment of Merlin's prophecy that a monarch will emerge to reunite Britain – rather than the self-styled 'King of Great Britainne' that he would declare himself by royal proclamation on 20 October 1604.[44]

To the Maiestie of King James congratulates James not only on his accession to the throne of England but also for the reunification of England and Scotland that the union of the crowns has effected:

> Two famous Kingdoms seperate thus long,
> Within one Iland, and that speake one tongue,
> Since *Brute* first raign'd (if men of *Brute* alow)
> Neuer before vnited vntill now,
> What power, nor war could do, nor time expected,
> Thy blessed birth hath happily effected.[45]

If Drayton had read *Basilikon Doron*, then he would have known that James favoured some form of union between England and Scotland. How does Drayton respond to the fact that James was now ruler of not only Scottish but also English subjects? Is Drayton's poem in any way committed to the kind of union (political, cultural) that James favoured and that would be vociferously debated in Parliament in the coming years? As is the case with much of the Jacobean succession literature, Drayton's poem foregrounds Anglo-Scottish sameness, in particular linguistic proximity. The kingdoms of England and Scotland are 'vnited' geographically, linguistically and through the personal, dynastic union brought about by James. Whilst Drayton's evocation of the Brutus myth ostensibly sustains a vision of a reunited Britain, the placement of '(if men of *Brute* alow)' within parentheses seems to highlight rather than downplay the poet's disbelief. Drayton was not the sole author of succession literature to invoke the Brutus myth with a hint of scepticism, as Henry Chettle's *Englands Mourning Garment* reveals: '[b]eginne with *Brute*, (if that of *Brute* be true)/As I'le not doubt, but giue old Bards their due'.[46] As Drayton's and Chettle's poems reveal, accompanying the euphoria captured in the English poems that greeted James is an invocation of a myth that most English writers viewed as highly suspect.[47] Writers such as Chettle and Drayton nevertheless invoke the Brutus myth in 1603 precisely because it is a cultural discourse that allows them to celebrate King James VI and I and to come to grips with the novelty of a three-nation island that finds itself under the rule of a single monarch. Britain is a subject that Drayton returns to again and again throughout his career, but after 1603 he does so under a composite monarch of an entire island. Nine years later, Drayton would be heralding a Tudor/Stewart reunification of Britain, yet again drawing upon the Brutus myth: '[b]y whom three seuer'd Realmes in one shall firmlie stand,/ As *Britain*-founding *Brute* first Monarchiz'd the Land'.[48]

In the lines that immediately follow the reference to Brutus, Drayton's 'gratulatorie' poem calls upon England's new sovereign to bring about a British revival:

> O now reuiue that noble Brittaines name,
> From which at first our ancient honors came,
> Which with both nations fitly doth agree
> That Scotch and English without difference be,
> And in that place wher feuds were wont to spring
> Let vs light Iigs, and ioyfull Pæans sing.[49]

It could be argued that these lines anticipate the 19 May proclamation's call for 'one people, brethren and members of one body'. But just as the poem desires such a revival, or invention, it posits distinct 'Scotch' and 'English' identities. Not unlike other early Jacobean panegyrics, Drayton's 'gratulatorie' poem struggles to articulate coherently a sense of cultural or national union. The poem even reminds its readers of past (and present) Anglo-Scottish violence: 'that place wher feuds were wont to spring' refers to the ever-troublesome Borders. Even the line 'O now reuiue that noble Brittaines name' is far from straightforward. The poem's most recent editors offer '[o]h now revive that noble Britain's name';[50] but given the reference to Brutus four lines earlier, 'that noble [Briton's] name' is plausible and less invested in Britain.

Just under a year after the publication of *To the Maiestie of King James*, Drayton found himself singing a very different 'ioyfull Pæan': namely, *A pæan trivmphall Composed for the Societie of the Goldsmiths of London: congratulating his Highnes magnificent entring the Citie. To the Maiestie of the King*. Entered into the Stationers' Register on 20 March 1604, *A pæan trivmphall* says very little about King James; it celebrates instead the City of London's civic culture. Crucially, this pageant contains not one reference to 'Britain'. England and London in particular receive all the attention: 'England yeelds to goodly London this,/That she her chiefe and soueraine Citie is'.[51] If, as Richard Dutton argues, civic pageants played a crucial role in 'early modern negotiations of national, civic, and personal identity', then Drayton's first and only contribution to Jacobean civic pageantry signals a conspicuous resistance to a British identity.[52] In the same year, Drayton, in *The Owle*'s prefatory 'To the Reader', writes of 'vndertaking then in the generall joye of the Kingdome, and my zeale to his Highnesse, to write his Majesties descent in a Poeme gratulatorie'.[53] This, of course, is a reference to Drayton's *Gratulatorie Poem*. But rather than praising England's new monarch, Drayton, just one year into James's English reign, was, the story goes, now a staunch critic. Many literary historians agree that *The Owle* is one of the most trenchant critiques of James and his court from the early Jacobean period. Jean Brink notes that Drayton 'never wrote for the Jacobean court and addressed no verse to James after 20 March 1604'; moreover, '[t]he first editions of *To his Majestie* ... and *A paean triumphall* (1604) were also the last'. Drayton, Brink adds, 'never reprinted either of these tributes to James in later collections of his poetry'.[54] Although Drayton did retain his encomiastic sonnet 'To the high and mighty Prince, Iames, King of Scots', first published in 1600, in subsequent editions of his poems, he, significantly, left the title of the poem unaltered.

Drayton returns to the topic of his failure to secure James's patronage in a 1627 elegy written to George Sandys:

> It was my hap before all other men
> To suffer shipwrack by my forward pen:
> When King JAMES entred; at which ioyfull time
> I taught his title to this Ile in rime:
> And to my part did all the Muses win,
> With high-pitch *Pæans* to applaud him in:
> When cowardise had tyed vp every tongue,
> And all stood silent, yet for him I sung.[55]

After 1603 Drayton may have no longer 'sung' for James, but he did continue to reflect deeply on 'this Ile', especially under the patronage of Prince Henry. In his 1606 'To the Virginian voyage' Drayton follows a reference to '[y]ou braue Heroyque mynds/ Worthy your Countries name' with '*Britans* you stay too long'.[56] To what extent does Drayton view his country as Britain and his countrymen as 'Britans'? Nicholas Geffe's *The perfect vse of silk-wormes* (1607) includes a telling commendatory poem from Drayton. Whereas Geffe purports to discourse on the benefits of silk worms to 'England', Drayton's commendatory poem names the home of 'our people' as 'the Brittish soyle'.[57] In the ode that follows 'To the Virginian voyage' – 'To my frinds the Camber-britans and theyr harp' – the title heralds Drayton's association with and admiration of the Welsh, but the poem celebrates England's famous victory over the French at Agincourt. The poem concludes with a rather nostalgic nationalist pronouncement:

> O when shall Englishmen
> with such acts fill a pen?
> O[r] *England* breed agen
> such a king *Harry*?[58]

On one hand, these lines voice a desire for a militant English king in the mould of King Henry V; on the other hand, they offer a trenchant critique of King James and his pacifist policies. Moreover, they can be read as celebrating 'such a king *Harry*' in the form of James's eldest son. Indeed, in his *Pæan trivmphall* written just a couple of years earlier, Drayton had nominated 'the fair Prince' as a future King Henry V:

> Where might be seene in his fresh blooming hopes,
> *Henry* the fifth leading his warlike troupes,
> When the proud French fell on that conquered land.[59]

If 'To my frinds the Camber-britans and theyr harp' concludes with an assertion of Englishness that appears to be directed at James and his pacifist policies, the poem's title and its allusion to the Scottish prince (and future Prince of Wales) renders it a much more complex reflection on 'Englishmen' and '*England*' than traditional accounts of a disgruntled Jacobean Drayton afford. Early Jacobean opposition to James did not necessarily take the form of English chauvinism. Writers such as Drayton participated in communicating oppositional strategies by reinscribing and reworking the inherited fictions of Britain and Britishness.

Writing in 1603, Henry Chettle makes reference to Drayton's in-progress '*Poly-Albion*'.[60] Five years earlier, Francis Meres wrote 'so *Michael Drayton* is now in penning in English verse a Poem called *Polu-olbion* Geographical and Hydrographicall of all the forests, woods, mountaines, fountaines, riuers, lakes, flouds, bathes and springs that be in England'.[61] What we now know is that just as Drayton was celebrating 'faire England' as 'our natiue Ile' he was simultaneously at work on an epic poem, begun during Elizabeth's reign, that took not only England but also Wales as its subject matter, and this poem ranks among the greatest reflections on 'Olbion' in the Jacobean period.[62] Given the poem's theme – the history and geography of England and Wales – it would make sense for Drayton to dedicate it to James just as John Speed dedicated his *Theatre of the Empire of Great Britaine* (1612) to the king. The title page of the 1612 edition presents the reader with an allegorical representation of 'Albion' or 'Great Britaine'; however, the two editions of *Poly-Olbion* that appeared in 1612 and 1622 were dedicated to Prince Henry (1612) and Prince Charles (1622). In his prefatory 'To the Generall Reader', Drayton responds to those who might criticise him for 'publish[ing] only this part of it' by stating 'many times I had determined with my selfe, to haue left it off, and haue neglected my papers sometimes two yeeres together, finding the times since his Maiesties happy comming in, to fall so heauily vpon my distressed fortunes, after my zealous soule had labored so long in that, which with the general happinesse of the kingdom, seem'd not then impossible somewhat also to haue aduanced me'.[63] Unlike Speed's *Theatre*, Drayton's epic did not incorporate Scotland, leading Andrew Hadfield to label *Poly-Olbion* 'a text that conspicuously failed to represent the multiple kingdoms governed by James'.[64] Drayton may or may not have intended to include a third section of his epic dedicated to Scotland.[65] What we do know is that Drayton had close ties with Scottish poets, especially William Alexander, David Murray and William Drummond of Hawthornden, two of whom he names in his 1627 elegy written to Henry Reynolds.[66] A major impact of James's accession, then, was the emergence of poetic circles and knowledge communities that crossed borders, and Drayton, so long viewed as a bitter Elizabethan in a Jacobean age, is a prime example of an English poet whose intellectual network included fellow Scottish and Welsh subjects. We are accustomed to viewing *Poly-Olbion* as a text that in its pronouncements and silences reveals antagonism toward King James.[67] Drayton's masterpiece of bardic patriotism also offers us a prime example of the ways in which James's subjects produced alternative imaginings of Britain in the early seventeenth century.

'Shake hands with Vnion, O thou mightie State'

The Renaissance, James Garrison notes, 'found a serious purpose behind panegyric: instruction of the monarch'.[68] Drayton's *To the Maiestie of King James* does not hesitate to use the medium of print to counsel England's new monarch: '[b]ut from thy Court', Drayton writes at the close of his poem, echoing James's advice to his son in *Basilikon Doron*, 'banish quite/The foole, the Pandar, and the Parasite'.[69] Whilst these lines may seem forward and impolitic, such instruction was integral to early modern encomiastic verse. Francis Bacon's essay 'Of Praise' sheds valuable light on the seriousness of purpose underpinning praise. 'Some praises', Bacon acknowledges, 'proceeds meerely of flattery'; '[s]ome praises', he adds, 'come of good wishes and respects, which is a forme due in ciuility to *Kings* and great persons, *Laudando praecipere*; when by telling men what they are, they represent to them, what they should bee'.[70] Drayton's praise of England's new monarch is grounded in a sober commitment to the social role of the poet as advisor, a commitment shared, we shall see, by Ben Jonson and, especially, Samuel Daniel. More so than any other poem on James's accession, the multiple copies of Daniel's 1603 *Panegyrike* temper encomium with a strong resistance to constitutional innovation. Consider, for example, the title pages of the two folio editions of Daniel's *Panegyrike*: both copy the title page used for Daniel's 1601/2 *Works*, which included Queen Elizabeth's crest, crown and motto, *semper eadem*. One of the ways in which Daniel's *A Panegyrike Congratvlatorie to The Kings Maiestie* eases fears of the arrival of a foreign monarch, therefore, is by framing James's accession in the political symbolism of England's former monarch. Moreover, as is the case in much of the succession literature, James is Tudor through and through: '[t]hus hath the hundreth yeare brought backe againe/The sacred bloud lent to adorne the North'.[71] Daniel's poem eases fears of James's accession by figuring it not as the arrival of a foreign king but as a homecoming.

'This mighty worke of vnion'   69

In many ways Daniel's lengthy *Panegyrike* is the least occasional text produced in celebration of James's accession. According to John Pitcher, 'immediately before and after the accession of King James [Daniel] was meditating deeply on the social and intellectual roots of law, rebellion, monarchy and civil war'.[72] As evidenced by the multiple editions of his epic poem on the Wars of the Roses, Daniel was particularly preoccupied with civil war, so it is little surprise that he hails James's peaceful accession as a second union modelled upon the union of the houses of Lancaster and York. Nevertheless, Daniel's seventy-three-stanza *Panegyrike* seizes upon the opportunity afforded by the moment of regnal transition to offer serious reflection on monarch–subject relations, reflection informed if not determined by James's foreignness as well as the publication of James's *Basilikon Doron* and *The Trve Lawe of Free Monarchies*. James's rule was guaranteed to bring about some sort of political change, for he was now, as Daniel describes him in 1606, '*Brittaines* mightie Monarch'.[73] More so than any other panegyric poem of 1603, Daniel's both fears and cautions against change in the form of alterations to the state and to its fundamental and immemorial laws. Although Daniel informs James that he will find in his English subjects '[a] people tractable, obsequious,/Apt to be fashion'd by thy glorious hand',[74] the panegyrist is far from tractable. Consider, for example, the following lines, less lofty praise than stern advice:

> Thou wilt dispose, change, forme, accommodate
> Thy kingdome, people, rule, and all effect,
> Without the least convulsion of the State.[75]

Semper eadem indeed. Of particular interest here is Daniel's use of the word 'State', which appears in singular and plural form with an upper case 'S' seventeen times in the first print version of the poem.[76] The historian D. R. Woolf notes that whilst traveling in France Samuel Daniel was introduced to the works of the French absolutist Jean Bodin, whose *Six livres de la république* was housed in the young King James VI's library.[77] It is important to recall, however, that Bodin placed ample emphasis on the law of the land: 'the first and chiefe law of all Commonweales, is this, SALVS POPVLI SVPREMA LEX ESTO'.[78] According to Woolf, Daniel's use of the word 'State' to signify 'the sovereign association of prince and people under the law' is especially indebted to Bodin, who, for all his absolutism, championed a state 'fast knit together by an

Aristocratique and Popular kind of gouernment'.[79] In a verse epistle published with the *Panegyrike* to Thomas Egerton, then England's lord keeper and soon to be lord chancellor, Daniel writes 'this is that great blessing of this land,/That both the Prince and people vse one Barre'.[80] The following lines from Daniel's *Panegyrike* reveal a shift from advising to admonishing England's new monarch, and in doing so they anticipate the inflexibility that would come to dominate English, especially Parliamentary, responses to Anglo-Scottish union in subsequent years:

> We shall continue one, and be the same
> In Law, in Iustice, Magistrate, and forme,
> Thou wilt not touch the fundamentall frame
> Of this Estate thy Ancestors did forme,
> But with a reuerence of their glorious fame
> Seeke onely the corruptions to reforme,
> Knowing that course is best to be obseru'de
> Whereby a State hath longest beene preseru'd.[81]

Consistent with succession literature of 1603, Daniel celebrates James's peaceful accession and the concord it has brought about, but his *Panegyrike* reveals a more cautious, even reformist, approach to England's new 'imperiall Prince'. Daniel's '[w]e' does not have the ring of inclusivity to it, for it seems to designate James's new English subjects only. When Daniel hails James as 'King of this great Nation' – the only occurrence of the singular 'Nation' – the use of the deictic directs the compliment to the English nation rather than the king.[82] Just as the poem clearly welcomes James, it, paradoxically, evinces resistance to any change that his rule may bring to a nation 'populous,/Stout, valiant, powrefull, both by Sea and Land'.[83] When Daniel speaks of 'this Empire of the North', the sense is that, like Wales, Scotland has been or will be incorporated into England.[84]

Daniel's *Panegyrike*, his first Jacobean poem, shares with Drayton's 'gratulatorie' poem a celebration of 'Vnion', as is evident in the following lines from the 1603 folio, the first print version of the poem:

> And now she is, and now in peace therefore
> Shake hands with Vnion, O thou mightie State,
> Now thou art all great *Brittaine*, and no more,
> No Scot, no English now, nor no debate:

No Borders but the Ocean, and the Shore,
No wall of *Adrian* serues to separate
Our mutuall loue, nor our obedience,
All subjects now to one imperiall Prince.[85]

Given the invocation of 'Vnion', the heralding of 'great *Brittaine*', the apparent erasure of English and Scottish identities as well as national borders – reinforced by the poet's use of anaphora – it is not surprising that the these lines (indeed the entire poem) have been read as celebratory of union.[86] In his influential essay 'The Stuarts and their style', S. T. Bindoff cites this stanza as evidence of the enthusiastic English reception to James's accession, and a host of historians and literary historians have followed suit, resulting in impoverished readings of Daniel's complex *Panegyrike*. More importantly, such readings have also resulted in a limited and limiting picture of the texts printed in England in the wake of James's accession. Daniel's poem, I want to argue, evinces the rigidity and insularity of English national consciousness in this period, an insularity present in Daniel's multiple editions of his epic poem on England's civil wars, where the narrator pleads with Neptune to '[k]eepe vs meere English'.[87] It is tempting to read Daniel's '[n]o Scot, no English now' as a profound, inclusive reimagining of Anglo-Scottish or British national and cultural identities. But perhaps these lines reflect less an instance of profound reflection than the occasional nature of this poem. 'Many of the poets who celebrated James's accession or lauded him in the first years of his reign', Philip Schwyzer argues, 'were keen to associate the new monarch with the triumph of British nationalism'.[88] The invocation of 'great *Brittaine*' certainly marks a peculiarly Jacobean rewriting of Daniel's earlier Elizabethan representation of Great Britain (or is it England?) as 'faire *Albion*, glory of the North'.[89] Absent from Daniel's poem, however, is any pronouncement of a common British identity, the logical response, one would think, to '[n]o Scot, no English now'. The 'State' (or, as he terms it in an earlier version of the poem, 'Ile')[90] is now 'great Brittaine', but where are the signs of British subjects?[91]

Daniel's complex poem registers a fundamental contradiction: it contributes to a body of work that welcomed England's new monarch, but it does so from an ideological position that anticipates the political and legislative resistance, especially in relation to any possible union between England and Scotland, that James would face from English MPs. Although Daniel's *Panegyrike* never gives voice to anti-Scottish sentiments, it boldly cautions the monarch not to alter the political body of which he is now head. Resistance to change would emerge in the ensuing years as a central issue in Parliamentary union debates and in manuscript tracts and treatises. Consider, for example, this following passage from Henry Spelman's 'Of the Union'. Spelman, a member of the lower house and a founding member of the Society of Antiquaries, vociferously rejects any alteration of the name of his native land: 'if the honorable name of England be buried in the resurrection of Albion or Britannia, we shall change the goulden beames of the sonne for a cloudy day, and drownde the glory of a nation triumphant through all the worlde to restore the memory of an obscure and barberous people'.[92] Not surprisingly, Spelman refrained from publishing his manuscript treatise, even, the evidence suggests, in scribal form. The single holograph in the British Library, which is without any prefatory or dedicatory material, suggests a very limited audience for Spelman's text.[93]

If we know little about Spelman's readers, what do we know about Daniel's readers? To whom was Daniel's poem addressed? I have been discussing this poem as it if was addressed to the king, which, obviously, it was; however, James was not the poem's only intended reader. Critical discussions of this poem often posit a close and closed writer–reader relationship between Daniel and his new monarch. In his study of 'panegyric negotiations' in early Jacobean culture, Curtis Perry details the ways in which Daniel's first Jacobean poem maintains his public role as 'Elizabethan poet-advisor'.[94] As we will see, material evidence in the form of a manuscript version of the poem exists to support Perry's reading, although he does not discuss the manuscript version. Other material evidence invites consideration of how Daniel's status as 'Elizabethan poet-advisor' was negotiated not only through the medium of verse but also through the publication and transmission of his printed poems.

Daniel's *Panegyrike* was entered in the Stationers' Register on 30 May 1603.[95] But this date does not mark the poem's first appearance. Earlier in the year – on 23 April (St George's Day) to be exact – a handwritten version of Daniel's *Panegyrike* was 'deliuered' to England's new monarch. The occasion was James's stay at Burley on the Hill in Rutland, the home of John and Anne Harington of Exton, whilst the king was progressing south from Edinburgh to

London, and the enabling force was Daniel's connection to the Haringtons' daughter, Lucy Harington, countess of Bedford, one of the leading patrons in the period. The poem that was 'deliuered' to James exists in the form of an undated fifty-eight-stanza holograph fair copy in the British Library.[96] John Pitcher describes the manuscript and the circumstances of its delivery as follows:

> Daniel has transcribed and signed the poem in his small but elegant italic hand. Given the manuscript's provenance, and what we can learn from the printed texts of the *Panegyrike* (that it was 'deliuered to the Kings most excellent maiesty at *Burleigh Harrington*'), it seems reasonable to suppose that Daniel himself presented this particular manuscript to the king on 23 April.[97]

Pitcher goes on to ask what exactly 'deliuer' means in this context: in other words, did the poet hand over the handwritten poem to James, or does 'deliuer' signal the poet's reading of the poem in James's presence? Noting that the 'first recorded use of the noun "panegyric" in the English language occurs in the title of Samuel Daniel's poem on the Stuart succession', Garrison suggests the 'title indicates that Daniel not only conceived of his poem as a verse oration, but also that he actually read the poem directly to the king'.[98] Whether or not Daniel read his manuscript poem in James's presence, it is likely, given the manuscript's fair italic hand, its red ink borders and its formal title page, that this was meant as a presentation copy for the monarch: 'delivered' meaning, therefore, 'presented to'. Daniel's handwritten 'Panegyrick' made its way into the Royal Library, which seems to confirm that such a transaction transpired. The social life of Daniel's poem does not, however, end here, for Daniel's 'occasional' text 'acquired a second life', to borrow Malcolm Smuts' phrase, 'through the relatively durable medium of print'.[99] If the circumstances of the presentation of Daniel's manuscript 'Panegyrick' appear to reinforce a top-down model of cultural production, then the publication and reception history of Daniel's printed *Panegyrike* reveals the poem's entrance into a broader political community.

Daniel's manuscript 'Panegyrick' was followed by the publication of lengthier print versions of the poem in the form of two folio issues (STC 6258, 6259) and an octavo edition (STC 6260). There is ample evidence that the folio issues of the *Panegyrike* also served as presentation copies. 'The Folio', Pitcher tells us, 'is printed on high quality paper, with the same typeface, ornaments, and layout as Daniel's collected edition, the 1601/2 *Works* Folio'. 'The *Panegyricke* Folio', he continues, 'was evidently designed to be bound separately, but also to complement and be added to copies of this *Works* edition, for either sale or presentation'.[100] Of the two folio copies in the British Library, for example, one is bound with other poems of praise to James in Latin and in French; the other is included as an addition to the 1602 *Works of Samuel Daniel*. Included among the prime recipients of presentation copies of the *Panegyrike* were 'members of the Jacobean court elite',[101] including those to whom Daniel wrote verse letters that were published under the title *Certaine Epistles* and accompanied all three print versions of the *Panegyrike* (these epistles do not accompany the manuscript version of the poem). The recipients of *Certaine Epistles*, the product of a burgeoning print culture and a nascent Republic of Letters, were Sir Thomas Egerton, Lord Henry Howard, Lucy, countess of Bedford, Margaret, countess of Cumberland, Lady Anne Clifford and Henry Wriothesley, earl of Southampton. In fact, two folio copies housed in the Huntington Library – one of the first issue and one of the reissue – clearly belonged to the Egerton household (they were part of what would come to be known as the Bridgewater Library) and one – bound in the original limp vellum with gilt tooling on the covers – was most likely a presentation copy to Thomas Egerton, who was one of Daniel's patrons and who in July of 1603 was appointed lord chancellor, subsequently playing a seminal role in union matters, especially in relation to Calvin's Case, which decided that those born in Scotland after James's accession to the English throne were no longer regarded as aliens in England.[102] The presence of these two books (and there are more of Daniel's books – eleven in all – in the Bridgewater collection) suggests that Daniel's 'panegyric negotiations' were restricted neither to manuscript culture nor to a single monarch. That Daniel exploited print culture to foster social and literary circles and networks is well documented. What I wish to suggest is that the publication and transmission of *A Panegyrike Congratvlatorie to The Kings Maiestie. Also certaine Epistles* is not only a culturally and socially significant act but also a politically significant act, one that reflects a less monarchical, more republican or quasi-republican conception of the state in which authority is invested not solely in the monarch but dispersed among the nation's cultural and political elite – in this particular instance select recipients of *Certaine Epistles*. That is to say, we could point to *A Panegyrike Congratvlatorie to The Kings Maiestie*. *Also certaine Epistles* as a product of and productive of if not a 'monarchical republic' then certainly a 'mixed polity', for in both content and form this publication proposes political mediation between England's royalty, aristocracy and, especially, Parliament.[103]

In thinking through Daniel's politics in the wake of James's accession, it is important not to overlook the author's *Defence of Ryme*, which first appeared in the second-issue folio of the *Panegyrike* (STC 6259). Daniel's reflections on the English language – a topic that he returns to again and again – intersect nicely with his ideological position in the *Panegyrike*; moreover, they buttress Pitcher's point that the poet was reflecting on such topics as law and monarchy around the time of the succession.[104] In the *Defence*'s concluding paragraph, Daniel writes

> we always bewray our selues to be both vnkinde, and vnnaturall to our owne natiue language, in disguising or forging strange or vnvsuall wordes, as if it were to make our verse seeme an other kind of speech out of the course of our vsuall practice, displacing our wordes, or inuesting new, onely vpon a singularitie: when our owne accustomed phrase, set in the due place, would expresse vs more familiarly and to better delight, than all this idle affectation of antiquitie, or noueltie can euer doe. And I can not but wonder at the strange presumption of some men that dare to audaciously aduenture to introduce any whatsoeuer forraine wordes, be they neuer so strange; and of themselues as it were, without a Parliament, without any consent, or allowance, establish them as Free-denizens in our language.[105]

This passage, with its ideologically charged invocation of 'Parliament', establishes fruitful connections between two seemingly disparate texts. When, in his *Panegyrike*, the residually Elizabethan Daniel chastises those who follow a 'greedy course of eminencie, gaine,/And private hopes' for 'weighing not what is done/For the Republicke', the temptation to invest the word 'Republicke' with real political significance is hard to resist.[106] Daniel's use of the word 'republic' is not infrequent; he uses it, for instance, when discussing the good of the country in his 1609 edition of *The Civile Wares*, and the following stanza in this same poem uses 'Common-wealth' and 'State' as synonyms for 'Republique'.[107] That William Camden describes Daniel in his *Remaines of a Greater Worke, Concerning Britaine* as 'our *Lucan*' lends further weight to such a reading.[108] 'Lucan's epic', David Quint reminds us, 'had depicted the struggle of an aristocratic patriciate to preserve its control over the Roman republic against the threat of imperial monarchy'.[109] Lucan's *Pharsalia* was a text well known to Daniel, as is evident in his various editions of, to cite its 1595 title, *The First Fowre Bookes of the ciuile warres betweene the two houses of Lancaster and Yorke*, which, like so many Elizabethan texts on the Wars of the Roses, is concerned as much with the future succession as past broils.[110] Of course, Daniel, like Drayton, like Jonson, was no staunch opponent of monarchy. Among his patrons after 1603 were Prince Henry and Queen Anne, whom he addresses as 'ANNE of Denmark, Queene of England, Scotland, France and Ireland' in contradistinction to other writers, like Aemilia Lanyer, who address Anne as 'great Britaines Queene'.[111] Moreover, his 1601/2 *Works* includes a dedicatory poem to Queen Elizabeth. But even as Daniel proclaims James 'King of our Loue', he does so in politically charged language:

> God makes thee King of our estates, but we
> Do make thee King of our affection,
> King of our Loue, a passion borne most free,
> And most vn-subiect to dominion.[112]

Daniel's representations of English subjects as 'most vn-subiect' grants them a citizen-like status under their new and foreign king, a king who had consolidated his Scottish rule at the expense of Scotland's nobles as well as the Presbyterian church. In his *A Souldiers Wish vnto His Soveraigne Lord King Iames*, Pricket sounds a note that resonates through much of the Jacobean succession literature: '[t]hy kingdome England: knowes thy true dissent,/ And yealds it selfe vnto thy gouernment'.[113] Daniel's complex and contradictory *Panegyrike* strikes a much less accommodating note. Indeed, in its invocation of 'dominion' the poem bears witness to an uneasy relation between England's national sovereignty and the sovereign authority of England's new monarch.

Is there a danger, however, of investing Daniel's use of 'Republicke' with too much political force? Have I, as other historians and literary historians have been accused of doing, 'found "republican" strands' in Daniel's poem 'that are simply not there'?[114] James himself uses the term 'Republicke' when advising his son on good kings and tyrants, and the duties of monarchs.[115] In fact, it could be argued that much of Daniel's advice for James echoes James's own advice for his son in *Basilikon Doron*, where James presents the 'good king' as committed to 'the well-fare and peace of his people' and as 'subjecting his owne priuate affections and appetites to the weale and standing of his subjects'.[116] If Daniel's description of the English and Scots as '[a]ll subjects now to one imperiall Prince' contains within it a hint of caution (here 'imperiall' could mean 'majestic' as well as 'imperious'),[117] then it is no surprise that James's imperial status is tempered by a republican-inflected rhetoric of judgement and justice:

> Religion comes with thee, peace, righteousnes,
> Iudgement and Iustice, which more glorious are
> Then all thy Kingdomes, and arte more by this,
> Then Lord and Sou'raigne, more than Emperor.[118]

This is a far cry from Robert Pont's account of 'the now moderne state of Brittish affayres': 'this our Great Brittaine, Ireland and the adjoying Brittish isles', writes James's countryman Pont in a treatise published in Edinburgh and London in 1604, 'are now reduced to the monarchicall obedience of one emperor'.[119] 'Daniel's version of national sovereignty', Woolf argues, emphasises 'the supremacy of the law rather than the independence and freedom of the monarch', a sentiment reflected in the passage above.[120] What Daniel says of King Henry VII – '[h]ee, of a priuate man, became a King' – has in common with Shakespeare's history plays a demystification of sacred monarchy.[121] Consider, for example, Warwick's line spoken in *The third Part of Henry the Sixt*: '[f]or who liu'd King, but I could digge his Graue?' (TLN 2822). In 1609 Daniel puts the historical figure of Warwick to similar political use:

> But greatest in renowne doth *Warwicke* sit;
> That braue King-maker *Warwicke*; so farre growne,
> In grace with Fortune, that he gouerns it,
> And Monarchs makes; and, made, againe puts downe.[122]

If Daniel had read *Basilikon Doron*, most likely he did, then he would have been aware of James's proprietary references to 'this whole Ile'.[123] In fact, in the manuscript version of the 'Panegyrick', Daniel seems to follow James in his use of 'Ile': '[s]hake handes w^t Vnion, ô thou mightie Ile'.[124] But in all three of the 1603 printed versions of the *Panegyrike* 'Ile' is replaced by Daniel's preferred 'State'.

If the folio versions of Daniel's *Panegyrike* bear all the signs of an author, a Stationer (Simon Waterson), a printer (Valentine Simmes) and a bookseller (Edward Blount) creating a commodity for an elite readership, the 1603 octavo reveals an author, working closely with printers and booksellers, placing his book within a more public sphere.[125] The obvious sign is the physical nature of the book: the smaller octavo would have been much cheaper than the folio, especially given the quality paper used for the first-issue folio. However, Daniel's octavo *Panegyrike* was not just physically different from the folio; its content underwent revision. One significant variant in particular stands out. In the octavo, the first six lines of stanza 30, cited earlier from the folio, have been revised. In the octavo, these lines now read:

> We shall continue and remaine all one,
> In Law, in Iustice, and in Magestrate,
> Thou wilt not alter the foundation
> Thy Ancestors haue laide of this Estate,
> Nor greeue thy Land with innouation,
> Nor take from vs more then thou will collate.[126]

Whereas the folio text admonishes James to keep his hands off 'the fundamentall frame', the octavo strikes a more commanding note. Contrasting the manuscript and printed versions of Daniel's panegyric, Richard McCabe argues that the latter 'offers a rather different authorial persona, that of a mature counsellor to kings'.[127] As the lines above attest, the folio and octavo editions of the poem also offer a different authorial persona in the form of a hardening of opposition to change. This is another instance of Daniel's anticipation of the English antiquarian and Parliamentarian resistance that James's rule would face, especially from common-law lawyers. 'This land', Edward Coke would write, 'the Brittayns first then the Romaynes then the Brittayns agayne, then the Saxons then the Danes and then the Normans [inhabited] yet none of them had ever changed or extinguished the fundamental lawes of England ... The king cannot change the natural lawe of a nation. This foundation is a firme foundation.'[128] In Coke's words and in Daniel's lines the monarch is very much subject to an English constitution. '*Law*', Daniel remarks in his epistle to Egerton, is 'the most combining band,/The strongest fasting of societie ... whereon all this frame of men doth stand'.[129] Of particular interest in the octavo's revised stanza is Daniel's insertion of 'vs'. To whom does 'vs' refer? The reference is surely to James's English subjects, the same subjects who were the intended readers of the octavo poem. Whereas Daniel's monumental 1601/2 *Works* was dedicated '[t]o her sacred Maiestie', his Jacobean books were increasingly offered to new and wider reading publics.[130] Daniel's 1607 octavo *Certaine Small Workes*, his fourth collected edition, contains, for the first time, an intimate poem, 'To the Reader', addressed to a general readership. If the 1603 octavo *Panegyrike* continues Daniel's self-presentation as a national poet, it also evinces Daniel's awareness of and attention to a national readership, specifically an English readership.[131]

Given that Daniel worked closely with stationers, printers and booksellers to prepare his books for patrons as well as for the public, we can take meaning not only from the content of his poems but also from the material form in which they appeared. Like the folio *Panegyrike*, the octavo can be found bound with other publications: the Bridgewater copy in the Huntington Library, for example, is bound with the 1605 octavo *Certaine Small Poems Lately Printed: with the Tragedie of Philotas*.[132] According to Pitcher, the octavo version of the *Panegyrike* was printed to be bound with the 1605 *Certaine Small Poems*. Compared to Daniel's epic poem on the Wars of the Roses, the *Panegyrike* is a 'small' poem, so its inclusion in *Certaine Small Poems* is not out of place. But I want to suggest that the smaller octavo form complements the textually altered poem. That is, the *Panegyrike*'s physical reduction from folio to octavo anticipates English hostility towards what would increasingly be viewed as James's absolutism, especially in relation to Anglo-Scottish union debate. Interestingly, the *Panegyrike* was not included in the 1607 and 1611 octavo editions of *Certaine Small Workes*. The last appearance that the *Panegyrike* made in print during Daniel's lifetime was in 1607 when it was bound with his play *The Tragedy of Philotas*, which literary historians have traditionally read as a play sympathetic to Robert Devereux, second earl of Essex, but which one critic has recently read as addressing 'anxieties surrounding the accession of James I'.[133] Perhaps it is not insignificant that the poem's final publication in Daniel's lifetime is in the form of a tiny duodecimo.

Daniel's manipulation of print as a cultural agent calls attention to the crucial role that the Jacobean book played in reaching and shaping wider political communities. The various readerships for Daniel's printed verse – presentation copies for elite culture; cheaper copies for public consumption – point to the ways in which the publication of his verse opened up questions of the novelty of James's composite monarchy as well as the king's 'nuanced, moderated absolutism', to borrow a phrase from Johann Sommerville, to a socially heterogeneous readership.[134] Centred on the life of the author, as much as on a stable text, traditional readings of Daniel's *Panegyrike* represent the poem as the product of a poet who sought but was unsuccessful in his attempts to secure James's favour. Informed by the history of the book, a revisionary reading attentive to the production and transmission of Daniel's *Panegyrike* sheds valuable light on the author's contestatory cultural politics as well as his deft handling of panegyric.

'[A] new Bodie of people'

Conventional literary history presents Daniel and Drayton as unsuccessfully handling the transition from Elizabeth's reign to James's, especially in terms of securing royal patronage. Drayton, despite his efforts (including, apparently, a trip to Scotland in 1599), found little favour from James, but he went on to write 'Britain' like no other Jacobean. What about Daniel? Thanks to Lucy, countess of Bedford, Daniel was recommended to produce one of the first Stuart masques, *The Vision of the 12. Goddesses*. Performed on 8 January 1604 at Hampton Court, and patronised by the queen, Daniel's masque inaugurated the Stewart tradition in England of the Christmas masque. In a dedicatory epistle to the countess, the author describes 'the intent and scope of the project' as 'to present the figure of those blessings, with the wish of their encrease and continuance, which this mightie kingdome now enioyes by the benefit of his most gratious Maiestie, by whom we haue this glory of peace, with the accession of so great state & power'.[135] Of particular interest is the masque's representation of the goddesses Concordia and Tethys. '*Concordia*', Daniel informs the countess, appears 'in a partie coloured Mantle of Crimson and White (the colours of *England* and *Scotland* ioyned) imbrodered with siluer, hands in hand, with a dressing likewise of partie coloured Roses, a Branch whereof in a wreath or knot she presented'.[136] If elements of the masque invite a celebration of Anglo-Scottish union, Daniel does not pursue them fully. Concordia's obvious nod to the newly unified kingdoms of England and Scotland does not result in any mention of Britain. Is Daniel's 'this mightie kingdome' a reference to James's British isle or England? Daniel's 'Tethis' or 'Tethes' lends herself to pro-union iconography; however, she is presented not as Great Britain's but rather as '*Albions* fairest loue'.[137] Is Albion synonymous with Britain or, more likely, a conscious refusal to use a geopolitical term favoured by James? Daniel's masques are often placed alongside Jonson's especially to highlight the latter's ability to mythologise James's political vision of a united Britain and to be rewarded for doing so. 'Daniel's hostility to pomp and ceremony', David Norbrook has suggested, 'was too deep-rooted to make him a very effective court poet'.[138] Daniel's investment in England and Englishness, I would add, did not lend itself to James's vision of Great Britain.[139] Performed at the Banqueting Hall in Whitehall on 6 January 1605, Jonson's *The Masque of Blackness* initially uses '*Albion*' to refer to the island but then opts for 'Britania': '[t]his isle hath now recovered for her name ... that great name *Britania*'.[140] The success of Jonson's 1605 masque established Daniel's court rival as the Jacobean period's premier producer of the court masque.

Daniel, however, would continue to be part of the Jacobean court's masque culture: he received Queen Anne's patronage, and he would write for and dedicate works to Prince Henry.[141] As Perry remarks, 'the relative autonomy of Queen Anne and Prince Henry, each with a separate court, created new sources of patronage and protection on the margins of James's court'.[142] Such patronage and protection also allowed Daniel to imagine the state otherwise than Jonson, who would produce altogether different masques for James in the early years of his English reign, ones much more in line with James's commitment to Anglo-Scottish union. Daniel's contribution to Prince Henry's investiture as Prince of Wales in June 1610, a masque titled *Tethys Festival: Or the Qveenes Wake*, supplies a fine example of the sharp contrast between Daniel's and Jonson's court masques. Set upon the 'sweete, and pleasant Shores of Cambria', Daniel's masque celebrates the Prince in the guise of Meliades and the Queen in the guise of Tethys, wife of Neptune.[143] The masque's action begins from a place of historical significance: Milford Haven, '[t]he happy Port of Vnion, which gaue way/To that great Heros *HENRY*, and his fleete'.[144] Just as he did in his *Panegyrike* in relation to James, Daniel, by invoking Henry VII, is highlighting Prince Henry's Tudor roots. Although Meliades/Henry is 'Prince of th'Iles (the hope and the delight,/Of all the Northerne Nations)', little or nothing by way of British iconography is mapped on to the Prince.[145] Indeed, the word 'Britain' is absent from the masque. In an epistle to Prince Henry written around the same time as *Tethys Festival*, Daniel again makes no mention of the Prince's nationality.[146] At the same time that Daniel was writing to and for Prince Henry he was at work on *The First Part of the Historie of England*, which also tells the story of 'the generall dissolution of ... Britayne':

> Wherefore, wee are now heere to beginne with a new Bodie of people, with a new State, and gouernment of this Land, which retained nothing of the former, nor held other memory but that, of the dissolution thereof: where scarce a Citie, Dwelling, Riuer, Hill, or Mountayne, but changed names. Britayne it selfe was now no more Britayne, but New Saxonie, and shortly after either of the Angles (the greatest people of the inuadors) or of Hengist, called Engist-Land, or England. The distance, made by the rage of warre, lay so wide betweene the conquering and conquered people, that nothing either of lawes, rites and customes, came to passe ouer vnto vs from the Britaynes: nor had our Ancestors any thing from them, but their countrie: which they first diuided into eight kingdomes: all which, continued to the last extermination of the Britaynes.[147]

Camden, too, writes that 'the Angles, Englishmen or Saxons, by Gods wonderfull providence were transplanted hither', labelling them a 'warlike, stiff, stout and vigorous nation' who by 'subduing the Britans, and driving them into the mountanous Westerne parts, made themselves by a most compleate conquest'.[148] Camden is less explicit or celebratory regarding the dissolution of Britain than Daniel, whose historiography is informed by a burgeoning antiquarian interest in England's Saxon roots, especially exemplified in the Antwerp-based Counter-Reformation polemicist Richard Verstegan's *A Restitvtion of Decayed Intellengence* (1605). Just as Verstegan, English-born of Dutch stock, was rejecting '*Eneas* and his Troyans' as 'the supposed anceters of king *Brute* and his Britans' in favour of the Saxons, 'the true originall of Englishmen', Daniel's 'New Saxonie' posits a national genealogy at odds with the fictions of a British past that were emerging from the Jacobean court.[149]

Daniel's masques, too, are at odds with those, in particular Jonson's, that place Britain and Britishness at the core of their panegyric; his dig at Jonson in his 'Preface to the Reader' in *Tethys Festival* signals not just authorial rivalry but also rival visions of nationhood.[150] If Daniel the historian, as the title of his historiographical tract implies, invested little energy in resurrecting the concept of Britain, the same is true, especially in comparison to Drayton and Jonson, of Daniel the poet.

'Triumph, my *Britaine*'

It has been suggested that 'for most, certainly in England, 1603 was less an opportunity to be taken and more a threat against which the body politic needed protection'.[151] For Ben Jonson, 1603 marked an opportunity to be seized, and seize it he did. Jonson, who failed to attract Queen Elizabeth's attention, enjoyed ample success, however uneven, under James; in fact, literary history remembers Jonson as James's unofficial poet laureate. An anonymously published song on the subject of Elizabeth's death and James's accession commands

> You Poets all braue *Shakspeare,*
> *Iohnson, Greene,*
> Bestow your time to write
> for Englands Queene.
> Lament, lament, &c.
>
> Returne your songs and Sonnets
> And your sayes:
> To set foorth sweete
> *Elizabeths* praise.
> Lament, lament, &c.[152]

As far as we know, Jonson produced no elegaic verse on the subject of Elizabeth's death. Writing in 1610, Bacon says of the last years of Elizabeth's reign 'a new court and a new reign were not by many unwelcome'; Jonson was one of those 'many'.[153] Unlike Daniel and Drayton, Jonson never published a poem in 1603 on James's accession or coronation. Jonson did, however, play his part in early Jacobean panegyric. His *A Particvlar Entertainment of the Qveene and Prince their Highnesse to Althorpe* probably marks Jonson's earliest encounter with England's new royals. The Althorp entertainment was published along with *B. Ion: His Part* of King Iames his Royall and Magnificent Entertainement through his Honorable Cittie of London as well as B. I. His Panegyre. On the happie entrance of IAMES our Soueraigne to his first high Session of Parliament in this his Kingdome the 19. of March. 1603 in a composite quarto of 1604.[154] The context for Jonson's private Althorp entertainment was Queen Anne and Prince Henry's stay at the Northamptonshire household of Sir Robert Spencer in late June 1603 as they progressed from Edinburgh to London. The context for Jonson's *Royall and Magnificent Entertainment* was the 15 March 1604 royal entry to the City of London, a formal welcoming of England's new monarch originally scheduled for 25 July 1603 (St James's Day) but postponed because of an outbreak of the plague. Very much a product of London's civic culture, not to mention its playwrights, the royal entry included seven triumphal arches stretching from Fenchurch Street to Temple Bar, the site of James's first entry into London in 1603. Jonson's *Panegyre* celebrates the King's ceremonious progress to Westminster Hall and his opening of Parliament four days later. Both Jonson and Dekker were chosen to write material to be delivered at as well as inscribed on the triumphal arches through which the royal procession would pass on its journey from the Tower to Westminster. That *B. Ion: His Part of King Iames his Royall and Magnificent Entertainement* was entered in the Stationers' Register on 19 March 1604 suggests a desire on Jonson's part to present himself ahead of the likes of not only Dekker but also Daniel and Drayton as the King's poet. It is not difficult to hear in Electra's '[t]his from that lowd, blest *Oracle*, I sing,/Who here, and first pronounc'd, thee *Brittaines* King' Jonson staking a claim as panegyrist to the new monarchy.[155] It has been suggested that 'an important function of these welcoming ceremonies was to invest James with the symbolism of the old Queen'.[156] The dominant image of the Soper Land End triumphal arch in Cheapside is that of James as phoenix.[157] Jonson's March 1604 festival texts, however, reveal little interest in connecting James with Elizabeth. Just a few weeks after the royal entry, the king and queen witnessed Jonson's *A Private Entertainment at Highgate*. 'A little more than a year after James's accession', Robert Evans writes, 'Jonson had begun to achieve the kind of official recognition that had eluded him under Elizabeth'.[158]

What enabled this 'official recognition'? Certainly one enabling force was the ties to the new monarchy provided by the circles of knowledge and patronage to which Jonson belonged. For example, as early as 1603 Esmé Stuart, Lord Aubigny, third duke of Lennox, who accompanied James from Edinburgh to London and who secured a place in James's royal bedchamber, took Jonson into his household.[159] Jonson, moreover, managed to please James almost immediately in a way that Daniel and Drayton never really did or desired to. In other words, Jonson's masques and poems on the themes of monarchy and union (political as well as matrimonial) and the subject of Britain intersected nicely with the king's public statements on these topics. To be sure, Jonson's early Jacobean work is heavily invested in Britain as well as Anglo-Scottish union. Literary historians usually point to a number of Jonson's masques as evidence of his participation in the production and dissemination of Britain and Britishness: *The Masque of Blackness*, *Hymenaei*, *The Masque of Beauty*, *The Irish Masque at Court*, for example. At the same time that Jonson was composing or thinking about composing his festive texts, he wrote his 'Ode ἀλληγορική [Allegorical]'. Jonson penned this dedicatory ode for his friend the Welshman Hugh Holland, fellow Catholic and former Westminster School pupil, and the one who most likely facilitated Jonson's connection with the Welsh MP and patron and poet John Salusbury. The ode is prefixed to Holland's *Pancharis*, which was entered in the Stationers' Register on 1 August 1603.[160] Holland's incomplete epic romance, very much a belated Elizabethan text, celebrates the Welsh origins of the Tudors, although its full title reveals the ways in which Tudor mythology could easily be refigured to address a Stewart king.[161] Jonson's ode traces the 'Coast to Coast' flight of a black swan, symbolising Holland, from London to Wales and then to Ireland, on to Scotland, returning, eventually, to London. Jonson inscribes a multi-island and multination imagining of Great Britain and Ireland and adjoining islands that not only is the product of a particular cultural moment but also works to circumscribe a British-Irish geopolitical entity put in place by James's accession to the English throne.[162] Although the swan's flight takes it initially to Wales, Jonson's native island's prime site of Britain and Britons, the poet's 'Ode' never invokes the word 'Britain'. Crucially, neither do the words 'England', 'Ireland', 'Scotland' and 'Wales' appear. The black swan's flight over and around Great Britain and Ireland commences and concludes on the Thames, but the circuitous route goes from the liminal space of Anglesey, back to mainland Wales, over to

Ireland, on to select Scottish Isles, returning to mainland Scotland and, finally, England. On his journey, the swan encounters 'Mône' (Mona, Anglesey), 'Cluid', (Clwyd, Denbighshire), 'Iërna main' (the Irish Sea), 'Eugenian dale' (Munster), '[t]he Hebrid Isles', 'Orcades' (Orkneys), 'vtmost Thule' (Shetlands?), 'Caledon' (Caledonia), 'Grampius mountaine', 'Loumond lake', 'Twedes blacke-springing fountaine', the rivers 'Tine', 'Humber', 'Owse' and 'Trent' before returning to the Thames.[163] These place names may come across as poetic, but they are also distinctly Celtic and Latinate, likely informed by Jonson's copy of Camden's 1600 Latin edition of *Britannia*. If this ode marks Jonson's first articulation of the archipelagic geopolitics of James's composite monarchy, then it reveals a reimagining of the polity to which Jonson belonged. That terms such as empire, kingdom, land, nation, realm and state are absent from the poem is striking, especially given their prominence in succession literature. It is precisely the absence or evacuation of these key nomenclatures and political terms that reveals Jonson's rejection and rewriting of dominant (Protestant) Elizabethan discourses of nationhood. Also, London's status as the beginning and end of the swan's coast-to-coast journey suggests just how vital a civic identity was to the proud Londoner, Jonson. If it is possible to dissociate the two identities, then it would not be an exaggeration to say Jonson's civic identity as a Londoner took precedence over his national identity as an Englishman.

As early as March 1604 Jonson begins to put in place a discourse on the 'GENTIVM. CONIVNCTARVM' (conjoined nations) of England and Scotland heretofore absent in his writings.[164] Jonson's account of a female 'MONARCHIA BRITANNICA' at the royal entry's opening arch at the Londinium (the Latin name for London) triumphal arch in Fenchurch Street draws heavily upon contemporary (Camden) and classical sources (Claudian, Virgil) on Britain:

> Shee was a woman richly attir'd in cloth of golde and tissue; a rich mantle; ouer her state twoo Crownes hanging, with pensile shieldes thorow them; the one lim'd with the particular Coate of *England*, the other of *Scotland*: on either side also a Crowne, with like Scutchions, and peculiar Coats of *France* & *Ireland*. In her hand she holdes a Scepter; on her head a fillet of gold, inter-wouen with Palme and Lawrel; her haire bound into foure seuerall points, descending from her Crownes; & in her lappe a little Globe, inscrib'd vpon

> ORBIS BRITANNICVS.
> And beneath, the word
> DIVISVS AB ORBE.
> To shew, that this Empire is a world diuided from the world, and alluding to that of * Clau.
> –Et nostro diducta Britannia mundo.
> And Virg.
> –Et penitus toto diuisos orbe Britannos.[165]

These lines may not reveal an original imagining of the British monarchy, but they do signal the commencement of Jonson's decidedly British (and decidedly classicist) political compliment of, severally and together, King James, Queen Anne and Prince Henry. We can appreciate Jonson's British iconography (as well as Jonson's royal favour) if we contrast it to how Dekker's Genius would have greeted the new monarchy in his Bishopsgate pageant. Readers of Dekker's *The Magnificent Entertainment* are informed that this device 'should haue serued at his Majesties first accesse to the Citie' (apparently a reference to James's May 1603 London entry), but, for whatever reason, it was not performed (in 1603 or 1604). Dekker still supplies the text, and these lines from the Genius's speech mark a stark contrast to Jonson's addresses to the new monarchy:

> This little world of men; this precious stone,
> That sets out *Europe*: this (the glasse alone,)
> Where the neate Sunne each Morne himselfe attires,
> And gildes it with his repercussiue fires.
> This Iewell of the Land; *Englands* right Eye.[166]

Whereas Jonson employs a British-themed discourse, Dekker reinscribes Elizabethan or Gauntean imaginings of England, evident not only in the use of anaphora but also in the obvious echoes of Gaunt's speech: '[t]his little world', 'this precious stone'. At the royal entry's sixth arch, produced by Dekker, Thomas Middleton's Zeale speaks of '[t]he populous Globe of this our *English* Ile'.[167] At Jonson's Londinium arch, King James (and Queen Anne and Prince Henry) would have encountered no instances of the use of England or English, but would have seen/heard numerous instances of Britain and British (in English, in Latin) and one of Britons.[168] In the pageant's remaining six arches, the word 'Britain' surfaces just twice – both instances occurring at the Cheapside arch.[169] One year later, in his *Masque of Blackness*, Jonson, unlike Dekker, at once alludes to and amends Gaunt's '[t]his blessed plot' when he writes 'this blest Isle/Hath wonne her ancient dignitie, and stile': 'this blest Isle' signifying not Richard II's (or Elizabeth I's) England but rather James's 'Britania'.[170]

At the Fleet Street arch, which Stephen Harrison terms 'The Device called *Cozmoz Neoz*, New World', Middleton's Zeale speech registers one of the pageant's three invocations of Brutus:

> And then so rich an *Empire*, whose faire brest
> Containes foure *Kingdomes* by your entrance blest,
> By *Brute* divided, but by you alone
> All are againe united, and made one.[171]

The two other occurrences are at the Soper Lane End arch and Jonson's Londinium arch. Jonson's invocation of Brutus as founder of Britain/London is, however, half-hearted. 'Rather then the Citie shuld want a Founder', he writes in a marginal note, 'we choose to folowe the receiu'd story of *Brute*, whether fabulous, or true'.[172] Jonson's naming of Brutus, however formulaic, has much in common with numerous writers, including Anthony Munday, who celebrated the new monarchy as well as union in the early years of James's English reign.[173] What distinguishes Jonson's discourse on the subject of Britain in the early years of James's English reign is its refusal to reinscribe received narratives of Brutus. According to Martin Butler, Jonson 'conspicuously ignored any reference to Queen Elizabeth, or to the English patriotic mythology which claimed Brute as the founding father of Britain and of the Tudors in particular, and which, by implying that the English were the senior partners, was so offensive to the Scots'.[174] Not surprisingly, Craig makes clear his aversion to the Brutus myth, describing Brutus's 'asserted division of Britain among his three sons, to the eldest of whom, Locrin, he gave superiority' as 'an error of judgment; for it is a woeful tale of disasters and civil wars'.[175] Jonson would, of course, come to occupy a, if not the, central place in the Jacobean cultural production and dissemination of British ideas and themes in his many court masques, which have been read as celebratory of a multinational Jacobean court. Scholarship on Jonson's masques, especially criticism attentive to the British contexts of the performances, has highlighted the contestatory strains embedded in them. Whilst acknowledging that 'the arrival of a Scottish king at

Whitehall necessitated the invention of an iconography to articulate the realm's changed identity', Butler argues eloquently for readings of Jacobean masques, including Jonson's, that view them not as propaganda vehicles but rather as 'a series of attempts to respond creatively to some novel opportunities and problems'.[176] I want to argue that Jonson's early Jacobean poetry – not only his *Panegyre* but also his Epigram V, 'On the Vnion' – invite readings attentive to Jonson's creative and pragmatic response to James's composite monarchy as well as a burgeoning British and Irish contact zone at the Jacobean court.[177]

A crucial contributing factor in the difference between Jonson's early Jacobean writings and Daniel's and Drayton's is their date of composition: whereas Daniel and Drayton published their panegyrics shortly after James's accession, Jonson's earliest 'panegyric negotiations' were published in 1604, just as James was 'striving to the utmost to secure the support of his Estates in both kingdoms for the perfecting of his project'.[178] 'On the Vnion' first appeared in print in Jonson's 1616 folio *The Workes of Beniamin Jonson*, whereafter Jonson received a royal pension, 'establishing him in fact if not in name as Britain's poet laureate'.[179] The editors of the Cambridge edition of Jonson's works posit 1603–04 as the date of composition.[180] At the opening of Parliament on 19 March 1604 King James delivered a speech that sought to legitimate in the eyes of his subjects his vision of a perfect union. In the speech, James compares the union of England and Scotland to a marriage: '[w]hat God hath conioyned then, let no man separate. I am the Husband, and all the whole Isle is my lawful Wife.'[181] James's speech was published shortly after its delivery, so Jonson would have had access to it; in fact, Jonson's 'On the Vnion' employs a similar marriage trope. Here is the poem as it appeared in Jonson's 1616 folio *Workes*:

> WHen was there contract better driuen by *Fate*?
> Or celebrated with more truth of state?
> The world the temple was, the priest a king,
> The spoused paire two realmes, the sea the ring.[182]

The general consensus among Jonson scholars is that this epigram was written shortly after and in response to James's speech. The poem has even been described by one of Jonson's biographers as a 'coda' to James's speech.[183] Perry's appraisal of this poem captures the dominant critical view: '"On the Union"', he writes, 'picks up a metaphor from James's first speech in parliament and nicely encapsulates it. This sort of propaganda is one thing a poet can do for his monarch.'[184] Perhaps a more productive way of approaching this poem, one that challenges an inflexible and reductive top-down model, is to consider Jonson's investment in the concept of Britain, even though the word 'Britain', as is the case in Jonson's 'Ode ἀλληγορική', is absent from this brief poem. Unlike Drayton's and Daniel's early Jacobean poems, Jonson turned to James's accession and the topic of union as an opportunity for the poet, who claimed Scottish ancestry, not to assert an entrenched sense of Englishness but rather to reimagine his place as a subject of Britain, just as a host of close associates to Jonson were also doing. Robert Cotton, a fellow Westminster School student, traced his lineage to Robert the Bruce, rechristening himself in 1603 Robert Bruce Cotton.[185] On the title page of the 1604 composite quarto Jonson, for the first time in print, omits the 'h' from his surname.[186] A new identity, not only authorial but also communal, is beginning to emerge.

That Jonson seized the opportunity of James's accession to reimagine his place as a subject to Britain's monarch comes across forcefully in his *Panegyre*, a poem that shares Daniel's and Drayton's emphasis on the poet's role as advisor to the prince but not their deep-seated English patriotism.[187] In the midst of a scene of public euphoria in Jonson's *Panegyre*, which Butler labels 'perhaps Jonson's most considerable political poem', Themis, Goddess of Justice, draws the king aside and 'to his mind suggests/How he may triumph in his subiects brests'.[188] Remembering the monarch's destination (Westminster Hall), Themis provides James with a brief history of English or, more accurately, Henrician government:

> She shewd him, who made wise, who honest Acts;
> Who both, who neither: all the cunning tracts,
> And thriuing statutes she could promptly note;
> The bloody, base, and barbarous she did quote;
> Where lawes were made to serue the Tyran' will;
> Where sleeping they could saue, and waking kill;
> Where Acts gaue Licence to impetuous lust
> To bury Churches, in forgotten dust,
> And with their ruines raise the Pandars Bowers:
> When, publique Iustice borrow'd all her Powers
> From priuate Chambers; that could then create
> Lawes, Iudges, Consellors, yea Prince, and State.[189]

These lines call attention to Jonson's confessional identity at the time of this poem's composition.[190] Surely Jonson, a Catholic convert, found the kind of national identity proclaimed by the likes of the Protestant Daniel and Drayton uncomfortable and unappealing.[191] When Daniel uses the words 'we' and 'us', the reference is to fellow English subjects, but to whom do Jonson's 'we' and 'us' refer when, in an early 1604 epigram to King James, he writes 'we haue now no cause/Left vs of feare'?[192] It may be no accident that the word 'England' never surfaces in the *Panegyre*. Englishness was by no means a stable and fully inclusive, monolithic identity in this period – one's gender, religion and/or social status could result in forms of exclusion. To what extent, then, were claims to a British identity in the early seventeenth century a response to these forms of exclusion? Given that the target of the lines cited above is Henry VIII and the destructive forces of the Reformation, Jonson is launching a remarkable attack on what many of his fellow English subjects regarded as an, if not the, foundational moment in the formation of the English 'state'. Not surprisingly, Jonson, unlike Drayton and Daniel, makes little effort to place James within the Tudor line; moreover, his reformist agenda contrasts sharply with the Protestant reformism of the other poets.

Drayton's and, even more so, Daniel's early Jacobean poems, we have seen, voice an anxiety over the changes that James's accession will or threaten to bring about: namely, promoting the power of the sovereign at the expense of the state. In his distinctly titled *Panegyre*, Jonson is less anxious about James's rule than he is about 'publique Iustice'. In other words, Jonson, of Scottish descent, who, in 1618, walked from London to Edinburgh 'to revisit his family's homeland', is much more accommodating to England's Scottish monarch and accepting of a potential alteration in nationhood.[193] Jonson's 1604 festive texts make no attempt to anglicise James; in fact, the focus is on 'his Maiesties seuerall pedigrees *Eng.* and *Scot*'.[194] The *Panegyre* concludes with the following acclamation from the people: '*let blest* Brittaine *aske (without your wrong)/Still to haue such a king, and this king long*'.[195] It is no simple task to fix the meaning of 'Brittaine' in this period. For a poet, a playwright, a member of the Society of Antiquaries or of Parliament (the two often overlapped), a Calvinist, or a Catholic, Britain could and did carry various cultural, devotional, historical and political meanings and significations. Jonson was writing at a moment when conflicting and competing meanings of Britain were in place. But what did Britain mean to Ben Jonson? Did it simply mean a land mass that was home to two kingdoms and three nations, or did it signify a united polity? Did Britain come to signify or hold the possibility of a more inclusive identity for Jonson than Englishness did? At Jonson's Londinium arch, the actor Edward Alleyn in the guise of 'Genivs' proclaimed

> Time, Fate, and Fortune haue at length conspir'd,
> To giue our Age the day so much desir'd.
> What all the minutes, houres, weekes, months, and yeares,
> That hang in file vpon these siluer haires
> Could not produce, beneath the Britaine stroke [rule],
> The Roman, Saxon, Dane, and Norman yoke,
> This point of Time hath done.[196]

In the printed text's margins, 'Britaine stroke' is glossed by Jonson as follows: '[a]s being the first, free, and naturall gouernment of this Iland, after it came to ciuilitie'.[197] A gloss on '[t]he Roman, Saxon, Dane, and Norman yoke', on the other hand, reads '[i]n respect they were all Conquests, and the obedience of the subiect more enforced'.[198] Jonson's '[t]his point of Time' does more than herald James's rule; it inscribes a cultural memory at odds with Daniel's privileging of Anglo-Saxon England. References a few lines later to 'the *Isle*', '[h]is [Prince Henry's] Countries' and 'this Land' contrasts his contemporaries' often Anglocentric use of these terms, given that Jonson's praise is directed to an isle-encompassing monarchy.[199] 'Vnder whose shade, may *Brittane* euer be' is how Jonson's Genius heralds Prince Henry.[200] In 1605, Jonson hailed William Parker, Baron Monteagle, who informed King James of the Gunpowder Plot, as 'sauer of my countrey'.[201] The Monteagle epigram refers three times to 'my country'. To which country is Jonson referring? The obvious answer is England, but might it be Britain? In Epigram XIV, 'To William Camden', Jonson salutes the learned and cosmopolitan antiquary, author of *Britannia* – a text that Jonson draws upon copiously in his *Royall and Magnificent Entertainment* – as well as *Remaines of a Greater Worke, Concerning Britaine* and his former schoolmaster at Westminster School as the one 'to whom my countrey owes/ The great renowne and name wherewith shee goes'.[202] Jonson's country, it seems, is Britain. In a poem prefixed to the First Folio of Shakespeare Jonson famously writes '[t]riumph, my *Britaine*'.[203] To what extent, then, does Jonson's 'On the Vnion' ideologically echo James's speech to Parliament? Warning against representing Jonson as an uncritical mouthpiece of royal policy, Norbrook argues that Jonson 'developed a knack of praising the king without compromising his own integrity by adapting James's favourite political metaphors and subtly varying them'.[204] Subtle yet signal differences exist between James's 1604 speech and Jonson's poem. In James's speech to Parliament, the king is the husband and the entire island is his wife. Thus, James's hold on the entire island is underwritten by intertwining monarchical and patriarchal ideologies. Jonson's poem borrows James's metaphor, but not as a simple act of cultural reproduction. Instead of presenting James as absolutely empowered husband, 'On the Vnion' refigures him as priest: '[t]he world the temple was, the priest a king,/The spoused paire two realmes, the sea the ring'. I would hesitate to say – in the manner of Helgerson's reading of Drayton's *Poly-Olbion* – that the land has displaced the king: Jonson's classically balanced lines do not afford such a reading.[205] This is not to say, however, that the priestly king's hold over the land has not been diminished. To suggest that the king's agency has been reduced to a participatory role would not be an overstatement. In this, Jonson's poem shares with Daniel's a critical engagement with the realities of Jacobean kingship, although with a significant difference: Jonson's response, at least in this instance, manifests an openness to political change that is strikingly absent from Daniel's poem.[206]

'The spoused pair two Nations'

Another significant difference distinguishes Daniel's *Panegyrike* and Jonson's 'On the Vnion'. Whereas print culture provides fertile ground for documenting the transmission of Daniel's poems, manuscript culture, or rather the intersection of print and manuscript cultures, is where we need to look to examine the rich social life of Jonson's 'On the Vnion'. Unlike Daniel's 'Panegyrick', no autograph copy of 'On the Vnion' exists; however, according to the *Catalogue of English Literary Manuscripts 1450–1700*, sixteen manuscript copies of the poem survive.[207] These multiple manuscript poems and their significant variants raise a number of questions about the composition and circulation of the poem. In his *Index to English Literary Manuscripts*, Peter Beal notes that '[t]here are numerous copies of Jonson's poems in miscellanies and other MS sources. Those texts often represent early versions which circulated in MS before being revised for publication.'[208] Although the extant manuscript copies of 'On the Vnion' are all post-1616 copies, most dating from the 1630s, we cannot discount the possibility that these copies represent engagement with earlier versions of the poem as it appeared in print in 1616. A few of the verse miscellanies can be connected to particular individuals, but determining who exactly participated in the transmission of Jonson's poem is not a simple task. Nor is it easy to determine how these readers came to possess the poem. Were they, for instance, readers of Jonson's poem as it appeared in his printed folio *Workes*, or did they come across a pre-publication copy of the poem through scribal transmission? If the latter, did 'On the Vnion' circulate through an open network or was it restricted to a select coterie? I offer these questions by way of an exploration of the surviving manuscript copies of 'On the Vnion'. Fortunately, material evidence in the form of transcribed copies of the poem supplies a sense of how readers of Jonson's poem participated in its transmission and, crucially, its revision.

Walter Ong's notion of 'participatory poetics' captures wonderfully the fluidity and vibrancy of the handwritten worlds of early modern Britain.[209] Evidence of participatory poetics in the extant manuscript copies of Jonson's 'On the Vnion' exists in the form of not only different headings – for example, 'Vppon the Vnion of Scotland & England', 'On the Vnion of great Britaine', 'Ben Johnson vppon kinge James his vnion of England and scotland' and even 'On the Vnion betweene Scotland and England by King James' – but also significant variants.[210] One handwritten poem housed in the British Library is titled 'In Vnionem Angliæ & Scotiæ', and the final line reads '[t]he spoused pair two Nations, the sea the ring' – a revision of the 1616 folio's '[t]he spoused paire two realmes'.[211] What is the significance of this scribe's substitution of 'Nations' for 'realmes'? It would not be inaccurate to suggest that 'Nations' privileges the people over the monarch. A coming together of 'realmes' constitutes a dynastic union; a coming together of people is an altogether different kind of union. The insertion of 'Nations', therefore, could be interpreted as supporting the idea of a perfect union: that is, a union not just of realms or kingdoms but also nations or people. It may be, as Butler argues, that the 'ideological premise of all Jonson's poetry is the centrality of the monarch to the state'.[212] By no means did those who transcribed Jonson's poems necessarily share the poet's politics. What they do share, however, is Jonson's serious reflection on state and identity formation in the period.

In one of the three copies that exists in the Bodleian Library, the second line, which in Jonson's 1616 folio is '[o]r celebrated with more truth of state?' reads '[o]r solemnized with more Royall state?'[213] Again, to make a precise pronouncement on these variants is difficult. The use of 'solemnized' rather than 'celebrated' makes sense given the poem's metaphor of marriage. But what about 'Royall state' in place of 'truth of state'? Might the scribe have chosen the adjective 'Royall' to expose the union as a self-interested and self-aggrandising monarchical project? Another scribe titles the poem 'On the Vnion betweene Scotland and England by King James', which, given the presence of 'by King James', points to dynastic union or the union of the crowns, but it can also be read as ascribing authorship to the king. Indeed, the epigram is followed by the ascription 'James Stuart K: of England'.[214] Given that Jonson's poem concerns the 'two realms' of England and Scotland, the reference here to James as king of England only is surprising. With little knowledge of the context of the production and dissemination of these manuscript poems, it is difficult to interpret them with any certainty. 'It is possible', Colin Burrow writes, 'that some at least of the MS variants are authorial, although miscellanies are often freer with short poems (which can be transcribed from memory)'.[215] In many instances of the extant handwritten copies of 'On the Vnion' we can only offer partial responses to Ong's fundamental question 'who is saying what to whom?'[216] From a cultural and historical perspective, however, these poems are invaluable documents, for they reveal reading and writing subjects engaged in dialogue on the subject of Britain, thinking through questions of dynastic and cultural union at a moment when various media impacted on the production, circulation and reception of new political ideas spawned by the composite monarchy of James Stewart. It has been suggested that James's 'union policy became one of the most unpopular of his reign, and was quietly shelved within a few years of his accession'.[217] The majority of James VI and I's subjects, however, continued throughout his dual monarchy, as Morrill argues, 'to recognise themselves as subjects of a British king, whilst also developing – in some but not all cases – new and varied senses of themselves as Britons'.[218] Daniel's reference in his *Panegyrike* to '[t]his mighty worke of vnion' was prescient, for it would be well over a hundred years before England and Scotland were to join in a constitutionally and politically incorporating union.[219]

Notes

1. According to the *OED*, the word 'panegyric' makes its English-language debut in the title of Daniel's 1603 *A Panegyrike Congratvlatorie to the Kings Maiestie*.
2. See Alastair Bellany, 'Writing the King's death: the case of James I', in Kewes and McRae (eds), *Stuart Succession Literature*, 37–59. As discussed in chapter 1, James's 1617 return to Edinburgh resulted in the publication of a number of panegyrics produced by his fellow countrymen, including William Drummond of Hawthornden, John Hay and David Hume of Godscroft.
3. On James's failure to effect more than dynastic union, Thomas Corns writes '[t]he "British" project remained largely an unrealized aspiration, though one frequently celebrated among writers looking to James for patronage and preferment': Thomas Corns, *A History of Seventeenth-Century English Literature* (Oxford: Blackwell, 2007), 34. For a sophisticated reading of panegyric within the context of James's English succession, see McCabe, 'Panegyric and its discontents'.
4. Russell, 'A Treatise of the Happie and Blissed Unioun', 85.
5. Of the numerous tracts and treatises on the Jacobean union listed in Galloway and Levack's appendix to *The Jacobean Union* only Bacon's *A Briefe Discovrse* was published before 1604.
6. Sandra Bell, '"No Scot, No English Now": literary and cultural responses to James VI and I's policies on union', *Renaissance Forum: An Electronic Journal of Early-Modern Literary and Historical Studies*, 7 (2004), para. 10. www.hull.ac.uk/renforum/v7/bell.htm. Accessed 12 May 2014.
7. Thomas Powell, *A Welch Bayte to spare Prouender* (London, 1603), D4^r.
8. England and Wales. Privy Council, *By the King forasmuch as the Kings Maiestie, in his princely disposition to iustice hauing euer a speciall care and regard to haue repressed the slaughters, spoyles, robberies and other enormities which were so frequent and common vpon the borders of these realmes* (London, 1603).
9. Gordon, *A Panegyrique of Congratulation*, B1^{r-v}.

10 Pont, 'Of the Union of Britayne', 21. According to Levack, 'the memory of bitter conflict that had taken place between the two states in the past, and continued tension in the Borderlands led Englishmen and Scots in 1603 to regard the members of the other nation as foreigners': Levack, *The Formation of the British State*, 180. For a fuller and richer account of these continuing Borders tensions in relation to the union, see Mark Netzloff, '"Counterfeit Egyptians" and imagined borders: Jonson's *The Gypsies Metamorphosed*', *English Literary History*, 68 (2001), 763–93.

11 Burgess, Wymer and Lawrence, 'Introduction', xiv. This proclamation, according to Paul Hughes and James Larkin, marks 'James's first formal statement in England on the Union': James F. Larkin and Paul L. Hughes (eds), *Stuart Royal Proclamations*. Volume I: *Royal Proclamations of King James I, 1603–1625* (Oxford: Oxford University Press, 1973), 18. In a later collection of royal proclamations this 1603 proclamation is retitled 'A Proclamation for the vniting of England and Scotland': see England and Wales. Sovereign, *A Booke of Proclamations, published since the beginning of his Maiesties most happy reigne ouer England, &c. Vntill this present Moneth of Febr. 3. anno Dom. 1609* (London, 1610).

12 James VI and I, *Basilikon Doron. Or His Maiesties instructions to his dearest sonne, Henry the prince* (London, 1603) (STC 14350), A8^r, E2^v.

13 *Ibid.*, E4^r, G3^r, H2^r, K8^v.

14 *Ibid.*, L1^r.

15 *Ibid.*, L1^r.

16 Jenny Wormald, 'James VI and I, *Basilikon Doron* and *The Trew Law of Free Monarchies*: the Scottish context and the English translation', in Linda Levy Peck (ed.), *The Mental World of the Jacobean Court* (Cambridge: Cambridge University Press, 1991), 53.

17 See STC 7231 (first state), STC 7231.2 (second state) and STC 7231.3 (another reissue). According to Bernard Newdigate, 'Drayton's "gratulatorie poem" *To the Majestie of King James* must have come hot from the press within a few days of [Elizabeth's] death': Newdigate, *Michael Drayton and His Circle* (Oxford: Basil Blackwell & Mott, 1961), 196. Perhaps the use of 'early' in the opening two lines of the poem – 'THE hopefull raigne of a most happy King,/Loe thus excites our early Muse to sing' (A3^r) – is in reference to the poem's hasty publication. Other succession literature texts borrow from Drayton's 'gratulatorie' poem: for instance, stanzas 5–8 of the anonymous *An excellent new ballad* (1603) echo, at times verbatim, *To the Majestie*'s account of James's lineage.

18 Richard F. Hardin, *Michael Drayton and the Passing of Elizabethan England* (Lawrence: The University of Kansas Press, 1973), 77. 'It is

possible', Anne Lake Prescott notes, 'that in 1599 Drayton visited Scotland: a resentful crane in *The Owle* who may speak for the poet mentions that it had gone in search of preferment "unto the happie North" and "there arriv'd, disgrace was all my gaine"': Anne Lake Prescott, 'Drayton, Michael', *ODNB*, https://doi.org/10.1093/ref:odnb/8042. Accessed 16 September 2015.

19 Michael Drayton, *To the Maiestie of King James: A Gratulatorie Poem* (London, 1603) (STC 7231), A3^r.

20 Here Drayton anticipates those select MPs in the 1614 English Parliament who 'dared to argue that James was in fact a king not only "by blood" but also by election "because in passing from Scotland to England he was called and to some extent chosen"': Doran and Kewes, 'Introduction', *Doubtful and Dangerous*, 12.

21 'Drayton's work', according to Andrew Hadfield, 'reveals him to be no straightforward lover of monarchs': Andrew Hadfield, 'Michael Drayton's brilliant career', *Proceedings of the British Academy*, 125 (2004), 144. Hadfield does not discuss *To the Maiestie of King James*; in fact, he mistakenly terms *The Owle* (1604) 'Drayton's first published poem in James's reign' (127). Might Drayton also be referring to Scotland's long history of elective monarchy before the advent of hereditary monarchy?

22 *The Trve Lawe of Free Monarchies. Or the Reciprock and mutuall dutie betwixt a free King, and his naturall Subiects* was entered into the Stationers' Register on 3 April 1603; of course, an anonymous copy was printed in Edinburgh in 1598. According to Jenny Wormald, 'the translation of James's Scottish writings into the English context ... contributed to, if they did not wholly create, an atmosphere of unease': Wormald, 'James VI and I, *Basilikon Doron* and *The Trew Law of Free Monarchies*', 48.

23 Drayton, *To the Maiestie of King James*, A4^v.

24 Much of my information on the *topoi* of praise comes from Thomas Cain's *Praise in 'The Faerie Queene'* (Lincoln: University of Nebraska Press, 1978).

25 England and Wales. Privy Council, *Forasmuch as it hath pleased almighty God*.

26 Drayton, *To the Maiestie of King James*, A4^v–B1^r. Drayton reiterates this prophecy in the Fifth Song of *Poly-Olbion*, but he does not name King James VI and I: see Drayton, *Poly-Olbion*, 76–7.

27 *Ibid.*, B1^v.

28 Bacon, *The Beginning of the History of Great Britain*, in Spedding et al., *The Works of Francis Bacon*, XI, 405.

29 Perry, *The Making of Jacobean Culture*, 1.

30 Drayton, *To the Maiestie of King James*, B1^v.

31 *Ibid.* McRae and West's edition of this poem supplies 'This Britain hope', accompanied by the following note: 'Drayton introduces the concept of a modern Britain as soon as he comes, in his historical narrative, to the birth of James VI and I': McRae and West (eds), *Literature of the Stuart Successions*, 43.
32 James VI and I, *Trve Lawe of Free Monarchies*, C2^v.
33 Hugh A. MacDougall, *Racial Myth in English History: Trojans, Teutons, and Anglo-Saxons* (Hanover, NH and London: University Press of New England, 1982), 13.
34 Mason, 'Scotching the Brut', 76. The Scottish historian John Monipennie, on the other hand, begins his chronology of Scottish kings, which ends with James VI, with King Fergus, who fashioned Scotland's warring tribes into a nation: see John Monipennie, *Certaine Matters Composed Together* (Edinburgh, 1594).
35 Harry, *Genealogy of the High and Mighty Monarch*, 39–40.
36 Drayton, *To the Maiestie of King James*, A4^{r-v}.
37 Michael Drayton, *The tragicall legend of Robert, Duke of Normandy, surnamed Short-thigh, eldest sonne to William Conqueror* (London, 1596), B4^r.
38 *Ibid.*, D7^r.
39 Michael Drayton, *Poems: by Michaell Draiton Esquire* (London, 1605), Ee7^v. In the 1619 version of this poem, the final line reads '[t]he *Camber-Britan*, hardy, big, and strong': Michael Drayton, *Poems: by Michael Drayton Esquire* (London, 1619), 330.
40 Michael Drayton, *Englands Heroicall Epistles* (London, 1597), 24.
41 Camden, *Britain*, 22. For some writers the preserve of Britishness was more expansive: one anonymous author writes of the 'Brittish of Walles and Cornewall': see 'The Diuine Providence in the misticall and reall union of England and Scotland both by nature and oth^{er} coherences w*i*th motives for reconcilinge such differences as may now seeme to hinder the same', British Library, Additional MS 38139, 42.
42 Drayton, *Englands Heroicall Epistles*, 41.
43 *Ibid.*, 43.
44 England and Wales. Privy Council, *By the King. As often as we call to minde the most ioyfull and iust recognition made by the whole body of our realme* (London, 1604).
45 Drayton, *To the Maiestie of King James*, B2^v.
46 Chettle, *Englands Mourning Garment*, F4^v.
47 Camden also rejects the Galfridian narrative of Great Britain's first inhabitants: '[a]nd verily this their beginning from Gomer and out of Gaule, seemeth more substantiall, ancient and true, than that from Brutus and Troie': Camden, *Britain*, 10–11. In his 'Ode 7', Drayton refers to London as 'greate *Brutes* first-builded towne'; however, the

invocation of Brutus serves poetic rather than historical purposes: see Michael Drayton, *Poemes Lyrick and Pastorall: Odes, Eglogs, the Man in the Moone* (London, 1606), C4^r. Of course, Brutus's arrival in Britain is central to *Poly-Olbion*; however, John Selden's sobering notes reveal the antiquarian's scepticism at the Brutus myth.

48 Michael Drayton, *Poly-Olbion*, 77.
49 Drayton, *To the Maiestie of King James*, B2^v.
50 McRae and West (eds), *Literature of the Stuart Successions*, 44.
51 Michael Drayton, *A pæan trivmphall Composed for the Societie of the Goldsmiths of London: congratulating his Highnes magnificent entring the Citie. To the Maiestie of the King* (London, 1604), B3^r.
52 Richard Dutton, *Jacobean Civic Pageants* (Edinburgh: Edinburgh University Press, 1996), 7.
53 Drayton, *The Owle*, A4^r.
54 Jean Brink, *Michael Drayton Revisited* (Boston, MA: Twayne, 1990), 14, 17–18. Curtis Perry writes of 'Drayton's increasingly oppositional politics': Perry, *The Making of Jacobean Culture*, 168.
55 Michael Drayton, *The battaile of Agincourt Fought by Henry the fift of that name* (London, 1627), Aa4^v.
56 Drayton, *Poemes Lyrick and Pastorall*, C4^v.
57 Nicholas Geffe, *The perfect vse of silk-wormes, and their benefit* (London, 1607), A1^r, A3^v.
58 Drayton, *Poemes Lyrick and Pastorall*, C7^v.
59 Drayton, *A pæan trivmphall*, A3^r, A3^v.
60 Chettle, *Englands Mourning Garment*, D2^r.
61 Francis Meres, *Palladis tamia Wits treasury being the second part of Wits common wealth* (London, 1598), 281.
62 Drayton, *Englands Heroicall Epistles*, 23.
63 Drayton, *Poly-Olbion*, A1^r.
64 Hadfield, 'Michael Drayton's brilliant career', 132.
65 On Drayton's intention to incorporate Scotland into *Poly-Olbion* according to William Drummond, see Newdigate, *Michael Drayton and His Circle*, 188–9. In his dedication to Prince Henry that prefaces the 1612 edition of *Poly-Olbion* Drayton writes '[m]ay I breath to arriue at the *Orcades* ... I shall leaue your whole British Empire, as this first and southerne part, delineated': Drayton, *Poly-Olbion*, π3^r.
66 Drayton, *The battaile of Agincourt*.
67 Drayton, Helgerson writes, 'dedicated the poem to Prince Henry, whose court was then a center of opposition to the king, and in the body of the poem itself he conspicuously stopped his catalog of the English kings with Elizabeth, thus omitting all mention of James': Helgerson, *Forms of Nationhood*, 128–9.

68 James D. Garrison, *Dryden and the Tradition of Panegyric* (Berkeley: University of California Press, 1975), 20.
69 Drayton, *To the Maiestie of King James*, B3ʳ.
70 Francis Bacon, *The Essaies of Sʳ Francis Bacon* (London, 1612), 205, 206.
71 Samuel Daniel, *A Panegyrike Congratvlatorie to The Kings Maiestie. Also certaine Epistles* (London, 1603) (STC 6258), B1ʳ.
72 John Pitcher, 'Samuel Daniel's letter to Sir Thomas Egerton', *Huntington Library Quarterly*, 47 (1984), 59.
73 Samuel Daniel, *A Funerall Poem Vppon the Death of the Late noble Earle of Deuonshyre* (London, 1606), A4ᵛ.
74 Daniel, *A Panegyrike Congratvlatorie to The Kings Maiestie*, A1ᵛ.
75 *Ibid.*, A4ᵛ.
76 The word 'state(s)', with a lower case 's', appears five times; 'Kingdome(s)' appears three times; 'Nation(s)' appears twice; 'Common-wealth' and 'Republike' once.
77 Johann P. Sommerville, 'Introduction', in Johann P. Sommerville (ed.), *King James VI and I: political writings* (Cambridge: Cambridge University Press, 1994), xxviii.
78 Jean Bodin, *The Six Bookes of a Commonweale*, trans. Richard Knolles (London, 1606), 471.
79 D. R. Woolf, 'Community, law and state: Samuel Daniel's historical thought revisited', *Journal of the History of Ideas*, 49 (1988), 71. Bodin, *The Six Bookes of a Commonweale*, 251. Daniel may have also been indebted to Pierre Charron's definition of the 'state' as 'the bond of societie': see Pierre Charron, *Of Wisdome Three Bookes Written in French by Peter Charron*, trans. Samson Lennard (London, 1608), 189. Charron's *De la sagesse* was originally published in Bordeaux in 1601.
80 Daniel, *A Panegyrike Congratvlatorie to The Kings Maiestie*, C4ʳ.
81 *Ibid.*, A4ᵛ.
82 Daniel, *A Panegyrike Congratvlatorie to The Kings Maiestie*, A1ᵛ. In his Jacobean history of England, Daniel describes England as 'the chiefest part of this Isle' and Scotland as 'being a part of the bodie of this Isle': Samuel Daniel, *The First Part of the Historie of England* (London, 1612), A3ʳ, 112.
83 Daniel, *A Panegyrike Congratvlatorie to The Kings Maiestie*, A1ᵛ.
84 *Ibid.*, A2ᵛ.
85 *Ibid.*, A1ʳ.
86 See, for example, Bindoff, 'The Stuarts and their style', 204–05; Levack, *The Formation of the British State*, 3; Galloway, *The Union of England and Scotland*, 54; Andrew Murphy, *But the Irish Sea Betwixt Us: Ireland, colonialism, and Renaissance literature* (Lexington: The University of

Kentucky Press, 1999), 128–9; Schwyzer, *Literature, Nationalism, and Memory in Early Modern England and Wales*, 151–2.
87 Samuel Daniel, *The Civile Wares betweene the Howses of Lancaster and Yorke* (London, 1609), 135.
88 Schwyzer, *Literature, Nationalism, and Memory in Early Modern England and Wales*, 151.
89 Samuel Daniel, *Delia. Contayning certayne sonnets: with the complaint of Rosamond* (London, 1592), G2^v. This line – in fact, this line and three subsequent lines of Daniel's verse – reappeared under the heading 'Of Albion' in Robert Allott's *Englands Parnassus* (London, 1600).
90 Samuel Daniel, 'A Panegyrick congratulatorie By Samuel Danyel', fol. F2^r.
91 According to David Norbrook, 'Daniel seems to have been the first person to use the term "Great Britain" in a panegyric': David Norbrook, 'Panegyric of the monarch and its social context under Elizabeth I and James I' (D. Phil, Oxford University, 1978), 171.
92 Henry Spelman, 'Of the Union', in Galloway and Levack (eds), *The Jacobean Union*, 170.
93 Henry Spelman, 'Of the Union', British Library, Sloane MS 3521.
94 Perry, *The Making of Jacobean Culture*, 25.
95 According to John Pitcher, the entry in the Stationers' Register is most likely a reference to the second issue of Daniel's *Panegyrike* (STC 6259): see Pitcher, 'Samuel Daniel, the Hertfords, and a question of love', *The Review of English Studies*, 35 (1984), 455.
96 Daniel, 'A Panegyrick congratulatorie By Samuel Danyel'.
97 John Pitcher, 'Editing Daniel', in W. Speed Hill (ed.), *New Ways of Looking at Old Texts: papers of the Renaissance English Text Society, 1985–1991* (Binghamton, NY: Medieval & Renaissance Texts & Studies, 1993), 65. A contemporary account gestures towards the occasion of the Haringtons entertaining James, but it makes no explicit mention of Daniel: '[t]he 23. day being Satterday ... his Maiesty tooke kinde leaue of the Earle of *Rutland*, his Countesse, and the rest, and set forward towards *Burleigh*, and by the way he dined at Sir *Iohn Haringtons*, where that worthy Knight made him most Royall entertainment': see T[homas]. M[illington]., *The True Narration of the Entertainment of his Royall Maiestie*, E3^r.
98 Garrison, *Dryden and the Tradition of Panegyric*, 12.
99 Smuts, 'Occasional events, literary texts and historical interpretation', 183.
100 Pitcher, 'Editing Daniel', 65.
101 John Pitcher, 'Samuel Daniel's gifts of books to Lord Chancellor Egerton', *Medieval and Renaissance Drama in England*, 17 (2005), 217.

102 The Huntington Library presentation copy is shelfmarked RB 60957. On Daniel's presentation of his poetry to Egerton, see Pitcher, 'Samuel Daniel's gifts of books to Lord Chancellor Egerton', 225–6. On Calvin's Case, see Thomas Egerton, *The Speech of the Lord Chancellor of England, in the Eschequer Chamber, touching the post-nati* (London, 1609).

103 Patrick Collinson, 'The monarchical republic of Queen Elizabeth I', *Bulletin of the John Rylands Library*, 69 (1987), 394–424. 'The development of the Privy Council', according to Kevin Sharpe, 'and more frequent meetings of parliaments made England a "mixed Polity"': Sharpe, *Remapping Early Modern England*, 201.

104 Noting that Daniel's *Defence of Ryme* 'emphasizes the crucial values of continuity over innovation', Richard McCabe adds that this text 'looks toward the preservation of traditional English values under a Scottish king': Richard McCabe, *'Ungainefull Arte': poetry, patronage, and print in the early modern era* (Oxford: Oxford University Press, 2016), 261.

105 Samuel Daniel, *A Panegyrike Congratvlatory Deliuered to the Kings most excellent maiesty at Burleigh Harrington in Rutlandshire. By Samvel Daniel. Also Certaine Epistles. With a Defence of Ryme, heeretofore written, and now published by the Author* (London, 1603) (STC 6259), I3^r.

106 Daniel, *A Panegyrike Congratvlatorie to The Kings Maiestie*, B2^v. It was difficult, of course, not to be residually Elizabethan in April or May of 1603. When using this term I wish to highlight the complex politics that Daniel shared with the deceased Edmund Spenser, a poet who wrote not only in praise of his monarch but in opposition to her policies, especially in Ireland.

107 Daniel, *The Civile Wares*, 205 – see stanzas 6 and 7.

108 Camden, *Remaines of a Greater Worke, Concerning Britaine*, 6. In 1598, Francis Meres wrote '[a]s *Lucan* hath mournefully depainted the ciuil wars of *Pompey* & *Caesar*: so hath *Daniel* the ciuill wars of Yorke and Lancaster': Meres, *Palladis Tamia*, 281.

109 David Quint, *Epic and Empire: politics and generic form from Virgil to Milton* (Princeton, NJ: Princeton University Press, 1993), 204. David Norbrook designates Lucan 'the central poet of the republican imagination' in the seventeenth century: David Norbrook, *Writing the English Republic: poetry, rhetoric, and politics, 1627–1660* (Cambridge: Cambridge University Press, 1999), 24.

110 For an in-depth analysis of the multiple editions of Daniel's War of the Roses epic and Lucan's *Pharsalia*, see Gillian Wright, 'What Daniel really did with the *Pharsalia*: The Civil Wars, Lucan, and King James', *The Review of English Studies*, 55 (2004), 210–32. Wright notes that

James is conspicuously absent from the one and only Jacobean edition of *The Civile Wares* (1609).
111 Samuel Daniel, *Hymens Triumph. A Pastorall Tragicomædie* (London, 1615), ¶2^r. Aemilia Lanyer, *Salve Devs Rex Ivdæorvm* (London, 1611), A3^r.
112 Daniel, *A Panegyrike Congratvlatorie to The Kings Maiestie*, A1^v.
113 Pricket, *A Souldiers Wish*, A4^r.
114 Doran and Kewes direct this accusation to the work of Markku Peltonen and Andrew Hadfield: see, Doran and Kewes, 'Introduction', 15.
115 James VI and I, *Basilikon Doron*, D5^v.
116 *Ibid.*, D4^r. Garrison notes that Daniel 'vigorously attempts to restrict James's rule by reference to the ideals affirmed in *Basilikon Doron*': Garrison, *Dryden and the Tradition of Panegyric*, 91.
117 Later in the poem Daniel does use 'Imperiall' ('an Imperiall lust') to mean 'imperious': see Daniel, *A Panegyrike Congratvlatorie to The Kings Maiestie*, B2^r.
118 Daniel, *A Panegyrike Congratvlatorie to the Kings Maiestie*, A1^v. In the earlier manuscript version of the poem, these lines read

> Religion comes w^t thee, peace, righteouness,
> Iudgment, and Iustice, w^c more glorious are
> Then all thy Empire, and art more by this
> Then king and sovraine, more then governo^r.

Daniel, 'A Panegyrick congratulatorie', fol. F2^v.
119 Pont, 'Of the Union', 4.
120 Woolf, 'Community, law and state', 71.
121 Daniel, *A Panegyrike Congratvlatorie to The Kings Maiestie*, A6^r.
122 Daniel, *The Civile Wares*, 146.
123 James VI and I, *Basilikon Doron*, A8^r.
124 Daniel, 'A Panegyrick congratulatorie By Samuel Danyel', fol. F2^r.
125 By no means do I wish to posit a too-rigid division of distribution: the octavo *Panegyrike,* for example, also made its way, most likely as a presentation copy, into the Bridgewater Library, where it is bound with *Certaine Small Poems* (1605).
126 Samuel Daniel, *A Panegyrike Congratvlatorie deliuered to the Kings most excellent Maiestie at Bvrleigh Harrington in Rvtlandshire. By Samuel Daniel. Also certaine Epistles, with a Defence of Ryme heretofore written, and now pvblished by the Avthor* (London, 1603) (STC 6260), A8^v.
127 McCabe, 'Ungainefull Arte', 260.
128 Sir Edward Coke, *The Fourth Part of the Institutes of the Laws of England* (London, 1648), 347.

129 Daniel, *A Panegyrike Congratvlatorie to The Kings Maiestie*, C1ʳ. The printed text's 'fasting' should read 'fastening'; indeed, in one British Library copy of this text an early modern reader has added a chevron-shaped caret below and an 'n' above the 't' and the 'i' in 'fasting'.
130 Daniel, *The works of Samuel Daniel newly augmented* (London, 1602), A2ʳ.
131 Pitcher describes Daniel's intended reader as 'unidentified and undifferentiated by social rank and learning and even gender, and only distinguishable by nationality, by being English': John Pitcher, 'Essays, works and small poems: divulging, publishing and augmenting the Elizabethan poet, Samuel Daniel', in Andrew Murphy (ed.), *The Renaissance Text: theory, editing, textuality* (Manchester: Manchester University Press, 2000), 16.
132 The Huntington Library shelfmark for the octavo *Panegyrike* is RB 60948; the shelfmark for *Certaine Small Poems* is RB 60949.
133 Daniel Cadman, '"Th'accession of these mighty States": Daniel's *Philotas* and the union of the crowns', *Renaissance Studies*, 26 (2011), 365. See also John Pitcher's entry on Daniel in the *ODNB*.
134 Sommerville (ed.), *King James VI and I: political writings*, xv.
135 Samuel Daniel, *The Vision of the 12. Goddesses, presented in a Maske the 8. of Ianuary, at Hampton Court: By the Queenes most excellent Maiestie, and her Ladies* (London, 1604), A3ᵛ.
136 *Ibid.*, A5ᵛ.
137 *Ibid.*, B5ʳ.
138 David Norbrook, *Poetry and Politics in the English Renaissance*, rev. ed. (Oxford: Oxford University Press, 2002), 157.
139 Martin Butler suggests that Daniel's masque presents James's 'multiple kingship not as nation-building but as dynastic ambition and territorial aggrandisement': Martin Butler, *The Stuart Court Masque and Political Culture* (Cambridge: Cambridge University Press, 2008), 103.
140 Ben Jonson, *The Characters of Two royall Masques* (London, 1608), B3ʳ, B3ᵛ.
141 'Daniel's reputation as a poet reached its highest point around the turn of the century': Pitcher, 'Essays, works and small poems', 13. *Pace* Pitcher, David Galbraith argues that Daniel 'was more successful at the end of the first decade of the new century than at any previous moment', and he adds that 'in comparison to Michael Drayton … Daniel managed the transition to the new reign quite adroitly': David Galbraith, *Architectonics of Imitation in Spenser, Daniel and Drayton* (Toronto: University of Toronto Press, 2000), 89.
142 Perry, *The Making of Jacobean Culture*, 154. See also Sharpe, *Remapping Early Modern England*, 207.

143 Samuel Daniel, *Tethys Festival: Or the Qveenes Wake* (London, 1610), E4^r.
144 Ibid., E4^v.
145 Ibid.
146 See John Pitcher, *Samuel Daniel: The Brotherton Manuscript, a study in attribution* (Leeds: Leeds Texts and Monographs, 1981), 131–7.
147 Daniel, *The First Part of the Historie of England*, 28–9.
148 Camden, *Remaines of a Greater Worke, Concerning Britaine*, 9.
149 Verstegan, *A Restitvtion of Decayed Intellengence*, †3^v–†4^r, ††1^r. On the anti-Scottish, Counter-Reformation politics of Verstegan's Saxon narrative of the origins of the English, see Christopher Highley, *Catholics Writing the Nation in Early Modern Britain and Ireland* (Oxford: Oxford University Press, 2008), 108–17.
150 Justifying his decision to publish his masque, Daniel states that he does so 'not, out of a desire, to be seene in pamphlets': Daniel, *Tethys Festival*, E1^4.
151 Burgess, Wymer and Lawrence, 'Introduction', xvi.
152 [Anon.], *A mournefull dittie, entituled Elizabeths losse together with a welcome for King Iames. To a pleasant new tune* (London, 1603).
153 Bacon, *The Beginning of the History of Great Britain*, 409.
154 Ben Jonson, *B. Ion: His Part of King Iames his Royall and Magnificent Entertainement through his Honorable Cittie of London, Thurseday the 15. of March. 1603* (London, 1604). All quotations from Jonson's *Panegyre* and *Royall and Magnificent Entertainement* will be from this text. Butler terms this publication a 'free-standing volume of festival texts celebrating the arrival of the new dynasty': Martin Butler, 'Introduction', in *The Cambridge Edition of the Works of Ben Jonson*, David Bevington, Martin Butler and Ian Donaldson (eds), 7 vols (Cambridge: Cambridge University Press, 2012), II, 423.
155 Jonson, *Royall and Magnificent Entertainement*, E1^v.
156 Graham Parry, *The Golden Age Restor'd: the culture of the Stuart court, 1603–42* (New York: St. Martin's Press, 1981), 1.
157 Stephen Harrison, *The Arch's of Triumph Erected in Honor of the High and Mightie Prince. James. the First of that name. King, of England. and the sixt of Scotland* (London, 1604), F1^r.
158 Robert Evans, *Ben Jonson and the Poetics of Patronage* (Lewisburg, PA: Bucknell University Press, 1989), 91.
159 '[W]hen James VI became king of England, Jonson, already connected to Welsh literary circles, got interested in his own Scottish-borders ancestors, moved into Scottish households in London, went on a walking tour to Edinburgh, and wrote masques about Anglo-Scottish union and the place of Ireland and Wales in the Jacobean system': Kerrigan, *Archipelagic English*, 11.

160 This poem has received little critical attention, although one notable exception is Murphy, who focuses on the incorporation of Ireland into 'the "geography" of union': Murphy, *But the Irish Sea Betwixt Us*, 132–8, 137.
161 Hugh Holland, *Pancharis: the first booke. Containing the preparation of the loue betweene Owen Tudyr, and the Queene, long since intended to her maiden Maiestie: and now dedicated to the inuincible Iames, second and greater Monarch of great Britaine, King of England, Scotland, France, and Ireland, with the islands adiacent* (London, 1603).
162 *Ibid.*, A8^r.
163 *Ibid.*, A8^r–A9^r.
164 Jonson, *Royall and Magnificent Entertainement*, A2^v.
165 *Ibid.*, A2^v.
166 Dekker, *The Magnificent Entertainment*, A2^r, A4^r.
167 *Ibid.*, H1^r.
168 The glosses that accompany Jonson's 1604 published version of this text also include (Latin) references to Britain.
169 'This *Pegme* presented it selfe aboue the great Conduit in *Cheape*: and caried the name of the *New Arabia*, vnder which title the whole Island of *Britannia* was figured'; 'In the most eminent place was aduanced a person, representing *Arabia Britannica*, and within a *Nesete* (beneath her) stood *Fame*': Harrison, *The Arch's of Trivmph*, F1^r.
170 Jonson, *The Characters of Two royall Masques*, B3^v.
171 Harrison, *The Arch's of Trivmph*, H1^r.
172 Jonson, *Royall and Magnificent Entertainement*, B3^r.
173 Munday hails James as 'our second *Brute*': Munday, *The Triumphes of Re-united Britania*, B2^r. See Tracey Hill, '"Representing the awefull authoritie of soveraigne Majestie": monarchs and mayors in Anthony Munday's *The Triumphes of Re-united Britania*', in Burgess, Wymer and Lawrence (eds), *The Accession of James I*, 15–33.
174 Butler, *The Stuart Court Masque and Political Culture*, 75.
175 Craig, *De Unione*, 208. Craig's dismissal of the Brutus myth is polemical: 'I hold the asserted political division of Britain by Brutus to be exceedingly improbable, since his alleged superiority over, even his rule in Britain, are not recorded until the time of the Lombards, nearly two thousand years after Brutus lived': *ibid.*, 208–09.
176 Butler, *The Stuart Court Masque and Political Culture*, 95, 99. As late as 1618, Butler adds, Jonson's masques evince 'the difficulty of finding a coherent language for describing brotherhood between three nations': *ibid.*, 92.
177 In a 1607 speech, James speaks of 'Irish, Scottish, Welsh, and English, diuers in Nation, yet all walking as Subiects and seruants within my

Court': [James VI and I], *His Maiesties speech to both the houses of Parliament*, E1r. Thomas Gainsford would later write 'looke how many nations and languages are under subjection: namely, *English, Scottish, Irish, Welch, Cornish, Ments, Ilanders* both *Hebrides* and *Orchades*, & the *French* of *Gersy* and *Jersy*: so that if the honour of a King consisteth in the multitude of his subjects, what Prince hath more, and such variety?': Thomas Gainsford, *The Glory of England, Or A True Description of Many Excellent Prerogatives and Remarkeable Blessing, whereby She Triumpheth over all the Nations of the World* (London, 1618), 246–7.

178 Craig, *De Unione*, 268. Although published in 1604, Jonson probably began working on his *Royall and Magnificent Entertainement* and *Panegyre* in advance of the planned 1603 royal entry, which was delayed by the outbreak of plague. If this was the case, it is likely that Jonson revised these two texts in 1604. The 1603 Althorp entertainment contains no references to Britain.

179 Ian Donaldson, 'Jonson, Benjamin [Ben]', *ODNB*, https://doi.org/10.1093/ref:odnb/15116. Accessed 21 October 2016.

180 Bevington, Butler and Donaldson (eds), *The Cambridge Edition of the Works of Ben Jonson*, V, 115.

181 [James VI and I], *The Kings Maiesties Speech, as it was deliuered by him in the vpper house of the Parliament to the Lords Spirituall and Temporall, and to the Knights, Citizens and Burgesses there assembled, On Munday the 19. day of March 1603.* (London, 1604), B2r.

182 Ben Jonson, *The Workes of Beniamin Jonson* (London, 1616), 770.

183 David Riggs, *Ben Jonson: a life* (Cambridge, MA: Harvard University Press, 1989), 197. It is possible that 'On the Vnion' was written in the wake of James's coronation (25 July 1603), for Jonson's rival Dekker was using language similar to that contained in Jonson's epigram: '*England* and *Scotland* (being parted only with a narrow Riuer, and the people of both Empires speaking a language lesse differing than english within it selfe, as the prouidence had enacted, that one day those two Nations should marry one another) are now made sure together, and king *Iames* his Coronation, is the solemne wedding day': Dekker, *1603. The Wonderfull yeare*, C1v.

184 Perry, *The Making of Jacobean Culture*, 36. Similarly, Rickard reads 'On the Vnion' as an instance of Jonson 'turning James's prose into poetry': Rickard, *Writing the Monarch in Jacobean England*, 76.

185 On Cotton's British interests, see Sharpe, *Remapping Early Modern England*, 294–341. Jonson and Camden were together at Cotton's country house in September of 1603. The Scottish poet Alexander Craig, who most likely followed King James to London and published his first collection of poems in London in 1604, presents himself

'This mighty worke of vnion' 109

as a 'Scotobritane': see Alexander Craig, *The Poeticall Essayes of Alexander Craige, Scotobritane* (London, 1604). Craig retains this identity on the title page of his subsequent collection of poems, also printed in London: see Alexander Craig, *The Amorose Songes, Sonets, and Elegies: of M. Alexander Craige, Scoto-Britane* (London, 1606).

186 Or, to be exact, from the first three letters of his surname: 'B. ION'. The 19 March 1604 entry in the Stationers' Register, however, lists the author of *A Part of the Kinges Maiesties right royall and magnificent Entertainement through his honorable city of London* as 'BENIAMIN JOHNSON': see Arber, *A Transcript of the Registers of the Company of Stationers of London*, III, 254.

187 Jonathan Goldberg describes Jonson's *Panegyre* as '[o]stensibly a poem of outright praise': Jonathan Goldberg, *James I and the Politics of Literature: Jonson, Shakespeare, Donne and their contemporaries* (Stanford, CA: Stanford University Press, 1989), 120.

188 Martin Butler, '"Servant, but not slave": Ben Jonson at the Jacobean court', *Proceedings of the British Academy*, 90 (1996), 73. Jonson, *Royall and Magnificent Entertainement*, E4^r.

189 *Ibid.*, E4^v.

190 Robert Miola's *Early Modern Catholicism* includes these lines from Jonson's poem, lines Miola describes as 'a Catholic perspective on the Henrician revolution': Robert Miola, *Early Modern Catholicism: an anthology of primary sources* (Oxford: Oxford University Press, 2007), 227. In their Introduction to *The Accession of James I*, the editors note that 'Jonson benefit[ed] from the greater toleration of Catholics in the brief Jacobean honeymoon which preceded the Gunpowder Plot': Burgess, Wymer and Lawrence, 'Introduction', xvii.

191 For a detailed study of the construction of cultural and national identity in the writings of English Catholics in the early modern period, see Highley, *Catholics Writing the Nation*.

192 Jonson, *The Workes of Beniamin Jonson*, 778. The same day that Jonson delivered his *Panegyre* to James, the king dismissively referred to Catholics as 'a priuate Sect, lurking within the bowels of this Nation', and he admonished Catholics that 'they presume not so much vpon my Lenitie': [James VI and I], *The Kings Maiesties Speech*, B4^r, C2^v.

193 Ian Donaldson, *Ben Jonson: a life* (Oxford: Oxford University Press, 2011), 52. 'For English writers', Kerrigan notes, 'the trappings of a British identity could be acquired by, for instance, claiming a Scottish ancestry, as Jonson did shortly after 1603': Kerrigan, *Archipelagic English*, 148. See also Donaldson, *Ben Jonson: a life*, 22–57. For Jonson's 'foot voyage' to Scotland, see James Loxley, Anna Groundwater and Julie Sanders (eds), *Ben Jonson's Walk to Scotland:*

An Annotated Edition of the 'Foot Voyage' (Cambridge: Cambridge University Press, 2015).
194 Jonson, *Royall and Magnificent Entertainement*, D4^r.
195 *Ibid.*, F1^v.
196 *Ibid.*, B2^v–B3^r.
197 *Ibid.*, B2^v.
198 *Ibid.*, B3^r.
199 *Ibid.*, B3^v, B4^r, B4^v.
200 *Ibid.*, B4^r. According to Butler, Jonson '[u]nlike many contemporaries, for whom the new name was a source of anxiety ... made it a symbolic centrepiece, the most visible sign of the transformed, king-centred State': Butler, '"Servant, but not slave"', 73.
201 Jonson, *The Workes of Beniamin Jonson*, 784.
202 *Ibid.*, 772. In his prefatory 'To the Reader', Camden speaks of 'the love of my Country' and 'the glory of the British name': Camden, *Britain*, *4^v.
203 Ben Jonson, 'To the memory of my beloued, The Avthor Mr. William Shakespeare: And what he hath left vs', in Hinman (ed.) *The Norton Facsimile: the First Folio*, 10.
204 Norbrook, *Poetry and Politics in the English Renaissance*, 161.
205 See Helgerson, *Forms of Nationhood*, 107–47.
206 Nasty references to the Scots in two extant copies of the second of two issues of the first quarto of *Eastward Hoe* (1605), entered in the Stationers' Register on 4 September 1605, landed Chapman and Jonson in prison. They include the following passage on Scots in Virginia: 'there are no greater friends to English men and *England*, when they are out an't, in the world, then they are. And for my part, I would an hundred thousand of 'hem were there, for wee are all one Countrey-men now, yee know; and wee should finde ten times more comfort of them there, then wee doe here': George Chapman, Ben Jonson, John Marston, *Eastward Hoe. As it was playd in the Black-friers. By the Children of her Maiesties Reuels. Made by Geo: Chapman. Ben: Ionson. Ioh: Marston* (London, 1605) (STC 4970; Qc), E3^v–4^r. Because the play is the product of multiple authors, determining who exactly wrote the anti-Scottish passages is difficult if not impossible. Jonson's letters to, among other nobles, the Scottish fellow Catholic Aubigny appear to have facilitated his release. Donaldson states that after James's accession, Jonson 'acted by turns as an apologist for the new King and as a satirist of his manners and countrymen': Donaldson, *Ben Jonson: a life*, 224. That royal proclamations were issued in 1603 and 1604 against those who were deriding and ambushing Scots reveals just how pervasive anti-Scottish sentiment was in London. Jonson did not include *Eastward Hoe* in his 1616

folio *Workes*. Craig, who as an Anglo-Scottish Union Commissioner would have been in London in 1604–05, remarks, 'in public representations of comedy a Scotsman is always treated as a fitting subject of ridicule': Craig, *De Unione*, 356.

207 See www.celm-ms.org.uk/authors/jonsonben.html. Accessed 21 April 2018.
208 Peter Beal, *Index of English Literary Manuscripts*, Volume 1: *1450–1625* (London: Mansell, 1980), 235.
209 Walter Ong, *Interfaces of the Word: studies in the evolution of consciousness and culture* (Ithaca, NY: Cornell University Press, 1977), 274–9. Ong opposes, perhaps too harshly, manuscript culture to the permanency of the printed word.
210 Numerous other manuscript poems on the question of union survive. One example of an extant pro-union poem is 'The Countreymans opinion touching the Uniting of the two Kingdoms England & Scotland', British Library, Additional MS 12497, 384–5.
211 British Library, Additional MS 15227, 8^v.
212 Butler, '"Servant, but not slave"', 69.
213 Bodleian Library, MS Rawl. Poet. 160, 34^v.
214 Trinity College Library, Dublin, MS 877, 243^r.
215 See Burrow's notes on the poem in *The Cambridge Edition of the Works of Ben Jonson*, V, 115.
216 Ong, *Interfaces of the Word*, 274.
217 McRae and West, 'General introduction', 15.
218 Morrill, 'The British problem', 2.
219 Daniel, *A Panegyrike Congratvlatorie to the Kings Maiestie*, B2^v.

3

'But when this island shall be made Britain': Hume, Bacon, Britain and Britishness

The Edinburgh publication of *Basilikon Doron* in 1599 made public, via the medium of print, James Stewart's desire that his son, Henry, would inherit not only Scotland's crown but England's, too. The father's advice to his eldest son reveals a Scottish monarch thinking through the rule of multiple kingdoms well in advance of his English accession. 'And incase it please God', a judicious James writes, 'to prouide you to all thir three Kingdomes, make your eldest son *Isaac*, leauing him all your kingdomes, and prouide the rest with priuate possessions: otherwayes by deuiding your Kingdomes, yee shall leaue the seede of diuisione and discorde among your posteritie'.[1] On 17 April 1603, Giovanni Carlo Scaramelli, Venetian secretary in England, wrote to the Doge and Senate stating that James 'is disposed to abandon the titles of England and Scotland, and to call himself King of Great Britain, and like that famous and ancient King Arthur to embrace under one name the whole circuit of one thousand seven hundred miles, which includes the United Kingdom now possessed by his Majesty, in that one island'.[2] Upon his accession to the English throne, James committed himself to securing a union of the kingdoms of England and Scotland that would transcend the personal, dynastic union of the crowns. The first year of James's English reign, however, produced little in terms of official Parliamentary or royal pronouncements on the topic of a union between the two kingdoms, a notable exception being the royal proclamation of 19 May 1603 (discussed in chapter 2, section headed '[O]ne people, brethren and members of one body'), which is generally considered James's first formal pronouncement on the union.[3] In that proclamation, James's English subjects learned of 'his Maiesties resolution for the vnion of the two Realmes', a resolution apparently shared by both his English and Scottish subjects, for

'*But when this island shall be made Britain*' 113

England's new king claimed to have 'found in the hearts of all the best disposed Subiects of both the Realmes ... a most earnest desire, that the sayd happy Vnion should bee perfected'.[4] How exactly was the 'happy Vnion' to be perfected? To proclaim the inhabitants of England and Scotland 'one people, brethren and members of one body' was one thing, to effect such a sea-change was another.[5] This chapter explores a sample of the print and manuscript tracts and treatises that played a vital role in early Jacobean debate on the Anglo-Scottish union. Some of the writings, to be sure, voice a strong resistance to union, but others reveal a profound commitment to imagining not only a united Britain but also a unified nation of Britons.

'[T]he Vnion of two ancient & famous Kingdoms'

In the second year of James's English reign, Anglo-Scottish union became a, if not the, central issue in English and Scottish political and public discourse, surfacing in royal proclamations, dominating English Parliamentary debate and circulating by way of printed and handwritten tracts and treatises produced by James's English and Scottish subjects. 'There is nothing now more in the mouthes of men', claimed the author of one manuscript tract, 'then discoursing the Vnion of *England* and *Scotland*'.[6] On the same day (19 March 1604) that Jonson's *Panegyre* was entered in the Stationers' Register, James delivered to both houses of Parliament a speech that voiced his desire to unite his two British kingdoms. Three of the king's speeches to England's Parliament addressed the topic of union: his 1604 and 1607 speeches in particular, less so his 1605 speech, which focussed on the Gunpowder Plot (his 1610 Parliament speech and his 1616 Star Chamber speech lament MPs' resistance to union). In his 1604 speech, James's initial invocation of union refers to King Henry VII's unification of the houses of Lancaster and York; but 'the Vnion of these two princely Houses', he adds, 'is nothing comparable to the Vnion of two ancient & famous Kingdoms'.[7] After acknowledging the union of the crowns, James's speech turns to other forms of union. Describing himself as 'no stranger to you in blood', James is quick to remind his English audience that the kingdom of England came about as a result of previous unions, including a conjoining (Saxon heptarchy) and an incorporating (Wales) union:

> Doe we not yet remember, that this Kingdome was diuided into seuen little Kingdomes, besides *Wales*? And is it not now the stronger by their Vnion? And hath not the Vnion of *Wales* to *England*, added a greater strength thereto? Which though it was a great Principality, was nothing comparable in greatnesse and power, to the ancient and famous Kingdome of *Scotland*.[8]

James's invocation of examples of earlier unions – a move made by many authors of pro-union tracts – is accompanied by a nod to divine sanction grounded in various forms of promixity, including linguistic, religious, cultural, and geographical:

> Hath not God first vnited these two Kingdomes, both in Language, Religion, and similitude of Manners? Yea, hath hee not made vs all in one Iland, compassed with one Sea, and of it selfe by nature so indiuisible, as almost those that were Borderers themselues on the late Borders, cannot distinguish, nor know, or discerne their owne limits? These two Countries being separated neither by Sea, nor great Riuer, Mountaine, nor other strength of nature, but onely by little small Brookes, or demolished little Walles, so as rather they were diuided in apprehension, then in effect, And now in the end and fulnesse of time vnited, the Right and Title of both in my Person, alike lineally descended of both the Crownes, whereby it is now become like a little World within it selfe, being intrenched and fortified round about with a naturall, and yet admirable strong Pond or Ditch, whereby all the former feares of this Nation are now quite cut off.[9]

This passage echoes sentiments expressed in the numerous texts that celebrated James's accession and coronation, and writers of union tracts and treatises will reiterate these points. 'Against outward inuasions nature hath cared', writes William Cornwallis (whose union treatise was printed in Edinburgh as well as London), 'we are enuironed by the sea, and so knit together both by religion, language, disposition, & whatsoeuer els can take away difference; as vnlesse we breed disagreeing affections, we are indissoluble'.[10] James's speech also has in common with Jacobean succession literature the use of a range of terms to designate the multinational polity that James's composite rule has brought into being. Consider the variety of terms that James invokes to signify Scotland and England: 'these two Kingdomes', 'one Iland', 'these two Countries', 'like a little World'. The reference to 'this Nation' is of particular interest. Since the auditors were members of both houses of Parliament, we can assume that James is consciously addressing an audience that consisted of representatives of the English nation. If 'this Nation' is indeed a reference to England, then 'the former feares' could include the question of Elizabeth's successor, the Catholic threat, the threat of Spanish or even Scottish invasion. In *The cronicle history of Henry the fift*, a version of which may have been performed at court in the early years of James's English reign, plans for an invasion of France are troubled by a fear of an incursion from England's northern enemy:

> We must not onely arme vs against the French,
> But lay downe our proportion for the Scot,
> Who will make rode vpon vs with all aduantages.[11]

In a passage included the First Folio version of this play, King Henry speaks of 'the Scot' as 'a giddy neighbour to vs', and he captures the nasty, brutish and long history of Anglo-Scottish relations in the pithy phrase 'th' ill neighbourhood' (TLN 292, 301). As a host of pro-union texts will do, James sought to promote neighbourliness between the historically antagonistic nations of England and Scotland. Pont, for instance, represents Scotland and England as 'neighbour nations and inhabitants of one iland'.[12] Might the king's use of 'this Nation' also refer to a larger entity? Given the allusion to Virgil – 'is now become like a little World within it selfe' – might James be using 'this Nation' to signify a united Britain? In other words, we can read 'this Nation' as signifying both a political reality (the English nation) and a political fantasy (a British nation). What is remarkable, or perhaps canny, is the absence of the word 'Britain' from James's speech. Whilst James makes references to 'this whole Kingdome', 'this Kingdome', 'this Nation', 'this State', 'this Isle', 'this Land', 'this whole Isle', he never refers to 'Britain' as he had in *Basilikon Doron*.[13] James informs his audience that 'God hath made *Scotland* the one halfe of this Isle to enioy my Birth, and the first and most vnperfect halfe of my life, and you heere to enioy the perfect and the last halfe thereof'; however, 'this Vnion' never translates into, even though it hints at, an explicitly British rule.[14] It would not be long, however, before the term Britain and the issue of Anglo-Scottish union would become the subject of heated debated both within and outside Parliament.

'[T]he Name of Great Britain'

Of the 1604 English Parliament, Galloway writes, 'the union was undoubtedly intended as the major issue of debate, and in fact occupied more parliamentary time than any other subject'.[15] A single reference in the *Commons Journals* dated 31 March 1604 reads 'Sir William Morrice beginneth the Motion for the Union, and for the Name of Great Britain'.[16] Not until mid-April did debate on union matters commence. An 18 April list of the 'Pro.' and 'Contra.' responses to 'Union with Scotland' registers the prevailing and contrasting attitudes of English Parliamentarians. Listed among the 'Pro.' statements are the following: '[t]hat God had made an Union'; '[f]or staying of Effusion of Blood'; '[f]or taking away Factions in several Names'; '[t]he King lineally descended both from the Blood of *England* and *Scotland* – By the name of *Britain* we return *ad priftinam dignitatem*, to Antiquity, which is most honourable'; 'the Uniting of Two ancient, valiant, and great Kingdoms'; '[n]o Separation between the Two Kingdoms; if any, imaginary'. The 'Contra.' statements include '[n]ames of Nations, and Titles of Kings, are in Question'; '[l]ong continued in the Name of *England*, glorious and famous'; '[i]n all Conquests the Kingdom of *England* continued his Name'; '[n]o man knows, whether *Scotland* will agree'; '[t]his Kingdom the more glorious, the more honourable'.[17] These *Commons Journals* entries bear witness to both a flexibility and an inflexibility on the part of English MPs, a willingness and an unwillingness to engage earnestly with the question of uniting the island's two kingdoms. These 'Pro.' and 'Contra' responses, moreover, adumbrate attitudes and ideas that the plethora of union tracts and treatises produced in 1604 and 1605 articulated and amplified.

The English Parliament was not really debating 'Union with Scotland' in April of 1604.[18] The king had invited both houses to consider, on one hand, the formation of an Anglo-Scottish Union Commission and, on the other, an alteration of the royal style from 'King of England, Scotland, France and Ireland' to 'King of Great Britain, France and Ireland'. The formation of an Anglo-Scottish Union Commission was achieved through the cooperation and willingness of both Houses, who granted the commissioners power to present proposals for a union of the two kingdoms to the English Parliament. The Anglo-Scottish Union Commission was made up of forty-eight Englishmen, headed by Cecil, and thirty-one Scots, headed by Seton, and it held its inaugural meeting on 20 October 1604. Any change in style, however, was acrimoniously and vociferously resisted by Parliament – principally on legal grounds but also on deep-rooted nationalist grounds – and was eventually withdrawn by the king. A committee appointed under Francis Bacon in late April compiled a list of objections (27 April 1604) to the change in style, and these objections exist in a plethora of extant manuscript copies, suggesting wide circulation; they were also reproduced in print, probably appearing in late May.[19] The lower house's objections to a change in the royal style are motivated not only by legal precedency (or lack thereof) but also, or especially, by a deeply entrenched Englishness. The 'English sense of their national identity was', Conrad Russell observes, 'strongly tied to their sense of legislative sovereignty'.[20] This comes across most forcefully in the third and, especially, fourth of the 'fowre severall natures or kinds' of objection: namely, 'Matter of estate forraine, or matter of intercourse' and 'Matter of honor or reputacion'.[21] The third objection listed under 'Matter of estate forraine, or matter of intercourse' laments that 'the glorie and good acceptacion of the English name and nacion wilbe in foereine parts obscured'. Anxiety about 'the English name' being obscured dominates the material on 'honor or reputacion', which lists four objections:

> The first is that noe wordlie thinge is more deare to men than their name: as wee see in private families that men disinherit theire daughters to Contineue theire names much in states and where the name hath bene famous and honorable:
>
> The second is that the Contracted name of Britaine will bring in oblivion the names of England and Scotland:
>
> The third is that whereas nowe England in the stile is placed before Scotland: in the name of Britaine that degree of prioritie or precedence wilbe loste:
>
> The fourth is that the Chaunge of names wilbe harshe in the popular opinion and unpleasing to the Countrey.[22]

In the face of such resistance, James abandoned his plans for Parliamentary ratification of the change in name of the royal style. He was not, however, content to let the issue lie. As the previously cited letter from the Venetian secretary in England attests, James's desire to proclaim himself King of Great Britain was firmly established at the time of his accession. With the English Parliament unwilling to ratify the change, James turned to royal prerogative. In a proclamation dated 20 October 1604, James proclaimed 'Wee haue thought good to discontinue the diuided names of England and Scotland out of our Regall Stile, and doe intend and resolue to take and assume vnto Vs in maner and forme hereafter expressed, The Name and Stile of *KING OF GREAT BRITTAINE*'.[23] As Bacon was to later write, 'the Kings Stile, is now no more of *England*, but of *Britaine*'.[24] The alteration in the royal style was just one of the means by which James sought 'to imprint and inculcate into the hearts and heads of the people, that they are one people and one nation'.[25]

'No British king or statesman of the seventeenth or eighteenth century', according to Levack, 'was as thorough, imaginative, or genuinely dedicated to the creation of a united national community or British people as James'.[26] No doubt this statement is meant as praise for James; indeed, it also takes revisionary aim at historians who represent James as vainglorious and deluded in pursuit of his 'pet project' of union.[27] Levack's statement, however, risks being misinterpreted as emphasising James's individual agency at the cost of the work of English and Scottish writers who played a crucial role in thinking through issues of union in the early years of James's reign. Not all historians are convinced that James's union ideas had purchase beyond Whitehall. In reference to James's 1607 speech to Parliament, John Morrill writes 'James then aims for perfect union, a new-modelled kingdom of Britain, brought about slowly, organically, via a union of hearts and minds. No one else (except perhaps Lord Keeper Ellesmere) shared his vision or his enthusiasm.'[28] Thanks to the pioneering work of Galloway and Levack, the assumption that Anglo-Scottish union was desired by the king only has been vigorously contested.[29] Many historians and literary historians, however, continue to treat early Jacobean pro-union discourse as the product of sycophants in search of royal favour. Consider, for example, the introduction to a groundbreaking collection of essays on the historical and cultural consequences of James's 1603 accession.[30] In many ways, this volume's work on the subject of union is to be welcomed as some of the best scholarship produced on union-related topics, for it contributes to a rethinking of long-held views that Jacobean discourse on Anglo-Scottish union was monopolised by James and his supposed sycophants. However, there are moments when those Jacobeans who wrote favourably on union matters are represented in a rather dismissive manner. Writing in reference to James's desire to cement the union, the editors state in their introduction '[h]is approach, and that of his propagandists, was both to talk up the areas of convergence that already existed between England and Scotland and to find ways of nudging both countries along a path of further convergence'.[31] 'James's plans [for Anglo-Scottish union]', they add, 'were supported by a chorus of politicians, clergymen, and civil lawyers; but the chorus did not seem to produce sympathetic echoes elsewhere in the political nation'.[32] Labelling those who wrote in favour of union – Francis Bacon, William Cornwallis, William Clerk, Thomas Craig, David Hume of Godscroft, Alberico Gentili, John Hayward, Robert Pont, John Thornborough – a 'chorus' and 'propagandists' necessarily denies that these authors committed themselves to engaging critically with questions of cultural, legal, national, religious and ecclesiastical union. Furthermore, these labels obscure the boldness and vibrancy of early seventeenth-century responses to the union.

'[T]hese British peoples': Hume's *De Vnione Insulæ Britannicæ*

Among the most profound union-inspired ideas to emerge from this period are those of David Hume of Godscroft. Hume, a graduate of the University of St Andrews, produced, probably between the first and second sessions of England's Parliament under James (7 July 1604–5 November 1605), two union tracts. Dedicated to 'Regi, Iacobo Brittaniarvm, Franciæ, & Hiberniæ, Regi', *De Vnione Insulæ Britannicæ Tractatus. 1*, his first tract, published in London in 1605 (and reprinted at Paris in 1639) offers a broad argument in support of Anglo-Scottish union.[33] Dedicated, significantly, 'Ad Lectorem', his second tract, 'De Unione Insvlæ Britannicæ Tractatvs Secvndvs', fleshes out the political and constitutional means by which the initial tract's general musings on union could be effected.[34] Unlike his first tract, Hume's second was never printed; his attempt to have it published anonymously in Bordeaux in 1610 proved unsuccessful. The second tract does, however, exist in multiple manuscript copies, suggestive of scribal publication: three manuscript copies are housed in the Edinburgh University Library; single manuscript copies are housed in the National Library of Scotland and the British Library.[35] Both tracts, but especially the first, respond to the plethora of objections to the union that English MPs voiced in 1604, objections with which Hume may have become familiar through a copy of Thornborough's *Discovrse*, which he acknowledges having read.

Hume's union tracts have received little critical attention, perhaps because they were published in Latin. Fortunately, Paul McGinnis and Arthur Williamson have published a fine bilingual edition of the two tracts (*The British Union*). In an essay titled 'Radical Britain: David Hume of Godscroft and the challenge to the Jacobean British vision', which extends many of the ideas expressed in the introduction to his and McGinnis's edition and translation of Hume's two tracts, Williamson cogently argues that Hume's early seventeenth-century union tracts are best appreciated and understood within the realm of a larger framework of a British civic culture that emerged in opposition to King James's absolutism, especially in Scotland. Williamson convincingly portrays Hume as a disciple of George Buchanan and Andrew Melville; in fact, some manuscript copies of the second tract include a dedicatory epistle from Melville to Hume, wherein Melville describes Hume's work as 'difficult and dangerous ... but both useful and necessary for these times'.[36] Given these connections, and given the fact that the second tract was refused publication, it makes little sense to treat Hume's union writing as the product of a subject desperately seeking James's favour. Hume, according to Williamson, 'regarded the 1603 regnal union and the prospect of a new Britain as a Machiavellian *occasione*, an altogether unique opportunity for immediate, far-reaching political innovation and creativity'. Hume's call at the close of the first tract to 'take the opportunity by the forelock, while it presents its forehead and while it isn't yet bald' draws upon emblematic as well as literary images of Occasion as an elderly woman bald except for a single forelock in order to incite his fellow Britons to seize this critical moment in England's and Scotland's history. 'Quite unlike any other unionist literature of the time,' Williamson adds, 'Hume's writings passionately urged a civic and reformed British commonwealth'.[37] Hume's tracts also passionately urge the formation of a unified kingdom and a single, collective British body politic: 'I insist', Hume writes, 'that when I hear or speak of union, I have had nothing else in mind than a union of kingdoms and peoples. I mean that from two kingdoms and two peoples there should finally come into being one kingdom and one people.'[38] 'The question on everybody's mind concerns the union of these British peoples'; how is it, Hume asks, that 'such diverse and adverse communities may agree to join together'?[39]

'But when this island shall be made Britain' 121

Aware of the vocal English resistance to any proposed change of the name of England – to Albion, Britain, Britannia – Hume devotes ample space to responding to this sensitive subject. The proposed change of name elicited emotive responses from Englishmen, not surprisingly in the form of manuscript rather than printed tracts. The following passage is just one of the many examples where an English author refuses to forsake their sense of Englishness:

> Kingdoms & Nations never alter their names but by the overflow of some forrain people of a strange language who giue their owne name to the country conquered, as the French did the name of France to the country of the Gaules, the Alemaynes to Germanie the Huns to Hungarie, the Lumbarde to Gallia Cisalpina. So tha^t we cannot be other than we are, being English we cannot be Brytaines: nations I say, giue the names to countries, & not contryes to the nations. O^{ur} Ancesto^{rs} put vs in possess[io]n of this kingdom by that name, & by that name we hold it, it is the inheritance of o^{ur} bloud, & we cannot but leave it in per*pet*uity to o^{ur} posteritie so long as they shall remayne inhabitants of this Island.[40]

Whilst the change in name ranks among the main objections expressed by English writers, not all Englishmen resisted. John Hayward's printed tract argues that 'the bearing of one name is a meane to knit men in affection and friendship'; 'difference in name doth often mainteine men in diuision of mind'. In a chapter titled 'What common name is most fit to comprehend the English and the Scots: and whether the like change of name hath been vsuall or no', Hayward declares 'no common name can be so fit to comprise as well the people as the countries of *England* and *Scotland*, as is the name of *Britaine*'.[41] Henry Savile, whose handwritten tract may have been produced at James's request, comes across as much more cagey when it comes to the topic of a name for a united kingdom. In a chapter titled 'Of assuming a third name for both', Savile's 'Historicall Collections' dances around the name 'Britain' without ever using that term. 'Of the third case (which now as I hear is the question with us), where both the former is extinct and a third name is assumed, I do hardly remember one example' is how he opens that chapter. 'I wish with all my heart', a pleading Savile later writes, 'his Majesty could be pleased the names of England and Scotland might still continue, as they have long done and are, following the example of all Christian kings this day in the world'.[42] Unlike Savile but like Hayward, Hume is open to the idea of a change in names: 'if it is determined to change the name, then it is for the better to adopt the more general name: Britannia'.[43]

Hume's response to what the 1605 printed text's marginal gloss terms 'Obiectiones circa nomen' reveals not only an openness to a new name but also an acknowledgement of subjects' or citizens' emotive attachment to their country, including his native Scotland.[44] 'In regards to the name', he writes,

> there remains a complicated problem which stems from the affection both the Scots and the English have for the old name of their country, not to mention its fame and popularity (so to speak), and its acceptance among foreigners. There's also the question of the dignity and the prerogative of the name as well as the strangeness and novelty of the name Britannia and its harsher sound (according to the common opinion).[45]

Attachment to one's native land is bound up with the historical name for that land. 'Name', Bacon writes to James in his earliest union text, 'carrieth much impression and inchantment'.[46] But in a wonderful piece of nomenclative archaeology, Hume reminds his readers that 'what is now called England was not always England, and they say that the name of Scotland was unknown to the earliest Scots'.[47] The (re)introduction of the name Britannia, therefore, constitutes the first step in not only eliminating Anglo-Scottish hostility and prejudice but also refiguring a sense of national belonging, community and neighbourliness. As Hume declares in his second tract, 'the citizens and people shall now be called British'.[48] In a congratulatory poem composed in honour of James's 1617 return to Edinburgh, Hume, like a host of Scottish writers after 1603, identifies himself as 'David Humius Scoto-Britannvs'.[49] If 'British' is a key word in the second tract, then so, too, is 'citizen', for Hume calls for an active engagement by Britain's population in order to form a 'British commonwealth' ('Reipublicæque Britannicæ').[50]

Hume's ideas on Britain and fashioning a British identity are grounded in the notion of commonality and community as well as what he terms 'the bonds of union'. These union bonds are to be effected through a variety of means: a common name for the kingdom; emblems and insignia (for instance, the coat of arms for Britain are to consist of the red lion rampant on a field of gold; the rose and the thistle in apposition constituting the ensign); a supreme council of Britannia made up of equal numbers of Scots and English, with York, Lancaster and Aberdeen playing greater roles in the new polity; a new seat of a singular British Parliament situated in York; standard coinage minted in Edinburgh and London; and free trade in commodities such as metals, food and drink, wool and weapons. In terms of cultural identity, a sense of Britishness is to be forged through Anglo-Scottish marriages: '[i]ntermarriage of the English and the Scots', Hume writes, 'shall be fostered as much as possible'.[51] In this, Hume anticipates Jacobean masques written by the likes of Ben Jonson and Thomas Campion that celebrated Anglo-Scottish marriages, though in all these masques the matrimonial unions were between Scottish husbands and English wives.[52] Education of the sons of Scottish and English nobles at, respectively, Oxford and Cambridge and Edinburgh, St Andrews and Glasgow is also proposed. In the second tract's longest chapter, religion emerges as a, if not the, key bond in forging a British kingdom/nation, and by religion Hume has in mind Scottish Presbyterianism. Hume's vision of a Presbyterian Britain probably explains the text's failure to appear in print, for Presbyterianism was not a confessional identity that James suffered lightly.

One subject upon which Hume and James did see eye to eye is internal colonisation. In the 1603 edition of *Basilikon Doron*, James offers the following comments on Scotland's non-Lowland inhabitants: '[a]s for the Hielands, I shortly comprehend them all in two sorts of people: the one, that dwelleth in our maine land, that are barbarous for the most part, and yet mixed with some shewe of ciuilite: the other, that dwelleth in the Iles, and are vtterly barbarous, without any sort of shew of ciuilitie'. The implementation of laws, according to James, will perform the work of civilising the Highlanders. For the Islanders, however, a root and branch reformation is called for, involving 'planting Colonies among them of answerable In-lands Subiects, that within short time may reforme and ciuilize the best inclined among them; rooting out or transporting the barbarous and stubborne sort, and planting ciuilitie in their rooms'.[53] Whereas James envisioned and indeed implemented a Lowland Scottish colonisation of the Isles, Hume champions an Anglo-Scottish or British colonisation:

> Colonies shall be sent out from the southern regions of Britannia (which are now the English part) to the Western Isles and to

Lochaber. Colonial administrators shall be placed in charge. If it shall seem convenient, these settlements shall include men and women from the more southerly regions of Scotland and, to whatever extent possible, they shall be encouraged to intermarry with the English settlers. The king shall grant whatever advantages there are in these newly established colonies especially to the English.[54]

Anticipating the Anglo-Scottish or British Jacobean plantation of Ulster, Hume's call for the colonisation of a predominantly Catholic Gaelic Scotland co-opts union in the name of a civilising mission: '[l]et the savagery of these regions begin to experience the power of union and its civilizing effect'.[55]

For Williamson, Hume's two tracts are distinguished by a sustained and surprisingly concrete vision of Anglo-Scottish union absent from any other contemporary pro-union tract. In its call for an end to Anglo-Scottish hostilities and its emphasis on the benefits that would accrue in the wake of fruitful cultural overlap, Hume's work is refreshingly progressive. But I would hesitate to label Hume's views on Highlanders and Islanders, as Williamson does, 'profoundly anti-racist'.[56] For all his talk of 'race', and 'one people', Hume's discourse is underpinned by an exclusive rhetoric of civility that privileges the English and Lowland Scots over Scotland's Gaelic community. The cultural sensitivity that accompanies Hume's discussion of the change of names is abandoned when his discussion turns to Scotland's native 'savages'. Detecting 'the voice of the Enlightenment' in Hume's union ideas, Williamson offers examples from the sixteenth century of other writers who, like Hume, anticipate 'Enlightenment attitudes', including Spenser: 'Edmund Spenser's view of the settlements in Ireland was similarly civic, and *pace* Irish nationalist historiography, similarly anti-imperial'.[57] Perhaps Williamson has in mind the following passage from Spenser's *A View of the Present State of Ireland* (c. 1596):

> since Ireland is full of her own nation that may not be rooted out, and somewhat stored with English already and more to be, I think it best by an union of manners and conformity of minds, to bring them to be one people, and to put away the dislikeful concept both of the one and the other, which will be by no means better than by this intermingling of them, that neither all the Irish may dwell together, nor all the English, but by translating of them, and scattering them in small numbers amongst the English, not only to bring them by daily

conversation unto better liking of each other, but also to make both of them less able to do hurt.⁵⁸

Although it invokes 'union' and the notion of 'one people', Spenser's account of Anglo-Irish 'intermingling' is underpinned by a desire for a translation and scattering of Ireland's indigenous inhabitants. The aim of Spenser's colonial 'reform' of Ireland, as one of his dialogue's speakers states, is to force the native 'quite to forget his Irish nation'.⁵⁹ In his attempt to render Hume radical – often the case when critics laud early modern authors belonging to the so-called 'Atlantic republican tradition' – Williamson risks investing his writings with values that simply are not there or obscuring values that are.

However unique Hume's two tracts are, they are not unique in the sense of being the only writings on union to have been published and to have circulated in manuscript form in the early seventeenth century; more than twenty-five print and manuscript tracts and treatises are extant. Hume, I want to suggest, was not alone in producing radical ideas in the wake of James's accession to the English throne; he was not the sole writer on union matters 'to think the whole matter through'.⁶⁰ One of the products of Anglo-Scottish union debate in the early seventeenth century was the emergence of new ideologies, new ways of thinking about state and identity formation. In response to James's union pronouncements, many English writers, to be sure, voiced a fear of an influx of Scots. In his 'Of the Union', the parliamentarian and antiquarian Henry Spelman betrays a deep-seated English insularity: '[t]he English ar our family; shall we then give awaye their breadde, which is their freedomes and libertyes, unto strangers?' 'Mak the Scottes free of Englande' he continues,

> what will be the sequele? First, many of their nobles and principall gentleman will strive to seate themselves as neare the Coorte as they cann. And good reason they shoulde, for who doth not desier the influence of the sonne. But our houses, our landes, our lyvings shall by that meanes be broughte upp in all places. The citty and cuntry shal be replenisshed with Scottes. The Courte shall abounde with them not as passingers but as commorantes.⁶¹

Not all of James's English subjects shared Spelman's sentiments. The writings of the polymath Francis Bacon on union are marked by an imaginative and political openness that demands critical re-examination.

'[T]he Vnion and commixture of bodies': Bacon

Like Hume, Bacon produced two tracts on Anglo-Scottish union, one printed shortly after James's accession, the other remaining unpublished until after Bacon's death. Unlike Hume, Bacon was fully immersed in the official Parliamentary business of union, especially as a member of the Anglo-Scottish Union Commission. His earliest tract and first Jacobean publication, *A Briefe Discovrse, Touching the Happie Vnion of the Kingdomes of England and Scotland Dedicated in Private to His Maiestie*, was entered in the Stationer's Register on 10 June 1603, and it was around this time that the *Briefe Discovrse* was printed. Numerous copies of this text survive, including manuscript copies, some of which are in contemporary handwriting – less an instance of scribal publication than the preparation of handwritten presentation copies.[62] Bacon's *Briefe Discovrse*, at just under 4,000 words, was the first union tract to appear in the wake of James's accession. It acknowledges the novelty of James's dual monarchy: 'Your Maiesty is the first King, which hath had the honour, to be *Lapis angularis*, to vnite these two mighty and warlike nations of *England* and *Scotland*, vnder one Soueraignety and Monarchy'.[63] This brief prose work reveals a British subject at once advising his king as well as seriously reflecting on cultural and national union. The bulk of Jacobean union tracts and treatises appeared between May and October of 1604, a period that followed the spring session of the English Parliament, the production of the Parliament's objections to union and the meeting of the Anglo-Scottish Union Commission in autumn. A second tract, *Certain Articles or Considerations Touching the Union of the Kingdoms of England and Scotland*, which Bacon did not publish but exists in a number of extant manuscripts, was most likely written in the summer of 1604 in advance of the Commission's autumn meetings. Given this manuscript's subtitle – 'Collected and dispersed for his Majesty's better Service' – and given the fact that on 18 August 1604 the king made Bacon a member of his learned counsel, or King's Counsel, Bacon's second union tract marks another instance of formal advice to the king. As a member of the House of Commons and as a member of the Anglo-Scottish Union Commission, Bacon held a prominent position in the lower house in relation to official union debate. The significance of union matters to Bacon's career is evidenced in the *Oxford Dictionary of*

National Biography's entry on Bacon, which includes as one of the entry's eleven subject headings 'Union of the kingdoms'.[64] More than any other name, Bacon's dominates the entries on union debate and discussion in the *Commons Journals*.

In his Preface to the Oxford edition of Bacon's *Major Works*, Brian Vickers says of two of Bacon's Elizabethan political writings – *An Advertisement touching the Controversies of the Church of England* and *Of Tribute* – 'I have chosen to illustrate Bacon's independence as a counselor, his ability to make a rational analysis of a given situation, rather than simply telling his superiors what they wanted to hear'.[65] Vickers goes on to describe Bacon's *Considerations Touching a War with Spain* (1624) as 'the last of his many treatises of advice to the Sovereign, a central genre in Renaissance political literature'.[66] Although Vickers is quick to point up Bacon's advisory prose, Bacon's brief union tracts are absent from his edition, perhaps because the editor regards those tracts as telling James what he wanted to hear.[67] Speaking of Bacon's Jacobean career, Vickers writes 'he was still only a tool of James, and the image that comes across is, rather like Eliot's "Prufrock", of one "Deferential, glad to be of use": conscientious, yet always implementing others' policies'.[68] The source for this statement is Vickers's reading of 'the five volumes of Spedding's monumental *Letters and Life* devoted to this period'; the 'period' under discussion is, of course, the period 'under King James', and the five volumes are volumes 3–7, which contain Bacon's union writing as well as Spedding's informative but dated commentary on Bacon's engagement with union matters.[69] In his notes to Bacon's essay 'Of Counsel', Vickers describes Bacon's *Briefe Discovrse* not as Spedding does – as 'a short philosophical treatise' – but instead as 'a detailed memorandum', a description that risks underestimating this text's place within the context of union ideas as well as Bacon's writings.[70]

The most detailed study of Bacon's work and writings within the context of Anglo-Scottish union debate remains Joel Epstein's 1970 article 'Francis Bacon and the issue of union, 1603–1608'. Epstein represents Bacon as an astute politician who 'champion[ed] James's policies in the Lower House'.[71] For Epstein, Bacon's interest in the union debates that marked the early years of James's reign was a purely self-serving one. Bacon, we are told 'was hopeful that a philosophical work on [union] might score favourably with His Majesty'.[72] Although Epstein describes Bacon's first union tract as 'a plea for patience and moderation', he still paints a portrait of Bacon as willingly accepting the 'task of trying to guide James's project through Parliament'; in fact, Epstein dismissively terms Bacon 'James's parliamentary agent for the promotion of a united kingdom'.[73] In doing so, Epstein elides one of the main conditions that Bacon's union tracts insist upon: namely, time. Again and again, Bacon warns James to leave the transformation of England and Scotland into a single polity to time. The voice that comes across in *Certain Articles*, for instance, is very much that of a counsellor rather than a servant. 'I have thought', Bacon says to his king,

> good to lay before you all the branches, lineaments, and degrees of this Union; that upon the view and consideration of them and their circumstances, your Majesty may the more clearly discern and more readily call to mind which of them is to be embraced, and which to be rejected; and of those which are to be accepted, which of them is presently to be proceeded in, and which to be put over to further time; and again, which of them shall require authority of Parliament, and which are fitter to be effected by your Majesty's royal power and prerogative, or by other policies or means; and lastly, which of them is liker to pass with difficulty and contradiction, and which with more facility and smoothness.[74]

Is this the voice of a subject slavishly adhering to his monarch's desires? Bacon presents himself as a subject willing to inform and advise James on serious matters of state. The 'true union', Bacon writes, 'must be the work of time'.[75] In an essay titled 'Of Innouations', Bacon describes innovations as 'the Births of Time'; 'Time' he adds, 'is the greatest *Innouatour*'.[76] In an obvious but unacknowledged reference to union debate, Bacon writes '[i]t is good also, not to try Experiments in States; Except the Necessity be Vrgent, or the vtility Euident'.[77] The final words here echo the list of objections that Parliament produced on 27 April 1604: under the heading 'Matter of generallitie, or Comon reason' is the objection '[t]hat in Constituting or ordayninge of any innovacion or Chaunge, there ought to be eyther urgent necescitie or evident utilitie'.[78] Thornborough's pro-union tract would recirculate this phrase in its title: *A Discovrse Plainely Prouing the euident vtilitie and vrgent necessitie of the desired happie Vnion of the two famous Kingdomes of England and Scotland: by way of answer to certaine obiections against the same*. Clearly Bacon was averse to any hasty approach to and handling of Anglo-Scottish union, and he certainly communicated this in his union tracts dedicated to James. Consider, for example, the following passage, which cautiously questions the evident utility or urgent necessity of Anglo-Scottish union:

> For the realm of Scotland is now an ancient and noble realm, substantive of itself. But when this island shall be made Britain, then Scotland is no more to be considered as Scotland, but as a part of Britain; no more than England is to be considered as England, but as a part likewise of Britain; and consequently neither of these are to be considered as things entire of themselves, but in the proportion that they bear to the whole.[79]

If this passage looks forward to a time 'when this island shall be made Britain', it also tempers such enthusiasm by calling to mind that Scotland/England will be 'no more'. Furthermore, Bacon is informing his monarch that because England constitutes two-thirds of the island and Scotland just one-third a future Britain will consist not of an equal partnershp of the two current kingdoms but instead will be dominated by England and the English. Bacon's early Jacobean political writings are frank, pragmatic and realistic, which is why they demand a critical reappraisal.[80]

In a letter to Henry Percy, earl of Northumberland Bacon offers his first impressions of the new king, and he broaches the topic of Anglo-Scottish union when he states that the king 'hasteneth to a mixture of both kingdoms and nations, faster perhaps than policy will conveniently bear'.[81] The fear of a too-hasty union underpins Bacon's *Briefe Discovrse*; in fact, the tract counsels James to proceed slowly in this monumental matter of state. Bacon frequently comes across in his letters and prose as a fawning and submissive subject to those above him, and there is little doubt that he is often angling for some form of promotion. 'Flattering the King's scholarly ambitions' is how Lisa Jardine and Alan Stewart describe Bacon's 'ideal gift' (*A Briefe Discovrse*) to James,[82] paradoxically resisting and reinscribing conventional narratives. Still, his investment of the role of the counsellor with seriousness and purpose should not be overlooked. 'The ancient times', Bacon writes in 'Of Counsel', 'doe set forth in figure both the incorporation, and inseparable coniunction of counsell with *Kinges*; and the wise and politike vse of Counsell by *Kings*'.[83] In a revised version of this essay, Bacon discusses counsel within the context of Anglo-Scottish union debate:

The *Councels*, at this Day, in most Places, are but Familiar Meetings; where Matters are rather talked on, than debated. And they run too swift to the Order or Act of *Councell*. It were better, that in Causes of weight, the Matter were propounded one day, and not spoken to, till the next day; *In Nocte Consilium*. So was it done, in the Commission of *Vnion*, between *England* and *Scotland*; which was a Graue and Orderly Assembly.[84]

Although Bacon will come to describe his role in his second union tract of 1604 as that of a 'remembrancer' rather than a 'counsellor', there is little doubt that he saw himself as advising his king in relation to the crucial work of effecting a union. Indeed, Bacon's reminders invest memory with cultural, ideological, political force.[85]

Like many of the union tracts and treatises written in 1604–05, Bacon's devote ample attention to historical precedents. However, the bulk of his *Briefe Discovrse* considers union matters generally, particularly a union of the inhabitants of the two kingdoms, in terms of the what he calls a congruity between nature and policy: that is, 'of making the gouernment of the world, a mirror for the gouernment of the state'.[86] Bacon immediately rejects the notion of a union by conquest or victory, 'when one body, doth meerely subdue another, and conuerteth the same into his owne *Nature*, extinguishing and expulsing, what part so euer of it, it cannot ouercome'.[87] Although Bacon's account of union by conquest supplies no historical examples, surely the Elizabethan Protestant reconquest of Ireland as well as the recent Nine Years' War exemplify such a union of countries by conquest: 'where the conquering State dooth extinguish, extirpate and expulse any parte of the estate conquered, which it findeth so contrarye, as it cannot alter and conuerte it'.[88] In a March 1599 letter to Essex on the eve of the earl's departure for Ireland, Bacon describes England's war with Ireland as 'no ambitious war against foreigners, but a recovery of subjects, and that after lenity of conditions often tried; and a recovery of them not only to obedience, but to humanity and policy, from more than Indian barbarism'.[89] The crucial word here is 'recovery': Bacon never posits any kind of union between Elizabeth's two kingdoms, one of which was in effect a colony. From the perspective of 1599, when manuscript copies of Spenser's *View* were in circulation, Ireland and the Irish, many English believed, could be recovered only by means of a violent reconquest.

Given that England and Scotland are separate kingdoms, although now united in sovereignty and subjection, Bacon shifts his attention from 'violent unions' to 'natural unions':

> It resteth therefore, but that, (as I promised) I set before your Maiesties Princelye consideration, the grounds of *Nature*, touching the Vnion and commixture of bodies; & the correspondence which they haue with the groundes of *Pollicie*, in the coniunction of states and kingdomes.[90]

Central to Bacon's intersection of natural and political philosophy in his reflections on Anglo-Scottish union is a vital distinction 'betweene *Compositio* and *Mistio*; putting together and mingling'.[91] Concerning *compositio* ('putting together') and *mistio* ('mingling') Bacon writes '[t]he one beeing but a coniunction of bodyes in place, the other in quality, and consent; the one, the mother of sedition and alteration, the other of peace and continuance: The one rather a confusion, then an Vnion, the other properly a Vnion'.[92] '*Compositio*', he continues, 'is the ioyning or putting togeather of bodyes, without a new Forme: and *Mistio*, is the ioyning or putting togeather of bodies, vnder a new Forme'.[93] And such a new form, according to Bacon, 'is *commune vinculum*' – a common bond.[94] Writing well after the publication of *A Briefe Discovrse*, Hume, discussing 'how useful it would be for these people to coalesce into one', acknowledges other published union tracts, noting 'there has already been said a great deal, and more cogently, than there is any need for me to say'.[95] McGinnis and Williamson suggest that Hume has in mind John Hayward and John Thornborough, but it is Bacon who, perhaps more than any other writer in the early seventeenth century, articulates most fully how the people of Britain may coalesce into a single collective identity.

In his *Certain Articles or Considerations Touching the Union of the Kingdoms of England and Scotland*, Bacon employs a standard humility *topos* when referring to his earlier *Briefe Discovrse*: 'I presumed at your Majesty's first entrance to write a few lines, indeed scholastically and speculatively, and not actively or politically'.[96] The key word here is 'speculatively', for, as Graham Rees argues, underpinning Bacon's philosophical enterprise is a certain doubleness: 'on the one hand, Bacon's philosophy offers itself to us as a program for constructing a body of scientific knowledge that was supposed to yield immense practical benefits and so release the human race from material privation. On the other hand, it manifests itself as a rather strange *corpus* of speculative science.'[97] The presence of this speculative science is precisely what distinguishes Bacon's union writing from that of his contemporaries. When Hume states '[h]ow easy it will be for this people to be mingled from here on' – 'Quam facile erit, sic genus adhuc miscere' – he seems to take the process of merging distinct national identities for granted.[98] Not that Hume does not supply a number of practical means by which to effect the creation of British people; as discussed earlier, he proposes Anglo-Scottish marriages; the education of Scots at Oxford and Cambridge and of the English at Edinburgh, St Andrews and Glasgow; and the colonisation of English settlers in remote parts of Scotland. Informed by a speculative model of scientific investigation, Bacon's theorising of the intermingling of James's British subjects is grounded in the study of natural bodies. The following passage is a remarkable instance of an early modern author thinking through union matters from the perspective of natural philosophy or science:

> Now, to reflect this light of *Nature*, vpon matter of estate: there hath beene put in practise in gouernment, these two seuerall kindes of pollicie, in vniting & conioyning of states & kingdomes. The one to retaine the auncient formes still seuered, and onely conioyned in Soueraingtie; the other, to superinduce a new forme agreeable and conuenient to the entire estate. The former of these hath beene more vsuall, and is more easie: but the latter, is more happy. For, if a man doe attentiuely reuolue histories of all nations, and iudge truly therevpon: hee will make this conclusion, that there were neuer any State that were good commixtures, but the *Romaines*: which because it was the best state in the worlde, and is the best example of this pointe, wee will chiefely insist therevpon.[99]

As this passage attests, Bacon approaches the concept of political union with a radically different vocabulary – not just 'mingling' and 'superinducing' but also 'conglutination' – than any other author, in part because he analyses the topic in not only historical but also, and predominantly, philosophical-scientific terms. A number of authors cite the example of the Romans and Sabines, including the anonymous author of 'A Treatise about the Union of England and Scotland' as well as Savile and Craig.[100] To my knowledge, Bacon is the only writer to employ the term 'superinduce' within the context of union debate and discussion; in fact, the *OED*, defining 'superinduce' as '[t]o bring in or add over and above, or on top of, something already present; to introduce (esp. something extraneous) in addition' (*v*.3), gives as the first usage of this word the passage cited above from Bacon's *Briefe Discovrse*. That Bacon is drawing upon scientific discourse becomes evident if we turn to Bacon's *Of the proficience and aduancement of Learning* (1605) where he uses the term 'superinduce' regularly (the *OED*'s second instance of this word's use comes from this 1605 text). For example, he writes 'whosoeuer knoweth any *forme* knoweth the vtmost *possibilitie* of *superinducing* that *Nature* vpon *any varietie of Matter*'.[101] Bacon was one of the few common-law lawyers in the House of Commons to lend his voice to James's vision of union. Other MPs supported the union, but they were members of the House of Lords, such as John Thornborough, or civil-law lawyers, such as John Hayward – not that Bacon was unfamiliar with civil law. What distinguishes Bacon from his fellow common-law lawyer MPs is his willingness and ability to think through union ideas relatively free of the insularity of English legal jurisdiction and, crucially, sustained by an intellect grounded in philosophical and scientific investigation and innovation.

As the passage just cited attests, there exists in Bacon's writing both before and after the production of his union tracts a commitment to new forms, and I believe that this commitment extends well beyond his scientific prose; indeed, it informs his discourse on state and identity formation. In his 'Letter and discourse to Sir Henry Savile, touching helps for the intellectual powers', which Vickers dates between 1596 and 1604 and describes as 'another example of Bacon using the genre of advice literature', Bacon notes 'how variously, and to how high points and degrees, the body of man may be (as it were) moulded and wrought'.[102] In his posthumously published *The New Atlantis*, Bacon returns to this idea. Within Salomon's House, the narrator of *The New Atlantis* is informed by the Father of Salomon's House that '[w]e have also parks and inclosures of all sorts of beasts and birds, which we use not only for view or rareness, but likewise for dissections and trials; that thereby we may take light what may be wrought upon the body of man'. One such trial involves 'means to make commixtures and copulations of different kinds; which have produced many new kinds'.[103] Although written toward the end of Bacon's life, *The New Atlantis*, as Markku Peltonen's *ODNB* entry notes, developed ideas that

Bacon had outlined thirty years earlier in the early 1590s. These ideas on the malleability of forms and subjects manifest themselves in Bacon's political writings, including those on Anglo-Scottish union. The following passage from his *Briefe Discovrse* exemplifies the way in which Bacon's speculative philosophy provides the conceptual glue that binds together his thoughts on a potential union of the two kingdoms:

> There remaineth onely, to remember out of the grounds of *Nature*, the two conditions of perfect *mixture*: whereof the former is *Time*. For, the naturall Philosophers say well, that *compositio*, is *opus homines*: and *Mistio*, is *opus Naturæ*. For it is the dutie of man, to make a fitte application of bodies together. But, the perfect fermentation and incorporation of them, must be left to *Nature* and *Time*: and vnnaturall hasting thereof, dooth disturbe the worke, and not dispatche it.[104]

Of particular interest here is Bacon's use of the words 'fermentation' and, especially, 'incorporation'. Numerous union tracts employ the word 'incorporation', but they do so to signify the incorporation of a political body. For example, Thornborough's discussion of Anglo-Scottish union invokes England's incorporation of Wales: 'as it was when the principalitie and countrie of Wales was by Parliament incorporated and vnited vnto the kingdome of England, and all the inhabitants thereof made equall in freedomes, liberties, rights, privileges, lawes, and in all other respects to the naturall subjects of England'.[105] As the presence of 'fermentation' suggests, Bacon uses 'incorporation' here, as he will again in his *New Atlantis*, to mean 'combine into new substances'.[106] Reflecting on the novelty of James's composite monarchy, Bacon's union tracts generate political ideas grounded in the idea of peoples and nations joining together.

If Hume's *De Vnione* 'comprises the Presbyterian response to the *True Law*, the patriotic riposte to the *Basilikon Doron*', then Bacon's tract shares little of Hume's radicalness.[107] If, as McGinnis and Williamson also suggest, Hume's tract envisions a Ciceronian republic, by no means does Bacon's lay the foundation for an Augustan empire. According to Markku Peltonen, 'Bacon's most important writings of the first decade of the new reign were not merely composed as answers to the central issue of the contemporary political debate – the Anglo-Scottish Union – they also utilized some of the chief themes of the classical republican tradition'.[108]

The radical Bacon that I wish to put forward has less to do with a radical republican tradition. Rather, I wish to highlight Bacon's articulation of fresh political ideas during this signal moment of British history. Like Hume, Bacon sees a potential union as a Machiavellian *occasione*. And no doubt Bacon sensed an opportunity for his own advancement. When, for instance, in *Certain Articles*, Bacon describes himself 'not as a man born in England, but as a man born in Britain', it is difficult not to associate Bacon's new-found British pedigree with political opportunism – as previously mentioned, Robert Cotton, upon James' accession to the English throne, rechristened himself Robert Bruce Cotton.[109] In fact, Bacon's opportunism becomes even more evident if we compare the previous statement with a similar one that he made in a 1592 letter to Lord Burghley, wherein Bacon presents himself 'not as a man born under Sol, that loveth honour; nor under Jupiter, that loveth business (for the contemplative planet carrieth me away wholly); but as a man born under an excellent Sovereign, that deserveth the dedication of all men's abilities'.[110] Bacon's nativity, it seems, can be moulded and wrought to suit the occasion. To dismiss Bacon's union writing as the product of a subject at once out of and in search of royal favour, however, risks foreclosing fruitful avenues of study. Bacon's political writings on Anglo-Scottish union bear witness to an author seriously engaging in early modern political thought; indeed, his union tracts can be read as a laboratory for thought about early modern notions of state and identity formation.

'[A]nother Britain': Planting Ulster

'Your majesty', Bacon addresses James, 'hath a royal and indeed an heroical desire to reduce these two kingdoms of England and Scotland into the unity of their ancient mother kingdom of Britain'.[111] In a Parliamentary response to Thomas Fuller's antiunion speech of 14 February 1607, Bacon cites 'Ireland reduced' as one of the benefits of James's triple monarchy.[112] If England and Scotland are children to a British motherland, then what place does Ireland occupy in this family history? In a letter to the king that accompanied his presentation copy of *Certain Considerations Touching the Plantation in Ireland*,[113] a text that provides what its title suggests, Bacon supplies an answer to this question: 'I was encouraged by my experience of your Majesty's former grace, in accepting of the like poor field-fruits touching the Union. And certainly I reckon this action [i.e. plantation in Ireland] as a second brother to the Union. For I assure myself that England, Scotland, and Ireland well united is such a trefoil as no prince except yourself (who are the worthiest) weareth in his crown.'[114] Just as nature and divine providence have combined to effect a union of England's and Scotland's crowns under James's rule, so, too, should Britain and Ireland, according to Bacon, be united: 'these islands of the western ocean seem by nature and providence an entire empire in themselves'.[115] Bacon presented his text on the plantation in Ireland to James in 1609; by this point the English Parliament had rejected James's proposals for union. Naturalisation had been granted to *post-nati* Scots, but England's Parliament had quashed any hopes of the uniting of England and Scotland into a single kingdom. How, then, was Ireland, which Bacon terms 'another Britain', to be incorporated within James's British empire?[116]

'It seemeth', Bacon begins his address to James in *Certain Considerations*, 'God hath reserved to your Majesty's times two works, which amongst the acts of kings have the supreme pre-eminence; the union and the plantation of kingdoms'.[117] The plantation here refers the English government's plans to pacify and plant, or colonise, not all of Ireland but rather the province that traditionally proved most resistant to English encroachment, Ulster. The Flight of the Earls in September 1607 meant that Ulster was no longer home to the mighty Gaelic lords who for years had led the Irish resistance against the English. Past attempts to colonise Ulster by Sir Thomas Smith and Walter Devereux, first earl of Essex, in the 1570s had failed miserably. But in 1609 the plantation of Ulster was a political reality. Indeed, Bacon's *Certain Considerations* imagines an earl-less Ulster as a *tabula rasa*: '[f]or most part unions and plantations of kingdoms have been founded in the effusion of blood: but your Majesty shall build *in solo puro et in area pura*, that shall need no sacrifices expiatory for blood'.[118] Bacon, of course, was fully aware that Ireland had seen its fair share of bloodshed. Writing to Essex, probably in March 1599, Bacon had described the Irish as 'a people barbarous and not reduced to civility, magnifying a kind of lawless liberty, prodigal in life, hardened in body, fortified in woods and bogs, and placing both justice and felicity in the sharpness of their swords'. 'Such', he adds, 'were the Germans and the ancient Britons'.[119] Like Hume's, Bacon's political writings are grounded in a rhetoric of civility. Bacon's plantation tract has nothing to say about the intermingling of James's British subjects and the Irish. Moreover, in labelling not only the Irish 'barbarous' but also the ancient Britons, Bacon shows little interest in reclaiming Britain or Britishness from antiquity. If Britain is to come into being, it must be invented rather than restored: 'unions and plantations are the very nativities or birth-days of kingdoms'.[120] Ireland, more specifically Ulster, is 'another Britain' precisely because its plantation by English and Lowland or 'inland' Scottish planters – some of whom were of Celtic descent and Catholic – under James gave rise to British subjects and British communities in a manner unmatched anywhere else in early modern Britain or Ireland.[121]

A quick glance at the titles of Ulster plantation literature reveal the use of an ethnically specific term to designate the incoming undertakers: for example, *Conditions to be Observed by the Brittish Vndertakers of the Escheated Lands in Vlster* (1610); *A Proclamation for the Brittish Vndertakers to repaire into Ireland* (1611). John Davies, writing in 1612, refers to James's '*British Vndertaker*' and speaks of a 'mixt plantation of *Brittish & Irish*'.[122] Who were these British undertakers? In a letter to Cecil dated 10 May 1610, Davies, then James's attorney-general in Ireland, writes

> we published by proclamation in each county, what lands were granted to British undertakers, and what to servitors, and what to natives: to the end that the natives should remove from the precincts allotted to the Britons, whereupon a clear plantation is to be made of English and Scottish, without Irish, and to settle upon the lands assigned to natives and servitors, where there shall be a mixed plantation of English and Irish together.[123]

In its designation of English and Scottish undertakers as 'British' and 'Britons', this passage reveals how a sense of Britishness came into being in opposition to the native Irish: Britishness was forged in Ulster as Irishness was being displaced and erased. If a union of English and Scottish subjects was to take effect in Ulster, then another union would be dismantled: namely, the political and cultural union forged between the native inhabitants of north-east Ulster and their fellow Gaels across the North Channel. In his 'Of the Union of Britayne', Pont predicted that a union would deliver a blow to the destabilising presence of 'wild and savadg Irish of the English dominion, and of the Scottish ilands the Hebridiani':

> These dout lest the English and Scottish once formed into one bodie, that they by force shalbe made subject to the lawes, when as before for every light and trifling matter ... they were readie to flie out and to ayde one another in their wicked defections. And if happely by any sleight or stratagem they were hemmed in or empaled, the Irish embarqued themselves for the Scotish iles, and these Hebridiani with their complices had a foorth into Ireland – which was no small troble and chardg to both nations. Which disease and distemper may now soone be wed, the whole state of Albion being reduced to the empire of one soveraigne, their being no place of refuge for the rebell, and the stubbornes of the seditions easily tamed, the power of the prince being doubled.[124]

Pont's vision of England and Scotland formed into one political body was never realised under James's rule. Ulster, however, emerged as a testing-ground for fashioning British subjects.

On 29 December 1613, the Jacobean court witnessed a performance of Jonson's *The Irish Masqve at Court*, performed in honour of Frances Howard's second marriage, this time to the King's favourite, the Scottish courtier Robert Carr, newly created earl of Somerset. What is striking about this production is its mystification of the 'civilising process': striking because it was produced at a time when James's Old and New, Catholic and Protestant English subjects in Dublin were engaged in an intense struggle for Parliamentary power – James had asked the Parliament in Dublin for legislative and financial support for the Ulster plantation, but the Old English, fearing yet more Protestant English settlers, were unsupportive. Jonson's masque opens with a band of uncouth and outlandish Irish servants who reveal that their lords, recently arrived from Ireland to take part in the nuptials, have lost their masquing apparel during a storm on the Irish Sea and therefore must 'dance forth a dance in their Irish mantles'. Antimasque gives way to masque as 'a civil gentleman of the nation' interrupts the four Irishmen and proclaims '[h]old your tongues./And let your coarser manners seeke some place/Fit for their wildnesse. This is none, be gone.'[125] Accompanying this 'civil gentleman' is a Bard who prophesies a transformation of the compliant, mantle-clad lords into newly fashioned British subjects:

> Bow both your heads at once, and hearts:
> Obedience doth not well in parts.
> It is but standing in his eye,
> You'll feele yourselves chang'd by and by,

> Few liue, that know, how quick a spring
> Workes in the presence of a king:
> Tis done by this; your slough let fall,
> And come forth new-borne creatures all.

'In this song', the text notes, 'the Masquers let fall their mantles; and discouer their masquing apparell. Then dance forth.'[126] Given the volatile political situation in Ireland, Jonson's *Irish Masqve* ranks among the more relaxed and mystified representations of colonial interaction in the early modern period. Yet it remains an invaluable text precisely because it enacts the process of British identity formation in Ireland. Although the words 'British' and 'Briton' are never uttered – 'great Britayne'[127] is – the roles of the submissive Irish lords in the masque were performed by five English and five Scottish courtiers. With its British ventriloquisation of Irish voices, Jonson's masque symbolises not only the briticising of Britain's and Ireland's nobles but also the Anglo-Scottish or British appropriation of Irish land and the supplanting of Gaelic culture. 'Union', Butler suggests, 'was the ideological crucible out of which [Jacobean] masques were made'.[128] Just a few years into James's English reign, not just union but its ideological brother, plantation, joined the matrix from which masques such as Jonson's emerged. Paradoxically, Anglo-Scottish sameness or Britishness was being promoted across the Irish Sea, where for so long English attempts at overcoming Anglo-Irish cultural differences had been greeted by fierce resistance from the native Irish.

In reference to his *Discoverie*, J. G. A. Pocock states that Davies 'with imperialist intentions, wrote an intercultural history, concerned with conflict and crossbreeding between societies differently based'.[129] Indeed, Davies is acutely aware of Ireland's heterogeneous body politic. Writing in 1613, Davies offers an optimistic account of an inclusive Irish Parliament, and he anticipates a time 'when all the inhabitants of the kingdom, English of birth, English of blood, the new British colony, and the old Irish natives, do all meet together to make laws for the common good of themselves and their posterities'.[130] The reference points here are to the New English ('English of birth'), the Old English ('English of blood'), Ulster-based English and Scots ('the new British colony') and the Gaelic Irish ('the old Irish natives'). This is a remarkable instance of an ethnic or racial classification of Ireland's native and non-native inhabitants, for it is grounded in notions of blood and birthplace as well as a coming together of distinct national identities – English and Scottish, not Irish. 'Ireland', writes Linda Colley (although in reference to a later historical period), 'was in many respects the laboratory of the British Empire'.[131] However, the majority of Ireland's inhabitants, according to Colley, were 'never swept into a British identity to the degree that proved possible among the Welsh, the Scots, and the English'.[132] But the Scots and the English were swept into a British identity in Jacobean Ulster: one result of the Jacobean plantation of English and Scottish settlers in Ulster was the emergence of a nascent British community and, eventually, collective identity. The 'Protestant people of Northern Ireland', Pocock reminds us, constitute 'the last of the historic nations formed in this part of the archipelago'.[133] The term the 'Jacobean plantation of Ulster' is apropos precisely because an Anglo-Scottish settlement could never have come about under Elizabeth. Furthermore, Jacobean Ulster played a crucial role in not only fostering Britishness but also consolidating Irishness.[134] Not surprisingly, a manuscript poem titled 'On the death of James King of England' remembers England's Scottish monarch as one who was able 'to plant Nations rather than destroy'.[135] Given the presence of the word 'plant', and given the fact that this poem is housed in Trinity College Library, Dublin, the poem seems to be acknowledging Ulster as the site of the emergence of a British nation.

The emergence of a British national community in Ulster was not immediate, and it never resembled an inclusive, non-violent coming together of peoples as imagined and desired in James's speeches or Bacon's writings on union or plantation. Instead, the Jacobean plantation of Ulster serves as a prime example of what Michael Hechter terms 'internal colonialism', a term that runs the risk of transhistoricising the local but serves to counter an upbeat narrative of the forging of Britishness by attending to the various cleansings – ethnic, yes, but also confessional and political – performed by the early modern state: from Ulster (and earlier) to the Cromwellian Settlement to the Highland Clearances.[136]

Notes

1 [James VI], *Basilikon dōron. Devided into three bookes* (Edinburgh, 1599), 99–100. In the 1603 London edition, the sentence cited from

the 1599 edition is followed by 'as befell to the Ile: by the diuision and assignement thereof, to the three sonnes of *Brutus, Locrine, Abanact,* and *Camber*': James VI and I, *Basilikon Doron*, 83.
2 *Calendar of State Papers and Manuscripts Relating to English Affairs, Existing in the Archives and Collections of Venice and in other Libraries of Northern Italy*, ed. Horatio F. Brown et al., 38 vols (London: Longman, Green, Longman, Roberts and Green, 1864–1947), X, 5.
3 Announcing his accession as James I to his Scottish subjects, James ordered 'the inhabitantis of baith realmes to obliterat and remove out of thair myndis all and quhatsumever quarrellis, eleistis or debaitis qhilk hes mentenit discord or distractioun of effectioun amangis thame in tyme past, and with ane universall unanimitie of harits conjoine thameselffis as ane natioun under his Majesteis authoritie': John Hill Burton and David Masson (eds), *The Register of the Privy Council of Scotland*, 14 vols (Edinburgh, 1877–98), VI, 516.
4 England and Wales. Privy Council, *By the King forasmuch as the Kings Maiestie.*
5 *Ibid.*
6 [Anon.], 'A briefe Replicacion to the Aunswers of the Obiections against the Vnion', British Library, Stowe 158, fol. 34^r.
7 [James VI and I], *The Kings Maiesties Speech*, A4^v.
8 *Ibid.*, B4^v, B1^{r-v}.
9 *Ibid.*, B1^v.
10 William Cornwallis, *The Miracvlovs and Happie Union of England and Scotland* (London, 1604) (STC 5782), D1^r. Cornwallis's text was entered in the Stationers' Register on 19 March 1604, the day of James's Parliament speech. This Sir William Cornwallis, the younger (*c.* 1579–1614), is not to be confused with his uncle Sir William Cornwallis (*c.* 1549–1611) at whose house Jonson's *A Private Entertainment at Highgate* was performed on 1 May 1604.
11 [Shakespeare], *The cronicle history of Henry the fift*, A3^r.
12 Pont, 'Of the Union', 20.
13 'Which may easily be done betwixt these two nations, being both but one Ile of *Britaine*, and alreadie ioyned in vnitie of Religion and language': James VI and I, *Basilikon Doron*, L1^r.
14 [James VI and I], *The Kings Maiesties Speech*, B3^r.
15 Galloway, *The Union of England and Scotland*, 19.
16 *Journal of the House of Commons*: Volume 1, *1547–1629* (London, 1802), 160.
17 *Ibid.*, 176, 177.
18 See Galloway, *The Union of England and Scotland*, 15–23.

19 See, for example, Huntington Library, Ellesmere MS 1226; British Library, Harleian MS 292; Bodleian Library, Tanner MS 75. A printed version of the list of objections appeared in some editions of John Thornborough's *A Discovrse Plainely Prouing the euident vtilitie and vrgent necessitie of the desired happie Vnion of the two famous Kingdomes of England and Scotland: by way of answer to certaine obiections against the same* (London, 1604). 'The Obiections' appear as prefatory text in one of the Folger Shakespeare Library's editions of Thornborough's *Discovrse* (copy 2) with the signatures a1^r–a2^v. In the Bristol Central Library's copy of Thornborough's *Discovrse* (shelfmark SR 4B), 'The Obiections' appear not as prefatory material but instead at the end of the work, although the signatures (a1^r–a2^v) remain the same. Thornborough's tract must have been in print by 26 May, for a complaint was raised in the lower house against Thornborough, who sat as a member of the House of Lords, for breaching Parliamentary privilege. Inscribed on the title page of a copy of the *Discovrse* housed in the National Library of Scotland – shelfmark 5.2475(4) – in a contemporary hand is the date 'maii 27.1604'.
20 Conrad Russell, '1603: the end of English national sovereignty', in Burgess, Wymer and Lawrence (eds), *The Accession of James I*, 1.
21 'Obiections agaynst the Chaunge of the name or Stile of England and Scotland into the name or stile of great Britaine to be moved and Debated in the Conference betweene the Lo: and the Comons, And to that end by the Comittees of the house of Comons collected reveved and reduced to order for theire better instruction', Huntington Library, Ellesmere MS 1226. The 'Obiections' can be found in Spedding, *Letters and Life*, III, 197–200 as well as in Galloway, *The Union of England and Scotland*, 28–9.
22 Ibid.
23 England and Wales. Privy Council, *By the King. As often as we call to minde.*
24 Francis Bacon, *The Essayes of Couvnsels, Civill and Morall, of Francis Lo. Vervlam, Viscovnt St Alban* (London, 1625), 215. Concerning 'the alteration of stile', Bacon in 1604 asked James 'whether it were not better to transpose the kingdom of Ireland, and put it immediately after Britain, and so place the islands together; and the kingdom of France, being upon the continent, last; in regard that these islands of the western ocean seem by nature and providence an entire empire in themselves; and also that there was never king of England so entirely possest of Ireland as your Majesty is; so as your stile to run King of Britain, Ireland, and the islands adjacent, and of France, etc.': Francis Bacon, *Certain Articles or Considerations Touching the Union of the Kingdoms of England and Scotland*, in Spedding (ed.), *Letters and*

Life, III, 226. James, it should be noted, never set foot in Ireland or Wales.
25 *Ibid.*, 227.
26 Levack, *The Formation of the British State*, 180.
27 Joel J. Epstein, 'Francis Bacon and the issue of union, 1603–1608', *Huntington Library Quarterly*, 33 (1970), 124.
28 Morrill, 'The fashioning of Britain', 18.
29 See, for example, Galloway, *The Union of England and Scotland*; Levack, *The Formation of the British State*; and Galloway and Levack's *The Jacobean Union*.
30 Burgess, Wymer and Lawrence, 'Introduction', xiii–xxvii.
31 *Ibid.*, xiv.
32 *Ibid.*, xv.
33 David Hume of Godscroft, *De Vnione Insulæ Britannicæ Tractatus. 1. Per Dauidem Humium Theagrium* (London, 1605), A2^r.
34 David Hume of Godscroft, 'Vincvla Vnionis Sive Scita Britannicæ id est De Unione Insvlæ Britannicæ Tractatvs Secvndvs. Per Davidem Hvmivm Theagrivm', Edinburgh University Library, MS Laing III, 249, 5^r.
35 Edinburgh University Library (EUL), MS Dc.5.50; EUL, MS Dc.7.46; EUL, MS Laing III, 249 (which is in the elegant italic hand of Esther Inglis); National Library of Scotland, Advocates MS 31.6.12; British Library, MS Royal 12.A.LIII.
36 Paul J. McGinnis and Arthur H. Williamson (eds and trans.), *The British Union: A Critical Edition and Translation of David Hume of Godscroft's De Unione Insulae Britannicae* (Aldershot: Ashgate, 2002), 137.
37 Arthur Williamson, 'Radical Britain: David Hume of Godscroft and the challenge to the Jacobean British vision', in Burgess, Wymer and Lawrence (eds), *The Accession of James I*, 56.
38 McGinnis and Williamson (eds and trans.), *The British Union*, 157. The phrase 'one kingdom and one people' is reiterated throughout Hume's two tracts.
39 *Ibid.*, 63.
40 [Anon.], 'Concerning the alteration of the name of England', Bodleian Library, Tanner MS 75, fol. 24^r.
41 John Hayward, *A Treatise of Vnion of the two Realmes of England and Scotland* (London, 1604), 34, 35.
42 Henry Savile, 'Historicall Collections', in Galloway and Levack (eds), *The Jacobean Union*, 202, 205–06.
43 McGinnis and Williamson (eds and trans.), *The British Union*, 109.
44 Hume, *De Vnione*, 16.
45 McGinnis and Williamson (eds and trans.), *The British Union*, 107.
46 [Bacon], *Briefe Discovrse*, B8^v–C1^r.

47 McGinnis and Williamson (eds and trans.), *The British Union*, 109.
48 *Ibid.*, 155. Hume's call for 'fines' for anyone who refers to themselves as English or Scottish is draconian, and his comment that 'giving offense on either side ... must be altogether avoided in conversion, in the performance of plays [*Eastward Hoe*?], and in social gathering', would have made him a rather dour Master of the Revels.
49 David Hume, *Regi suo, post bis septennium in patriam ex Angliâ redeunti, Scotiæ gratulatio* (Edinburgh, 1617), A4^v.
50 McGinnis and Williamson (eds and trans.), *The British Union*, 133; Hume, *De Vnione*, 24.
51 McGinnis and Williamson (eds and trans.), *The British Union*, 213.
52 For an in-depth study of the relation between Anglo-Scottish marriage and Jacobean masques, see Kevin Curran, *Marriage, Performance, and Politics at the Jacobean Court* (London: Routledge, 2009).
53 James VI and I, *Basilikon Doron*, 35–6.
54 McGinnis and Williamson (eds and trans.), *The British Union*, 217.
55 *Ibid.*, 223.
56 Williamson, 'Radical Britain', 61.
57 *Ibid.*, 62, 63.
58 Spenser, *A View of the Present State of Ireland*, 153.
59 *Ibid.*, 156. As Nicholas Canny and Andrew Carpenter note, 'the means that [Spenser] advocates for the reform of the Gaelic Irish involves their being reduced to the point where they would forget their very ancestry and their historical memory': Nicholas Canny and Andrew Carpenter, 'The early planters: Spenser and his contemporaries', in Seamus Deane (ed.), *The Field Day Anthology of Irish Writing* (Derry: Field Day Publications, 1991), I, 172.
60 McGinnis and Williamson (eds and trans.), *The British Union*, 57. In fact, Hume twice acknowledges other union tracts and treatises: see McGinnis and Williamson (eds and trans.), *The British Union*, 77, 157; the latter references James's speeches to Parliament, 'J[ohn]. H[ayward].', and 'the Bishop of Bristol' (Thornborough) as well as one unnamed source.
61 Spelman, 'Of the Union', in Galloway and Levack (eds), *The Jacobean Union*, 175.
62 The Huntington Library's manuscript copy (EL 1227 34 B 45) is in a neat italic hand and bound in a contemporary limp vellum binding which includes a printed label situated at the top left of the front pastedown ('34/B45'). Given what we know about the Bridgewater Library, this manuscript was most likely a presentation copy to Thomas Egerton, although it could have been intended for James. See Stephen Tabor, 'The Bridgewater Library', in William Baker and Kenneth Womack (eds), *Pre-Nineteenth-Century British Book Collectors and*

Bibliographers, 40–50. *Dictionary of Literary Biography*. Vol. 213. Detroit: The Gale Group, 1999.
63 [Bacon], *Briefe Discovrse*, A7ʳ.
64 See Markku Peltonen, 'Bacon, Francis', *ODNB*, https://doi.org/10.1093/ref:odnb/990. Accessed 19 February 2011.
65 Brian Vickers (ed.), *Francis Bacon: the major works* (Oxford: Oxford University Press, 2002), v.
66 *Ibid.*, xxii.
67 Bacon's writings on Anglo-Scottish union are also absent from Vickers's *The History of the Reign of King Henry VII and Selected Works* (1998), which was published in the Cambridge Texts in the History of Political Thought series.
68 Vickers (ed.), *Francis Bacon: the major works*, xviii.
69 *Ibid.*, xviii, xvii.
70 *Ibid.*, 741. Spedding, *Letters and Life*, III, 89.
71 Epstein, 'Francis Bacon and the issue of union', 121.
72 *Ibid.*, 122.
73 *Ibid.*, 123, 121, 125.
74 Bacon, *Certain Articles*, 220.
75 *Ibid.*, 224.
76 Bacon, *The Essayes of Couvnsels, Civill and Morall*, 139.
77 *Ibid.*, 141.
78 'Obiections agaynst the Chaunge of the name or Stile of England and Scotland', Huntington Library, Ellesmere MS 1226.
79 Bacon, *Certain Articles*, 228.
80 Bacon's political ideas are explored in some detail in Denise Albanese, '*The New Atlantis* and the uses of Utopia', *English Literary History*, 57 (1990), 503–28 and, especially, Willy Maley, *Nation, State and Empire in English Renaissance Literature* (Basingstoke: Palgrave Macmillan, 2003), 93–112.
81 Spedding, *Letters and Life*, III, 76–7.
82 Lisa Jardine and Alan Stewart, *Hostage to Fortune: the troubled life of Francis Bacon* (London: Gollancz, 1998), 272.
83 Bacon, *The Essaies of Sʳ Francis Bacon*, 59.
84 Bacon, *The Essayes of Couvnsels, Civill and Morall*, 122.
85 Bacon, *Certain Articles*, 219.
86 [Bacon], *Briefe Discovrse*, A6ᵛ.
87 *Ibid.*, B1ᵛ.
88 *Ibid.*, B2ʳ.
89 Bacon, 'A letter of advice to my Lord of Essex, immediately before his going into Ireland', in Spedding (ed.), *Letters and Life*, II, 130.
90 [Bacon], *Briefe Discovrse*, B2ʳ, A8ʳ.
91 *Ibid.*, B2ᵛ.

92 *Ibid.*
93 *Ibid.*, B3ʳ
94 *Ibid.*
95 McGinnis and Williamson (eds and trans.), *The British Union*, 77.
96 Bacon, *Certain Articles*, 218.
97 Graham Rees, 'Bacon's speculative philosophy', in Markku Peltonen (ed.), *The Cambridge Companion to Bacon* (Cambridge: Cambridge University Press, 2006), 121.
98 McGinnis and Williamson (eds and trans.), *The British Union*, 117, 116.
99 [Bacon], *Briefe Discovrse*, B4ᵛ.
100 See 'A Treatise about the Union of England and Scotland', in Galloway and Levack (eds), *The Jacobean Union*, 62–3; Savile, 'Historicall Collections', 200; Craig, *De Unione*, 395–6.
101 Francis Bacon, *The Twoo Bookes of Francis Bacon. Of the proficience and aduancement of Learning, diuine and humane. To the King* (London, 1605), Hh1ʳ.
102 Vickers (ed.), *Francis Bacon: the major works*, 573, 116.
103 *Ibid.*, 482.
104 [Bacon], *Briefe Discovrse*, C3ᵛ.
105 Thornborough, *A Discovrse Plainely Prouing*, 9.
106 Vickers (ed.), *Francis Bacon: the major works*, 798.
107 McGinnis and Williamson (eds and trans.), *The British Union*, 30.
108 Markku Peltonen, *Classical Humanism and Republicanism in English Political Thought, 1570–1640* (Cambridge: Cambridge University Press, 1995), 195.
109 Bacon, *Certain Articles*, 228.
110 Vickers (ed.), *Francis Bacon: the major works*, 20.
111 Bacon, *Certain Articles*, 218. Bacon would reiterate the phrase 'the aunceint Mother name of *Britainny*' in print in 1605: see Bacon, *Aduancement of Learning*, Dd1ʳ.
112 'Sir Fra: Bacons Answer to Mr Fullers Speach against Union Anno 4th Iacobi', British Library, Harl. MS 6842, fol. 3. 'This Scotland United, Ireland reduced, shipping Maintaind, and the Low Countries Combined, we need not fear the Spaniards Dreams of A Western Monarchy' (fol. 3).
113 'The Bridgewater collection contains a manuscript of Bacon's *Certaine Considerations Touching the Plantations in Ireland* (1609) [EL 1721], probably presented [to Ellesmere] by the author': Tabor, 'The Bridgewater Library', 41.
114 Francis Bacon, 'A letter to the King upon presenting my discourse touching the plantation of Ireland', in Spedding (ed.), *Letters and Life*, IV, 114.

'But when this island shall be made Britain'   147

115 Bacon, *Certain Articles*, 226.
116 Francis Bacon, *Certain Considerations Touching the Plantation in Ireland, Presented to His Majesty*, 1606, in Spedding (ed.), *Letters and Life*, IV, 119. *Certain Considerations* was composed in January of 1609 and not in 1606.
117 Bacon, *Certain Considerations*, 116.
118 Bacon, 'A letter of advice to my Lord of Essex', II, 131. Bacon would return to this theme is his 1625 essay 'Of Plantations', where he writes 'I like a *Plantation* in a Pure Soile; that is, where People are not *Displanted*, to the end, to *Plant* in Others. For else, it is rather an Extirpation, then a *Plantation*': Bacon, *The Essayes of Couvnsels, Civill and Morall*, 198.
119 Francis Bacon, 'A letter of advice to my Lord of Essex', 131.
120 Bacon, *Certain Considerations*, 116.
121 The 'vast majority of the Scottish undertakers came from the central lowland belt, especially the Edinburgh/Haddington area in the east and the Renfrew/north Ayrshire area in the west. Apart from a few undertakers from the east coast of Scotland north of Fife, the only other area from which significant numbers were drawn was the extreme south-west of the country between Dumfries and Portpatrick': Philip S. Robinson, *British Settlement in an Irish Landscape, 1600–1670* (Dublin: Gill and Macmillan; New York: St. Martin's Press, 1984), 80. On the Celticity and Catholicism of some Scottish settlers, see J. Michael Hill, 'The origins of the Scottish plantations in Ulster to 1625: a reinterpretation', *Journal of British Studies*, 32 (1993), 24–43.
122 John Davies, *A Discoverie of the trve cavses why Ireland was neuer entirely Subdued, nor brought vnder Obedience of the Crowne of England, vntill the Beginning of his Maiesties happie raigne* (London, 1612), 281.
123 Sir John Davies, *The Works in Verse and Prose of Sir John Davies*, Alexander Grossart (ed.), 3 vols. (Lancashire, 1869–76), III, 204–5.
124 Pont, 'Of the Union', 22.
125 Jonson, *The Workes of Beniamin Jonson*, 1003.
126 *Ibid.*, 1003–04.
127 *Ibid.*, 1002.
128 Butler, *The Stuart Court Masque and Political Culture*, 95.
129 J. G. A. Pocock, *The Discovery of Islands: essays in British history* (Cambridge: Cambridge University Press, 2005), 28.
130 Davies, *The Works in Verse and Prose*, III, 234.
131 Linda Colley, 'Britishness and otherness: an argument', *Journal of British Studies*, 31 (1992), 327.
132 *Ibid.*, 314.

133 J. G. A. Pocock, 'Conclusion: contingency, identity, sovereignty', in Alexander Grant and Keith J. Stringer (eds), *Uniting the Kingdom?: the making of British history* (London and New York: Routledge, 1995), 301.
134 Morrill speculates that 'there is a possibility that the growth of Irish identity was a product of the period we are studying in this book': Morrill, 'The British problem', 8.
135 Trinity College Library, Dublin, MS 877, fol. 479.
136 Michael Hechter, *Internal Colonialism: the Celtic fringe in British national development, 1536–1966* (Berkeley: University of California Press, 1975).

4

'Our downfall Birthdome': reimagining nationhood in *Macbeth*

'Like to his Iland, gyrt in with the Ocean' (*3H6*, TLN 2619)
Why would an English playwright whose plays not only depict intra-island warfare and border transgressions between the geographically contiguous nations that constitute Great Britain's political landscape but also include as stage props maps of all or parts of Britain delineate his native land an island?[1] Writing in 1604, Bacon informs King James of the 'points wherein the nations [England and Scotland] stand already united'; included among these points is '[i]n continent'. 'For the Continent', he adds, 'there are no natural boundaries of mountains, or seas, or navigable rivers'.[2] Shakespeare's plays often present not Britain but England in a continent-like manner, detached from neighbouring Scotland and Wales. By no means was Shakespeare alone among his contemporaries in giving voice to such imagined geographies.[3] Edmund Spenser addresses Queen Elizabeth in the Proem to book one of *The Faerie Queene* as 'Great Ladie of the greatest Isle'.[4] Does 'Isle' here signify England, or does 'the greatest Isle' refer to Great Britain? If the latter, then Spenser has amplified the dominion of a monarch whose rule did not encompass an entire 'Isle'.

Labelling Shakespeare's inscriptions of England as an island-nation or island-realm Anglocentric, as many critics have, offers a partial understanding of the cultural and historical significance of what Kate Chedgzoy terms 'the geopolitical metaphor of insularity'.[5] Shakespeare's use of this metaphor obscures England's, Scotland's and Wales's cohabitation of a land-mass that contemporaries struggled to assign a single name, describing it variously as Albion, Britain, Britannia, Great Britain, etc. Imagining England as an isle, as numerous characters in Shakespeare's plays do, seems even more incongruous given the historical context in which these plays were written. Although Wales had been politically incorporated into the English state under King Henry VIII, Scotland was a separate, sovereign, unconquered kingdom, notwithstanding a long history of English claims to suzerainty. The plays' geopolitical elisions are, of course, complicated by the powerful presence of characters representative of England's island neighbours and by the voices of a few of the playwright's non-English characters. Consider, for example, Nerissa's question to Portia concerning 'Fauconbridge, the yong Baron of England': '[w]hat thinke you of the Scottish Lorde his neighbour?'[6] And there is Glendour/Glendoure/Glendower's revision of the Gauntean islanding of England: 'the Sea,/That chides the Bankes of England, Scotland, and Wales' (*1H4*, TLN 1569–70), spoken in a scene set in Wales and in the presence of an onstage map. The words 'Wales', 'Welsh', 'Welshman' and 'Welshwoman', and 'Scotland', 'Scot(s)', 'Scotch' and 'Scottish', surface again and again in Shakespeare's plays as do references to non-English geographical place names within Britain, including Berwick (*3H6*), Brecknock (*R3*), Caernarvonshire (*H8*), Haverfordwest (*R3*), Milford Haven (*R3*, *Cym*), Monmouth (*1H6*, *H5* – geographically English, culturally and historically Welsh),[7] Pembroke (*R3*, *H8*), the rivers Wye and Severn (*1H4*, *Cym*), not to mention the various Scottish place names that surface in *The Tragedie of Macbeth*. Clearly Shakespeare had a better geographical knowledge of the three-nation island of Great Britain than he did of Bohemia.

The majority of the characters in Shakespeare's plays who represent England as an island-nation or island-realm give voice to an 'imagined political community' co-terminous with natural boundaries or, even more so, barriers in part because England's borders with Wales and Scotland in the early modern period were far from fixed.[8] As a cultural construct, the imagined island-nation or island-realm performs the ideological work of fixing the fluid national boundaries that constituted the Scottish and Welsh Marches in the Elizabethan period. When in *The third Part of Henry the Sixt, with the death of the Duke of Yorke* Warwicke promises the Lancastrian King Henry VI protection from his Yorkist foes, he does so with a simile that anticipates similar imaginings of an island-like England in Shakespeare's plays:

My Soueraigne, with the louing Citizens,
Like to his Iland, gyrt in with the Ocean,
Or modest *Dyan*, circled with her Nymphs,
Shall rest in London. (TLN 2620–3)

Earlier in the play, King Henry announces upon his return to England from the then Scottish town of (South) Berwick: '[f]rom Scotland am I stolne euen of pure loue,/To greet mine owne Land with my wishfull sight' (TLN 1411–12). Neither the historical King Henry VI nor Queen Elizabeth could claim that the 'Iland', Great Britain, was theirs. King James VI and I could and did make that claim, and as he passed through what was now the English town of Berwick on his journey from Edinburgh to London in 1603, he put an end to the 'warlike keeping of *Barwicke*'.[9]

My reference to 'Shakespeare's plays' should be qualified, for the plays in which England is termed an isle or island are the predominantly Elizabethan plays that the First Folio's catalogue labels 'Histories', the same plays in which references to the Welsh and Wales and the Scottish and Scotland appear most frequently – with the obvious exception of references to Scotland (twelve) in *Macbeth*. The First Folio's Elizabethan plays register twenty-two instances of 'ile', 'isle', 'iland', 'island': eighteen of those references are to the island of Shakespeare's birth, many of which explicitly or implicitly designate England an isle or island, the geographical nomenclature often preceded by a triumphant deictic.[10] Excluding *The Tragedie of Othello, the Moore of Venice* (set mainly on the island of Cyprus) and *The Tempest* ('[t]he Scene, an vn-inhabited Island'), there are less than ten occurrences of the words 'isle' and 'island' in the First Folio's post-Elizabethan plays, and only two of those occurrences – to which I will return at the end of this chapter – refer to the island of Shakespeare's birth. What can be gleaned from this diminution or absence of voicings of England as an island-nation or island-realm in Shakespeare's post-Elizabethan plays? If Shakespeare's Elizabethan plays, his histories especially, register a patriotic or a nationalist vision of England, then can his Jacobean plays be read as re-evaluating his earlier inscriptions of England and England's place within the island? Do Shakespeare's post-Elizabethan plays abandon English insularity for less exclusive, less Anglocentric, more inclusive, more Britocentric communal imaginings?

I wish to offer a partial response to these questions as a preamble to a reading of the decidedly Jacobean geopolitics of *Macbeth*, a play whose island references are much more localised – the Hebrides, 'the Westerne Isles' (TLN 31), Inchcolm, 'Saint *Colmes* ynch' (TLN 88) and Iona, 'Colmekill' (TLN 968) – and therefore alert to isles that are tied geographically and politically to Britain, and, the play reminds us, to Ireland. Set mainly in Scotland, with a key scene in England, *Macbeth*, usually dated 1606, situates a signal moment in Scotland's history within an archipelagic framework. The play's onstage and offstage battles include soldiers from not just a culturally heterogeneous Scotland but also Norway and England. In the wake of Duncan's murder, his eldest son flees to England, his youngest to Ireland – here Shakespeare is following his main historiographical source, *The Historie of Scotland* housed in the second edition of Holinshed's *Chronicles*. Although not referenced in the play, yet well known to contemporaries through chronicle histories, Banquo's son, Fleance, fled to Wales.[11] Given the play's archipelagic scope, perhaps it would be more accurate to say that the play turns to a signal moment in British and Irish history. By staging the reign of the historical Macbeth, or Mac Bethad *mac* Findláich (1040–57), Shakespeare returned to and rewrote a moment in British history whose cultural and political ramifications extended beyond national borders, which were much more permeable and porous in the eleventh century than they were in the seventeenth.[12] During the reign of the play's 'English' king, Edward the Confessor (1042–66) – England's penultimate Anglo-Saxon monarch and last undisputed king – England's political presence within the island was extended northward and westward through the acts of powerful supporters of 'the Holy King' (TLN 1503), including Siward, earl of Northumbria and Harold Godwineson, as Daniel describes in his Jacobean *The first part of the historie of England*:

> For the Earle *Syward*, would not be behind hand in effecting as braue deedes in the North, as *Harold*, Earle of *Westsex*, the sonne of the Earle *Godwyn* performed against the welsh in the west: For the first depriued of life and Crowne, *Macbeth*, an vsurper, and inuested *Malcolin*, in the kingdome of *Scotland*, the other defeated *Ris* [Rhys ap Rhydderch], and *Griffine* [Gruffudd ap Llywelyn], two brothers, Kings of *Wales*, and subdued that Prouince to this Crowne.[13]

'Even on the eve of the Norman conquest', R. R. Davies writes, 'the title *rex totius Britanniae* was accorded to Edward the Confessor in one group of his charters, and his near-contemporary biographer assumed that he was the ruler of Britain, nothing less'.[14] Although *Macbeth* incorporates elements of the Elizabethan history plays, it engages in a profound revision of the earlier plays' articulations of and reflections on nationhood. Much more so than Shakespeare's English histories, 'the Scottish play' is sensitive to England's shared place within the island of Britain. In *The Life of Henry the Fift* (i.e. the Folio version), the character designated '*Irish*' by speech prefixes, labelled '*Makmorrice*' in a stage direction and named '*Mackmorrice*' by Fluellen (or, as the speech prefixes label this character in this scene, '*Welch*') famously asks '[w]hat ish my Nation?' (TLN 1240).[15] Informed if not determined by the novel political situation of post-1603 Britain, *Macbeth* asks the question 'what is a nation?'

'You *Britaines* braue' (Hugh Holland, 'Vpon the Lines and Life of the Famous Scenicke Poet, Master William Shakespeare')

Shakespeare's turn to Scottish history is often cited as evidence of the playwright's much-heralded shift from matters English to matters British in the wake of James's accession to the English throne. As Kerrigan notes, 'a late-Elizabethan taste for English chronicle history gave way to such Stuart-British works as *King Lear*', a play which Kerrigan labels 'merely the most conspicuous example of [Shakespeare's] turn to British and archipelagic subject matter after 1603'.[16] Set in eleventh-century Scotland rather than ancient Britain, *Macbeth* is not a British play in the manner of *The Tragedie of King Lear* or *The Tragedie of Cymbeline*. Unlike these two plays, *Macbeth* contains no references to Britain, Britons or the British. Edward the Confessor may have been referred to as '*rex totius Britanniae*' in contemporary charters, but in the play he is 'gracious England' (TLN 2030). Like *King Lear* and *Cymbeline*, however, *Macbeth* reflects and reflects on the archipelagic geopolitics brought about by James's composite monarchy.

Shakespeare's shift to matters British, literary critics agree, is accompanied by an attenuation of the valorisation of Englishness and English nationhood. 'Shakespeare's political drama', according to Neil Rhodes, 'moves from a sense of England and Scotland as independent kingdoms into an alignment with the views of the Unionist King James'.[17] Perhaps Rhodes, who does not discuss *Macbeth*, is overstating the point; nevertheless, the play-texts, especially those published in the First Folio, appear to offer material support for an ideological shift on the part of the theatre company to which Shakespeare now belonged, The King's Men.[18] Noting that there 'are 159 instances of the word "England" in the sole author plays performed before 1603, compared to three in the plays from the later period, and [that] there are just twelve mentions of "Britain" in the early plays compared to thirty-four in the later ones', Hugh Craig suggests that under James Shakespeare's 'plays shifted attention to the new larger entity of Britain'.[19] 'There is little celebration of England and Englishness', Christopher Wortham remarks, 'in Shakespeare's plays written after the accession of James VI of Scotland to his English throne as James I in 1603'. 'There is', he adds, 'some reference to Britain and Britishness in the later plays, but mention of England is muted and infrequent'.[20] Not in *Macbeth*, however: 'the Scottish play' contains more occurrences of the word 'English' (six) than any of the First Folio's post-Elizabethan plays, and among the Jacobean plays it ranks second only to the co-authored *The Famous History of the Life of King Henry the Eight* for the most occurrences of 'England' (eight). Of the Folio's Jacobean plays only *King Henry the Eight* and *Macbeth* set scenes in England. Interestingly, in *Macbeth*, the earliest extant English tragedy on matters Scottish, England is always referred to simply as England; never is it referred to in the play by any other political term, be that country, kingdom, nation or realm; and certainly not isle or island.

That Shakespeare's Jacobean plays register a shift to matters British is acknowledged. How his post-Elizabethan plays handle 'Britain' has not resulted in critical consensus. Recent readings of *Macbeth* have produced nuanced interpretations alert to the play's handling of contemporary political debate, whether centring on the Gunpowder Plot, James's supposed absolutism or Anglo-Scottish union. For some critics, the play's main setting, its inclusion of witches and its allusion to King James's composite monarchy suggests that Shakespeare was indeed the King's man.[21] By producing a play that incorporated topics of keen interest to England's and Scotland's monarch, Cedric Watts argues, 'Shakespeare was flattering the monarchy of King James'.[22] Others wonder how a play that represents Scotland as *Macbeth* does could be viewed as a compliment to England's Scottish monarch. Pointing out that *Macbeth* is 'a tragedy, not a masque', Norbrook, alert to the play's republican subtext, warns against treating the play as 'crude propaganda'. 'The legitimists', he adds, 'are shown to need the aid of the English, and Scotland is represented as a wild and lawless country', leading Norbrook to ask whether 'the play really [is] an appropriate compliment to a Scottish king'?[23] Occupying a critical middle ground, Jonathan Baldo labels *Macbeth* 'a masterful piece of double-speak':

> While seeming to support James's case for union, it simultaneously telegraphs to English anti-unionists the hazards of joining their nation to one whose history, a monotonous tale of violence and regicide in the least charitable estimation, might have seemed to the most virulently xenophobic among them 'a tale/Told by an idiot, full of sound and fury,/Signifying nothing'.

For Baldo, the play's equivocal language results in a text that can be read as appealing to both sides of the union campaign: '*Macbeth* bore the potential to support anti-union pamphleteers and propagandists at least as much as it would have flattered James'.[24] Much more than Jonson's courtly masques, *Macbeth* continues to solicit complex and contradictory readings.

Another key point Baldo raises in relation to not only *Macbeth* but also Shakespeare's history plays deserves further attention, especially given this chapter's focus on key terms used in the play's articulation of nationhood. Baldo cites the work of Tudor historian John Guy and social scientist Liah Greenfeld on the terminological shift away from 'realm' and 'kingdom' to 'state' and 'nation' in the early modern period as evidence of 'the conceptual shift from dynastic realm to unitary nation whose identity and stability do not depend entirely on a principle of legitimate succession'. 'A similar terminological shift', Baldo suggests, can be traced in Shakespeare's chronicle histories: '"[n]ation" and "state" appear with increasing frequency in the later histories, gradually supplanting "realm", which predominates in the early *Henry VI* plays'. Attending to this conceptual shift from realm to nation, Baldo argues that *Macbeth* 'registers a convulsion within the idea of nationhood as England confronted a monarch and a history that seemed marginal, at best, to its own'.[25] Baldo's argument, then, is twofold: Shakespeare's history plays reveal a gradual shift from monarch- to nation-centred imaginings of community; furthermore, the playwright's Englishness necessarily results in a Jacobean play that struggles to accommodate Scotland as well as England's Scottish monarch. The result, I argue, is not a pro- or anti-union play but instead a play that invites its early modern viewers and readers to reassess Britain's intra- and Britain and Ireland's inter-island relations under the rule of doubly sceptred monarch.

Baldo's fine essay contributes to an ongoing critical reassessment of Helgerson's claim that 'Shakespeare's representations of England are ... the most exclusively monarchic that his generation has passed on to us'.[26] Ironically, since the publication of Helgerson's work Shakespeareans have been less attentive to the royal presence on the stage than to the plays' staging of nationhood and national identities.[27] Constructing a cultural narrative based on the appearance or absence of such terms as 'realm', 'kingdom', 'state' and 'nation' in the plays is, I want to argue, far from simple and straightforward precisely because it assumes a lexical linearity that is not supported by the play-texts. Consider, for example, the use of the word 'realm': it occurs frequently in the three Henry VI plays (over thirty times in the First Folio versions of those plays), and its use does diminish in the second tetralogy, where there are less than ten instances; it also appears infrequently in the Folio's Jacobean plays. Is this, then, reliable evidence of a conceptual shift from 'dynastic realm' to 'unitary nation' not only in Shakespeare's English histories but also within the historical context of their production? It certainly could be if not for the presence of other complicating matters: for example, the fact that 'kingdom' makes more appearances in *The Life of Henry the Fift* alone than in the three Henry VI plays combined. In *The First Part of Henry the Fourth*, when England is not referred to as 'England' it is termed a kingdom, a realm and a state but never a nation. Context is another complicating factor. Shakespeare's plays were produced during a crucial period in not just England's history, but also Ireland's, Scotland's and Wales's – the Nine Years' War (1594–1603) is the back-drop to many of the history plays. If Shakespeare's English histories are reflective and productive of a shift from 'dynastic realm' to 'unitary nation', then they are also acutely alert to the uneasy process of Elizabethan/Jacobean state-formation in the early modern period, a process triggered by the Tudor incorporation of Wales and Ireland and complicated further by James's composite monarchy, Anglo-Scottish union debate and

'Our downfall Birthdome'   157

the British plantation of Ulster. Shakespeare's Elizabethan and Jacobean inscriptions of nationhood reveal an awareness of the wider archipelagic framework that informed if not determined any 'terminological shifts' in this period.

'[T]his Kingdome?' (*Macbeth*, TLN 1648)

Throughout his career as a playwright, Shakespeare used a plethora of terms to designate the historical polities that his history plays brought to the stage, and he did so in order to reflect upon the polity to which he, under the rule of both Elizabeth and James, belonged. Included among these terms are commonweal, commonwealth, country, dominion, land, kingdom, nation, realm, state, territory, weal, etc. Of course, he also used these terms to designate other geographically and historically remote polities, including Athens, ancient Britain, Denmark, Rome, Scotland, Venice, Vienna and Wales. The importance of close, critical attention to Shakespeare's use of specific political terms to designate a polity cannot be underestimated, but a sole reliance on his word usage risks decontextualising the plays: in terms of their immediate cultural moment as well as in terms of genre, setting and topicality. What does it mean that a Jacobean Roman history such as *The Tragedy of Coriolanus*, arguably Shakespeare's most political play, uses the words 'country' and 'state' more than any of his other plays? 'Country' and 'state', however, are not the only terms that describe the ancient Roman polity: we also find 'the Weale a' th Common' (TLN 159), 'the Commonwealth' (TLN 2907), 'Nation(s)' (TLN 2420, 2835), 'Territories' (TLN 2792, 2942, 2990) and 'Weal' (TLN 950, 1581, 1878). The use of such distinct yet also overlapping and intersecting political terms cannot be ascribed to metrical regularity or a desire for lexical variety, especially as these words surface in a play that turns to an ideologically charged moment in the history of ancient Rome in order to probe contemporary political ideas.[28] Any consideration of *Macbeth*'s geopolitics must be sensitive to the play's political terminology, including the play's use of established political terms and, especially, newly coined terms, as well as more abstract language and images relating to nationhood. When writing *Macbeth*, Shakespeare returned to the same source text to which he had turned for his English histories: the voluminous histories of England, Ireland, Scotland and Wales that have come to be known as Holinshed's *Chronicles*, published in 1577 and revised and reissued in 1587. *The Historie of Scotland*'s entries on the reigns of Duncane, whose rule is invested with less legitimacy than in the play, and Mackbeth, whose reign, at least originally, is invested with more legitimacy than in the play, variously designate Scotland a 'common-wealth', 'countrie', 'estate', 'kingdome' and 'realme', the two latter terms occurring most frequently.[29] *Macbeth* also uses the terms country (most frequently, with ten occurrences), kingdom and realm as well as 'state' and 'weale' to designate Scotland. As we shall see, other novel terms surface in the play, terms that reveal a playwright reassessing and reconfiguring the concept, indeed the language, of nationhood.

One way to explore *Macbeth*'s reimagining of nationhood would be to situate Shakespeare's Jacobean appropriation of medieval Scottish history alongside his Elizabethan appropriations of medieval English history as manifested in his history plays of the 1590s. Shakespeare's representations of a warring and politically unstable, monarchical, medieval England in his Elizabethan histories are anachronistically but forcefully underpinned by their own cultural moment, in particular a burgeoning English national identity. Consider, as a prime example, the proto-Protestant and proto-nationalist representations of England's rejection of Catholic Rome's authority in *The life and death of King Iohn*, a play rich in references to 'this Ile/Isle/Iland'. Does a similar cultural appropriation of the past condition the representation of Scotland in *Macbeth*? Did the English playwright appropriate Scottish history in order to stage Scotland and Scottishness in the manner that, say, *Henry the fift* stages England and Englishness? Surely the answer to this question is no: that is, Shakespeare's nationalism was firmly rooted in Great Britain's English territory and people. Excluding stage directions and speech prefixes, *Henry the fift* includes fifty occurrences of 'England', forty-four of 'English', four of 'Englishman/men' and one of 'English-woman' – the sole use of 'Englishwoman' in his plays (used, ironically, in reference to a French princess). That Shakespeare's final English history play produced during Elizabeth's reign has traditionally been heralded as his most patriotic comes as no surprise. Numerous instances of the words 'Scots', 'Scotish' and 'Scotishmen' surface in the sections on the reigns of Duncane and Mackbeth in *The Historie of Scotland*, so it would not be unreasonable to expect these words to appear in 'the

Scottish play'. Remarkably, the words 'Scot', 'Scots', 'Scottish' and 'Scottishman'/'Scottishmen' never appear in *Macbeth*. Compared to *Henry the fift*'s inscriptions of England and Englishness, *Macbeth* seems strikingly devoid of Scottishness.

The absence from the play of the words 'Scot', 'Scots' and 'Scottish' could be cited as evidence of an erasure of Scottishness in favour of a British cultural identity. However, the fact that the word 'British' never surfaces in *Macbeth*, unlike in *Cymbeline* and *King Lear*, combined with the fact that 'English' does, suggests that the play's participation in the construction and dissemination of a British cultural or national identity, never mind British nationalism, is minimal at best. Around the time of *Macbeth*'s composition and original performance, William Warner, in a chapter on 'Makbeth' in his *Continvance of Albions England*, invokes Banquho's genealogy (especially Fleance's impregnation of 'King *Gruffyths* Daughter') to celebrate James's Britishness, even calling for a restitution of the name 'Britain':

> Great Monarke of great *Britaine* now, so amply neuer any:
> Long may he liue an happie King, of him may Kings be many.
> Boast of his triple royall blood from you yee *Cambrian Brutes*,
> Which to his high discents Else-where not lowest ranked sutes.
> For *Tudor* from *Cadwallader*, and *Iames* from *Tudor* claimes,
> From *Gruffyths* royall Daughter too himselfe a *Brute* he names,
> From *Gladys*, *Mortimer* his wife Prince *Dauids* sister and
> Vndoubted heire, he also hath in blood and ownes your Land.
> Great *Britaine*, sith a *Briton* doth remonarchize thy Throne,
> Remaund [recall] thy name: *Brute* had, *Iames* hath the whole, as els had none.[30]

Although *Macbeth* highlights James's connection to Banquo, the play resists the label pro-union just as much as it resists simplistic labels such as pro-James or pro-monarchy. Kerrigan describes *Macbeth* as a 'topical dramatization of medieval material that is calculated to explore the heterogeneity of the archipelago at the very moment (1605–6) when James VI and I sought to go beyond regal union and develop an integrated British state'.[31] In other words, the play is not committed to an official or unofficial political agenda or ideology, or an affirmation of national identities; rather, it captures the historical pressures in place at the time of its composition. If the play speaks to Pocock's idea of 'British history' – 'the plural history of a group of cultures situated along an Anglo-Celtic frontier and marked by increasing English political and cultural domination' – then it does so through an English playwright whose relationship to the king was marked by double trust: Shakespeare was subject to a Scottish sovereign who was also his acting company's patron.[32]

For many critics, England's national(ist) playwright's 'Scottish play' presents his monarch's native land in a negative light: namely, as a dysfunctional monarchy weakened by powerful warrior-chiefs that not only needs but even beseeches the support of 'gracious England' (TLN 1863).[33] Such readings tend to situate the play within the context of official (Parliamentary) and unofficial (print and manuscript tracts and treatises) debate on Anglo-Scottish union to argue that if the play commits itself to a such a union then the kind of union it proposes amounts to an aggrandisement of the English state at the cost of Scotland's independence. Some union tracts and treatises cite Tudor England's political incorporation of Wales as a precedent for a union between the two kingdoms. 'Wales' writes Cornwallis,

> is Englished, a country whose riches did not woe vs, nor her power, nor the fertility of the soyle; but the discommodities that we might receiue by them whilest they were held as Aliens, beeing matter to feed discontented or ambitious plottes, this was the furthest and onely aduantage we expected, which since it lay within the power of our incorporating to cure, and that nature had performed halfe the worke, with the alliance of countries so neerly knit together vpon one continent, wee performed.[34]

In other words, just as England has incorporated Wales so, too, should England incorporate Scotland. Although Kerrigan does not read the play in relation to union debate, his remarks on the play's 'contrast between insecure Scotland and stable, united England' capture the dominant critical perspective on the play's depiction of Scotland:

> That a core, unitary Scotland – 'O Nation miserable!' – exists in the play is not in doubt. But it is weakened (and left vulnerable to incursions) by magnate rivalries. Shakespeare's primary motive for removing from the narrative the many years of good government which Macbeth brought to Scotland before he sank into tyranny may have been dramaturgical ... but one consequence of the change is that

Scotland is never shown as a properly functioning state. It seems to be waiting for English intervention to stabilize it.[35]

Macduffe's 'O Natio*n* miserable!' (TLN 1930), on one hand grants Scotland nation status; on the other, the adjective 'miserable' laments that nation's political status at this point in the play. Shakespeare has reworked Macduffe's exclamation as it appears in the source material, where Makduffe proclaims '[o]h ye vnhappie and miserbale Scotishmen'.[36] Arguably, both source and play-text convey the same message, but the playwright's choice of 'nation' rather than the historian's 'Scotishmen' is telling. Shakespeare significantly revises his source material in order to highlight issues of nationhood in the play. What Frank Kermode has identified as *Macbeth*'s pronounced 'lexical habit' is of particular relevance to the play's political terms, nouns as well as adjectives.[37]

'Stands Scotland where it did?' (*Macbeth*, TLN 1999)

'Scotland is the least interesting feature of *Macbeth*, I think, the real Scotland.'[38] I think 'the real Scotland' is an interesting feature of this play, but so, too, is the play's imagined Scotland. For many critics, the label 'the Scottish play' is a misnomer: '[t]here was always something suspicious about *Macbeth* being called the "Scottish play"', writes Willy Maley, adding '[i]t was always the "Scottish play" in name only, and only to ward off evil spirits'.[39] Dismissing 'the Scottish play' as 'geopolitically hopeless', 'the British play' as 'anachronistic' and 'the Anglo-Scottish play' as 'too narrow', Kerrigan's tongue-in-cheek proposal for an alternative title that better reflects the play's geopolitics is 'The Archipelagic Tragedy'.[40] What makes this final option appropriate to *Macbeth*'s geopolitics is its insistence that the play invites and rewards readings alert to the two-island (Britain and Ireland), three-kingdom (England, Ireland, Scotland) and four-nation (England, Ireland, Scotland, Wales) framework within which it was produced and upon which it reflects.

'The British play', however, should not be dismissed too hastily, for the play's profound reflections on post-1603 nationhood are informed if not determined by the novelty of James's composite rule. What about 'the Scottish play'? After noting that 'Shakespeare set most of his tragedies somewhere other than England', Jean Howard adds 'Macbeth does unfold in Scotland, with a brief detour to the England of Edward the Confessor, but ... Scotland to the English was very much a foreign country'.[41] Was it, though, especially in the first decade of the seventeenth century when Scotland's monarch was also England's? Howard's reflections on the significance of English geography as evinced in Shakespeare's Elizabethan articulations of nationhood, which are informed by Helgerson's work and intersect nicely with Baldo's comments on a terminological shift from dynastic to national imaginings of community, bear critical scrutiny, for they not only direct attention to *Macbeth*'s political geography but also invite a comparison between Shakespeare's English histories and his Scottish history play:

> the farther Shakespeare advanced in the decade [1590s], the more details his plays drew from the actual geography of England: its cities, counties, mountains, and regions. In all the English histories, England is embodied and personified in its monarch, but gradually it also becomes recognizable, in a more modern, nationalist manner, as a bounded territory, a distinct geographic entity supposedly encompassing a shared language, customs, and history.[42]

If what Howard says about the relation between land and nation in the English histories is accurate, then might the same be said of *Macbeth*'s landscape and its imagining of Scotland?[43] By no means is Scotland's 'actual geography' absent from the play. Consider, for example, the play's various geographical references: 'the Westerne Isles' (TLN 31), 'Fiffe' (TLN 73, 972, 1704), 'Saint *Colmes* ynch' (TLN 88), 'Soris' [Forres] (TLN 138), 'Envernes' (TLN 329), 'Scone' (TLN 965, 971, 2528), 'Colmekill' (TLN 968). Various titles – Glamis, Cawdor, Lenox, Rosse, Angus, Menteth [Menteith], Cathnes [Caithness] – designate Scottish place names, and pronouncements of the variously spelt toponyms 'Great Byrnam Wood' and 'Dunsmane Hill' (TLN 1635) abound, resonating throughout the play's final act not unlike the geographically significant references to Dover in *King Lear* and Milford Haven in *Cymbeline*. And, of course, characters invoke 'Scotland' more times than in any other Shakespearean play. Clearly Shakespeare is drawing upon the actual geography of Scotland, to which the play is probably more true than it is to its actual or recorded history. Whatever Scotland is in the play, it is and it is not a 'bounded territory'. Scotland's real and imagined political geography is diverse, encompassing part of an island as well as offshore isles. Attempts to present Scotland as bounded do surface. When Macbeth says to the Doctor '[s]end out moe Horses, skirre the Country round,/Hang those that talke of Feare' (TLN 2255–6), his language works to demarcate 'the Country'. 'Skirre' here means 'to pass or go rapidly over (a stretch of land or water), esp. in search of something or some one' (*OED* v.3) – the *OED* lists this line as the earliest occurrence.[44] Macbeth's imperative, grounded in this neologism, and given the inclusion of 'round', imagines a finite, bounded space.

But if Scotland, like England in the Elizabethan histories, is 'embodied and personified in its monarch', to which monarch of Scotland would this apply, King Duncan or Macbeth, or the yet-to-be '[c]rown'd at Scone' (TLN 2528) Malcolme? Unlike Duncan, Macbeth never assumes the speech prefix 'King' in the play, and whereas the stage directions offer 'Enter King' for Duncan, Macbeth's act three, scene one entrance is heralded by the unsettling 'Enter Macbeth *as* King' (TLN 993, emphasis added). Significantly, the word 'Scotland' first appears in the play when the Captain refers to Duncan as 'King of Scotland' (TLN 47), but this title, though not the word 'Scotland', lies dormant until the close of the play. Only after Macbeth's death is Malcolme – Duncan's eldest son but also king by nomination and therefore heir to the Scottish throne based on two cultural practices: primogeniture and the Gaelic system of tanistry[45] – twice hailed, ominously, perhaps, as 'King of Scotland' (TLN 2510, 2511) in anticipation of his coronation. Furthermore, the signalling of royal authority in the stage directions – that is, 'Flourish' (TLN 278, 2478) – is limited to Duncan and Malcolm. Macbeth is addressed as 'King' just once in the entire play, and by one of the 'Weyard Sisters' (TLN 1686); there is one reference to Macbeth as 'your Maiesty' and two references to 'his Maiesty' (TLN 1258, 1401, 2098). In response to Macbeth's '[m]y name's Macbeth' (TLN 2,405), Young Seyward's '[t]he diuell himselfe could not pronounce a Title/More hatefull to mine eare' (TLN 2506–07) uses 'Title' as if to foreground a denial of the title 'King Macbeth'. If the play eventually refuses to legitimise Macbeth's kingship – I say eventually because both Rosse's '[t]hen 'tis most like,/The Soueraignty will fall vpon Macbeth' and Macduffe's '[h]e is already nam'd, and gone to Scone/To be inuested' (TLN 963–6) apparently accepts Macbeth's election – it does more than present Duncan's murderer as merely an 'vntitled Tyrant' (TLN 1931).

What the play offers in the figure of Macbeth, I want to suggest, is a nationalist. Whilst the play does not exactly figure Macbeth as Scotland's last Celtic king, it does mark him as a fierce and robust defender of his country.[46] 'Macbeth does not defend his kingship against rebels', Claire McEachern points out, 'so much as his kingdom against foreigners'.[47] Macbeth is indeed concerned less with retaining his crown, but is it actually 'his kingdom' that Macbeth defends from the oncoming English or Anglo-Scottish army, or is it instead what he terms 'my Land' (TLN 2274)? We might also ask whether Macbeth, as McEachern implies, adopts this stance only after becoming king. Early in the play we hear of Macbeth's (and Banquo's) combat against Norwegians as well as an Islander and a Highlander (Macdonwald and Cawdor), the historical Macbeth's fellow Celts. Is this combat performed in the name of king or country or, more likely, both? Determining whether the regicidal Macbeth's loyalty to country over the course of the play supersedes his loyalty to the office of the monarch is not easy, for any discussion of a nationalist Macbeth must keep in mind that he is Scotland's ruler. Nationalism is generally regarded as a phenomenon in which nationhood disassociates itself from monarchy; however, in the Elizabethan and Jacobean periods monarch and nation, crown and country often intersected in the language of national self-representation. As a Scottish King of England came to rule, however unevenly, English, Irish, Scottish and Welsh subjects, the discourse of nationhood was further complicated.

'Where Scotland?' (*The Comedie of Errors*, TLN 910)

Whilst Tudor chronicles, especially Holinshed's, were a prime source for Shakespeare when writing *Macbeth*, a somewhat underacknowledged 'source' is Shakespeare's Elizabethan English histories, to which the 'Scottish play' is much indebted.[48] There is a tendency to posit a discontinuity between the English/Elizabethan plays and the British/Jacobean plays, not just because of generic differences but also given the absence of 'England' and 'English' and the presence of 'Britain' and 'British' in the post-1603 plays. Is this another instance of when reliance solely on word usage can foreclose avenues of study? Residues of the earlier Elizabethan plays exist in the Jacobean ones: Shakespeare's reflections on nationhood within the context of the contingencies of state formation under

King James cannot be dissociated from his earlier imaginings of nationhood within a two-island (Britain and Ireland), two-kingdom (England, Ireland) and three-nation (England, Ireland, Wales) political context, an Elizabethan context in which the presence of the separate Kingdom of Scotland was often registered, whether – even in a single play – negatively ('the Weazell (Scot)' *H5*, TLN 316) or positively ('*Gower.* Here a comes, and the Scots Captaine, Captaine *Iamy*, with him./*Welch.* Captaine Iamy is a maruellous falorous Gentleman' (*H5*, TLN 1193–6)).

We might expect echoes of *The First Part of Henry the Fourth* in *Macbeth*, especially given the former play's numerous invocations of 'Scotland' (six), 'Scot' (fourteen) and 'Scottish' (two) – all occurring more than in any other of Shakespeare's Elizabethan plays.[49] To a certain extent, connections between the two plays exist. Specific terms used to praise the Scottish character whom the 1623 folio terms 'Dowglas' – 'braue *Archibald*,/That euer-valiant and approoued Scot' (*1H4*, TLN 57–8), 'my Noble Scot' (*1H4*, TLN 2221), '[t]he Noble Scot Lord *Dowglas*' (*1H4*, TLN 3154) – are also used to describe Macbeth at the play's opening: 'braue *Macbeth*' (TLN 36), 'O valiant Cousin' (TLN 43), '[n]oble *Macbeth*' (TLN 94). This connection is, of course, somewhat tenuous, for the words 'brave', 'valiant' and 'noble' are used to describe a host of Shakespearean warriors. In the wake of Duncan's murder and, especially, as the play nears its conclusion, the depiction of Macbeth shifts. Falstaff's description of 'that Fiend *Dowglas*' (*1H4*, TLN 1325) as a 'hotte Termagant Scot' (*1H4*, TLN 3079) anticipates other characters' accounts of Macbeth, including in act five, scene six Young Seyward's 'though thou call'st they selfe a hoter name/ Then any is in hell' (TLN 2403–04). *Macbeth* also has in common with the earlier chronicle histories the presentation of civil strife. In *Macbeth*, Scotland, not unlike England in many of Shakespeare's history plays, finds itself in a state of civil war: hence the use of 'the Reuolt' (TLN 19) and 'the Broyle' (TLN 24), not to mention the description of Macdonwald as 'a Rebell' (TLN 29, 220). Also like the earlier plays, the participants in *Macbeth*'s 'civil' wars are not, to quote from *The First Part of Henry the Fourth*, '[a]ll of one Nature, of one Substance bred' (TLN 15): Sweno is not Scottish just as Glendour(e)/Glendower and Dowglas are not English. In terms of genre as well as content, the history play to which *Macbeth* is most indebted is Shakespeare's *Richard the Third*.

Macduff's 'O Nation miserable!' (TLN 1930), for instance, echoes Hastings' 'O bloody *Richard*: miserable England' (TLN 2076), and Cathnes's 'the sickly Weale' (TLN 2207) reworks the Third Citizen's '[t]his sickly land' (TLN 1467). Given that these quotations mark the sole instances in Shakespeare's plays when 'miserable' and 'sickly' adjectivally qualify a noun designating a polity, it would seem that Shakespeare had *Richard the Third* on his mind when writing *Macbeth*. Other connections exist between the two plays, including the presence of the supernatural and, especially, prophetic figures: the 'weyward' or 'weyard' Sisters and Queen Margaret come to mind as does Richard's quarto-text line 'a Bard of Ireland told me once/I should not liue long after I saw Richmond'.[50] 'Beware Macduffe,/Beware the Thane of Fife' (TLN 1609–10); Macbeth does not live long after he sees Macduffe.

Perhaps the most striking connection between these two plays is the similarities between Richard III and Macbeth: both are termed tyrants and butchers by their enemies; both are bloody. As the action of *Richard the Third* advances to the play's climactic final battle scene 'in the Centry [centre] of this Isle' (TLN 3416) – another Anglocentric mapping – Richard's English army is pitted against 'the Britaine *Richmond*' (TLN 2748), whose army Richard terms a 'scum of Brittaines' and 'bastard Britaines' (TLN 3787, 3802). Editors tend to change the First Folio's 'Britaine(s)' to 'Breton(s)', for Brittany is the base from which the exiled Richmond approaches England – '[t]he Brittaine Nauie is dispers'd by Tempest' (TLN 3328).[51] But given that another of Richard's foes, Buckingham, is 'backt with the hardy Welshmen' (TLN 2757), and given that Richard also calls Richmond 'the Welchman' (TLN 3274), the possibility of a secondary meaning, Briton, should not be discounted.[52] Whatever Richmond's nation is – Brittany, Britain, Wales – Richard's is clearly England; indeed, he concludes his oration to his army with 'fight Gentlemen of England, fight boldly yeomen' (TLN 3809). What Schwyzer says about Shakespeare's Richard III – 'Richard himself is keen to depict his conflict with the rebellious Henry Tudor as an ethnic one, pitting the English against an invading Celtic enemy'[53] – rings true of how Macbeth imagines the play's final conflict. Even though 'blacke *Macbeth*' (TLN 1873) is fully aware that his forces confront an Anglo-Scottish army, he views the confrontation variously as a battle between his country's soldiers and an English army and as a battle between his force and an Anglicised Scottish army.

Early modern Scottish historians, Hector Boece in particular, bitterly lamented the period of Macbeth's death as ushering in a process of cultural degeneration. Here is how this historical moment is narrated in *The Description of Scotland*:

> In processe of time therefore, and cheeflie about the daies of Malcolme Cammor, our maners began greatlie to change and alter. For when our neighbors the Britons began, after they were subdued by the Romans, to wax idle and slouthfull, and therevpon driuen out of their countrie into Wales by their enimies the Saxons, we began to haue aliance (by proximitie of the Romans) with Englishmen, speciallie after the subuersion of the Picts, and through our dailie trades and conuersation with them, to learne also their maners, and therewithall their language ... wherof it came to passe that, some were named dukes, some earles, some lords, some barons, in which vaine puffes they fixed all their felicitie. Before time the noble men of Scotland were of one condition, & called by the name of Thanes.[54]

Shakespeare would not have been unfamiliar with this narrative, but, most critics agree, he chose not to reinscribe it; instead, his 'Scottish play' hails Macbeth's defeat at the hands of a combined English and Scottish army. For some, this revision of history signals the play's commitment to James's British project: 'Malcolm', Baldo writes, 'leads an English army against Macbeth in Act 5, suggesting a united purpose that the new monarch of a nominally united Great Britain no doubt applauded'.[55] At the play's close Malcolme declares

> My Thanes and Kinsmen
> Henceforth be Earles, the first that euer Scotland
> In such an Honor nam'd. (TLN 2515–17)

These lines bear witness to a remarkable instance of 'the *Scottish Englishing*'.[56] In reference to Malcolm's closing speech, Christopher Highley speaks of 'Malcolm's rejection of Gaelic culture for English-identified practices', which serves not only to Anglicise Malcolm but also to legitimate his rule.[57] It is an Anglicised and Anglicising Malcolm whom Macbeth confronts in the play. 'One way of looking at the [play's] action', Stephen Orgel writes, 'is to say that it is about the enforced Anglicization of Scotland, which Macbeth is resisting'.[58] Not surprisingly, in the First Folio 'Thane' is used to reference Macbeth more than any other character: seventeen of the play's thirty-one occurrences of 'Thane(s)' concern the historically Moray-based Macbeth.

Early in the play we learn of Macbeth's encounter with and eventual defeat of the rebel '*Macdonwald*' (TLN 28), who 'is supply'd' '[o]f Kernes and Gallowgrosses' 'from the Westerne Isles' (TLN 31–2). As a combined Scottish and English army advance upon the 'abhorred Tyrant' (TLN 2410) at the play's close, we learn that Macbeth is now supplied with Gaelic soldiers when Macduffe proclaims 'I cannot strike at wretched Kernes, whose armes/Are hyr'd to beare their Staues' (TLN 2419–20). Shakespeare learned of Macbeth's employment of kerns from the chronicle sources. In his *Rerum Scoticarum historia* (1582), George Buchanan, for example, records that Macbeth's army consisted of Gaels: '[Macbeth] sent his Friends into the *Æbudæ* [Hebrides], and into *Ireland*, with Money to hire Soldiers'.[59] The play hints that 'these skipping Kernes' (TLN 49) are in Macbeth's service even before Macduffe's reference to them in the final scene. In act four, scene two, when the 'Murtherers' term Macduffe 'a Traitor', his son replies '[t]hou ly'st thou shagge-ear'd Villaine' (TLN 1802, 1806, 1807). Editors tend to emend the folio's 'shagge-ear'd' to 'shag-haired' ('shag-hear'd'?), based most likely on Shakespeare's earlier uses of this and similar terms in his history plays. Shakespeare's Richard II, for example, speaks of 'those rough rug-headed Kernes' (TLN 803), and in the second of the Henry VI plays Richard, Duke of York compares Cade to 'a shag-hayr'd craftie Kerne' (TLN 1673). That the murderers of Macduffe's wife and son are kerns is a definite possibility.

Although Macbeth gains power without the assistance of kerns, his Machiavellian maintenance of power relies on their martial force. Just as his assumption of the Thane of Cawdor's title anticipates his Cawdor-like actions, Macbeth's employment of kerns consolidates his Macdonwald-like status. The historical 'Makdowald', according to Holinshed's *Chronicles*, was backed by Gaelic forces: 'for out of the westerne Iles there came vnto him a great multitude of people, offering themselues to assist him in that rebellious quarell, and out of Ireland in hope of the spoile came no small number of Kernes and Galloglasses'.[60] Shakespeare's rendering of Macbeth as like the rebel he earlier defeated rehearses a conventional narrative of his reign, one summarised by the Scottish historian John Monipennie: '[i]n the beginning of his raigne he behaued himselfe as a good and iust Prince, but after, he degenerated into a cruell Tyrant'.[61] Along with rendering him a rebel, does Macbeth's association with kerns and gallowglasses also bestow a specific cultural identity upon him? Highley thinks it does: 'Macbeth's isolation and descent into tyranny is presented as a process of Gaelicization'.[62] The historical Macbeth was a Gael, but *Macbeth*, at least originally, offers little distinction (in speech, in dress) between its eponymous hero and the play's Lowland or Anglicised Scots, such as Malcolme and, arguably, Macduffe.[63] Highley's suggestive observation about Shakespeare's Gaelicisation of Macbeth calls attention to how the play employs a rhetoric of civility to mark Macbeth's shift from loyal and obedient thane to savage and uncivil tyrant. I want to suggest that Macbeth's 'isolation and descent' is marked less by a 'process of Gaelicization' and more by his nationalist rhetoric.

In an essay on Scottish mercenary soldiers in the early modern period and as depicted in *1 Henry IV* and *Henry V*, Vimala Pasupathi notes that 'Shakespeare grants the Scots ... a tangible sense of military prowess while underscoring the unreliability (and even the lack) of political or emotional investment they bring to a given martial cause'. These Scottish soldiers 'embody a national identity at once forged through martial action and extricated from monarchical loyalty' and, Pasupathi adds, 'lacking a national affiliation entirely'.[64] In keeping with the absence of 'Scot', 'Scotch', 'Scottish' and 'Scottishman'/'Scottishmen', *Macbeth* never bestows an explicit national identity on its mercenary soldiers: they are, for sure, Gaels, but they are not specifically Irish or Scottish Gaels. The play associates the mercenary soldiers with the Western Isles, but Holinshed, as mentioned, traces Makdowald's support to two Gaelic sites: those 'out of the westerne Isles' and kerns and gallowglasses 'out of Ireland'. Buchanan also situates these soldiers in Scotland's west coast and Ireland: '[Mac-duald] called in the *Islanders* to his assistance, (who were always prone to Sedition) and also the forwardest of the *Irish*'.[65] Pont, too, distinguishes between 'the wild and savadg Irish of the English dominion, and of the Scottish ilands the Hebridiani, or Æbudiani'.[66] Given that Shakespeare's earlier history plays explicitly associate both kerns and gallowglasses with Ireland, *Macbeth*'s refusal to bestow a national identity upon them is all the more striking.[67] In light of Pasupathi's comments, perhaps the presence of kerns and gallowglasses in *Macbeth* serves to contrast (thereby highlighting) the mercenary soldiers' lack of 'a national affiliation' with Macbeth's nationalism, although his commitment to nation is similarly 'forged through martial action' and, paradoxically, 'extricated from monarchical loyalty': Macbeth is, after all, a regicide. Macbeth's nationalist rhetoric is, however, distinguished by the fact that it has little hold on his soldiers. What Macbeth achieves in the play is 'dominion but not connection'.[68] 'Those he commands, moue onely in command', remarks Angus, '[n]othing in loue' (TLN 2217–18). Mercenaries may have lacked loyalty, but, as Macduffe confirms, Macbeth's kerns stick with him until the bitter end; however, they do so, according to Malcolme, not out of love or duty:

> Both more and lesse haue giuen him the Reuolt,
> And none serue with him, but constrained things,
> Whose hearts are absent too. (TLN 2306–08)

Macbeth's Scottish soldiers, on the other hand, abandon him apace. Throughout act five, scene three, Macbeth's 'the Thanes flye from me' (TLN 2272) serves as an unsettling refrain.

Macbeth, Thane of Glamis and loyal subject to King Duncan, is praised at the play's opening for the vital role that he has played 'in his Kingdomes great defence' (TLN 203). Since the pronoun 'his' here refers to Duncan, Macbeth is figured early in the play as a loyal servant to Scotland's monarch: 'our Duties', Macbeth proclaims to his kinsman and monarch, 'are to your Throne, and State/Children, and Seruants' (TLN 308–09). 'State' here could mean a polity, but the primary meaning is probably '[a] person's high rank or exalted position' (*OED n.*15.a).[69] Initially, Macbeth is presented in opposition to rebels such as Macdonwald and the Thane of Cawdor, who, as Rosse states, 'labour'd/In his Countreyes wracke' (TLN 222). At the play's opening – and both appear just once – the only terms used to designate the Scottish polity are kingdom and country. As the play's early action is given over to 'the swelling Act/Of the Imperiall Theame' (TLN 239–40), references to Scotland as well as any other political term describing Scotland are muted. Not until act three, scene four does another political term designating Scotland, actually Scotland's nobility, surface: Macbeth, now king, speaks of 'our Countries Honor' (TLN 1304).[70] Even though this reference is exclusive, Macbeth's invocation of country rather than kingdom is significant, for this term and its variously spelt plural forms, voiced and contested by a host of the play's Scottish characters, will take pride of place among the play's political keywords in the lead-up to the final battle. Macbeth, who seems to presume the establishment of primogeniture in Scotland, does speak the word 'kingdom' when he demands '[s]hall *Banquo's* issue euer/Reigne in this Kingdome?'

(TLN 1647–8), a moment that marks Macbeth's sole utterance of 'kingdom'.[71] As we shall see, Macbeth commits himself at the play's close not to securing the crown, as Richard III attempts to do, but rather to defending and protecting Scotland. Macbeth, who at the play's opening is figured as serving Scotland's king, concludes the play, at least in his own eyes, as his country's protector.

'O Scotland, Scotland' (*Macbeth*, TLN 1927)

Not long after the sovereignty has fallen upon Macbeth does the subject of his usurpation of Malcolme's right to Scotland's crown surface. In act three, scene six, Lenox terms Macbeth a 'Tyrant', a title that will stick to him until the play's close. Not surprisingly, the play's representation of Macbeth as usurper is couched in a discourse of political legitimacy – '[f]rom whom this Tyrant holds the due of Birth' (TLN 1498) – but it is also grounded in a rhetoric of nationhood. Macbeth is not only '[d]iuellish *Macbeth*' (TLN 1945); Macduffe's and Malcolme's demonisation of him is also nation-specific: for instance, 'this fiend of Scotland' (TLN 2083). The play's incorporation of the supernatural draws our attention to 'fiend', but I am interested in the way in which the play figures characters in relation to a distinctly national identity and space. Macbeth is 'of Scotland', and he remains, at least in the play, within Scotland. But why 'fiend of Scotland' rather than 'Scottish fiend'?[72] *Othello* designates its eponymous hero 'of Venice', which may not equate to being Venetian: Iago's 'I know our Country disposition well' (TLN 1817) hints at Othello's exclusion from Iago's place of birth. Macduffe's labelling of Macbeth as 'of Scotland' similarly works to estrange Macbeth from his homeland. A disinherited Malcolme, we learn in act three, scene six, '[l]iues in the English Court' (TLN 1499), and in the same scene we hear that the Warwick-like kingmaker Macduffe is making his way to King Edward's court '[t]o wake Northumberland, and warlike *Seyward*' (TLN 1504) in order to bring aid to what Lenox terms 'our suffering Country' (TLN 1523) – Macduffe's wife's account of her husband as one who has flown 'the Land' (TLN 1712) casts a less heroic figure, a view of Macduffe reinforced by Malcolme's stinging interrogative '[w]hy in that rawnesse left you Wife, and Childe?' (TLN 1844). The play's shift from a Scottish to an English setting places two of its key figures, Malcolme and Macduffe, not to mention the unnamed 'exil'd Friends' (TLN 2519), outside of their native land. No wonder, then, that Macduffe's speech in this scene is punctuated by the rhetorical figure of apostrophe: 'O Scotland, Scotland'; 'O Natio*n* miserable!' (TLN 1927, 1930). In this crucial scene, the play's lengthiest, Malcolme and Macduffe's situatedness, 'banish'd ... from Scotland' (TLN 1940), becomes an ideologically enabling position: placed in England, their bitter laments of Scotland's current state are coupled with a profound longing to return home.

Dominating the play's English scene are the words 'Scotland' and 'Tyrant', Macbeth's tyranny having reduced Scotland to a wounded nation. The following lines, spoken by Macduffe, register the tenor of this scene:

> Bleed, bleed poore Country,
> Great Tyrrany, lay thou thy basis sure,
> For goodnesse dare not check thee: wear you thy wrongs,
> The Title, is affear'd. Far thee well Lord,
> I would not be the Villaine that thou think'st,
> For the whole Space that's in the Tyrants Graspe.
> And the rich East to boot. (TLN 1850–6)

To which Malcolme responds 'I thinke our Country sinkes beneath the yoake' (TLN 1859). Reminiscent of Richmond's pronouncement of England under King Richard III's rule as '[b]ruis'd vnderneath the yoake of Tyranny' (TLN 3407), Macduffe's and Malcolme's invocation of tyranny and the yoke are something of a Shakespearean commonplace, spoken by a host of characters – from Cassius to Cymbeline – who bewail present servitude, subjection or oppression under native or foreign tyranny. Invocations of 'the yoke' are often used to incite resistance by forging a sense of common cause; in the process, such invocations can also forge a group identity: consider, for instance, Cymbeline's 'Caesars Ambition ... Did put the yoake vpon's; which to shake off/Becomes a warlike people (TLN 1426, 1429–30). If Malcolme and Macduffe are now unwilling to recognise Macbeth's rule, then Macduffe also refuses to legitimate the space over which Macbeth rules by denying it any political specificity: an instance of what Peter Holland astutely terms 'power displaced from its geographical and conceptual boundaries'.[73] For Macduffe, Macbeth rules not a country, a nation, a kingdom or a state but rather the undefined and unlimited 'whole Space that's in the Tyrants Graspe'. The word 'Space' has the effect of evacuating from that undefined space any sense of national belonging or nationhood, as if under Macbeth's illegitimate rule or control Scotland cannot be Scotland, whether nation or kingdom or both. Scotland is, as Rosse states, '[a]lmost affraid to know it selfe' (TLN 2001). Rosse's pronouncement is prefaced by another kind of unknowing, for a moment of temporary confusion marks his entrance since Malcolme, unlike Macduffe, at once does and does not recognise Rosse:

> *Enter Rosse.*
> MACD: See who comes heere.
> MALC: My Countryman: but yet I know him no[t].
> MACD: My euer gentle Cozen, welcome hither.
> MALC: I know him now. Good God betimes remoue
> The meanes that makes vs Strangers. (TLN 1992–7)

Earlier in the play, following the stage direction *'Enter Rosse and Angus'* (TLN 66) and in response to Duncan's 'Who comes here?' (TLN 67), Malcolme, recognising his countryman, states '[t]he worthy *Thane* of Rosse' (TLN 68). Now, in a crucial scene, three Scots appear on stage as, paradoxically, countrymen, connected by ties to their homeland, but also as strangers, alienated not only from each other but also from their native land.[74]

Act four, scene three is also dominated by references to blood and tears, much more so than in Shakespeare's primary source. *The Historie of Scotland* depicts the meeting between Makduffe and Malcolme as follows:

> At [Makduffe's] comming vnto Malcolme, he declared into what great miserie the estate of Scotland was brought, by the detestable cruelties exercised by the tyrant Makbeth ... Malcolme hearing Makduffes words, which he vttered in verie lamentable sort, for meere compassion and very ruth that pearsed his sorowfull hart, bewailing the miserable state of his countrie, he fetched a deepe sigh; which Makduffe perceiuing, began to fall most earnestlie in hand with him, to enterprise the deliuering of the Scotish people out of the hands of so cruell and bloudie a tyrant ... Though Malcolme was verie sorowfull for the oppression of his countrimen the Scots ... yet doubting whether he were come as one that ment vnfeinedlie as he spake, or else as sent from Makbeth to betraie him, he thought to haue some further triall.[75]

Shakespeare's reworking of the source material augments Scotland's misery, Lenox's earlier use of '[o]ur suffering Country' anticipating act four, scene three's lament for the Scottish nation. The phrase 'poore Country' (TLN 1869, 1960, 2000), spoken by Macduffe, Malcolme and Rosse, echoes throughout this scene, magnified by Malcolme's 'the poore State' (TLN 1874). Malcolme's description of a feminised Scotland summarises his and this scene's attitude to his country: '[i]t weepes, it bleeds, and each new day a gash/Is added to her wounds' (TLN 1859-60). Commenting on the presence of blood and tears in relation to generic differences in Shakespeare's plays, Adrian Poole observes that in 'Shakespeare's histories and tragedies the liquid in which things get regularly "steeped" is of course blood and the action hardens memory into indelible griefs and grudges. In the comedies the predominant liquids are clearer, they enter and leave the body more freely in the form of water and wine and tears and sweat, and their action dissolves memory into new forms of readiness.'[76] Act four, scene three's invocations of blood are, to be sure, accompanied by 'indelible griefs and grudges'; however, this scene's numerous references to cries, groans, shrieks, sighs, tears, wailing and weeping also gives rise to 'new forms of readiness'. The opening exchange between Malcolme and Macduffe sets the tone for the oscillation between lamentation and incitation that underpins the scene:

> MALC: Let vs seeke out some desolate shade, & there
> Weepe our sad bosomes empty.
> MACD: Let vs rather
> Hold fast the mortall Sword: and like good men,
> Bestride our downfall Birthdome: each new Morne,
> New Widdowes howle, new Orphans cry, new sorowes
> Strike heauen on the face, that it resounds
> As if it felt with Scotland, and yell'd out
> Like Syllable of Dolour. (TLN 1814-22)

This dynamic of deflation and inspiration continues as Malcolme's misrepresentation of himself as devoid of 'King-becoming Graces' (TLN 1917) disconcerts Macduffe, leading the latter to proclaim 'O Scotland, Scotland' and 'O Nation miserable!' Macduffe's lamentations here are not too dissimilar from Gaunt's 'this sceptred Isle' (*R2*, TLN 681) speech: although Macduffe never figures Scotland as an isle, he does speak of Scotland as 'bloody Sceptred' (TLN 1930). Malcolme's acknowledgement of his 'false speaking' (TLN 1958), coupled with the news that 'Old *Seyward* with ten thousand warlike men/Already at a point, was setting foorth' (TLN 1962–3) begins to buoy Macduffe until Rosse brings news of his wife and children having been '[s]auagely slaughter'd' (TLN 2050), which reduces Macduffe's speech to a slew of interrogatives. Malcolme's 'let griefe/ Conuert to anger: blunt not the heart, enrage it' (TLN 2078–9) marks the scene's final shift from paralysing grief to rousing action as Macduffe does give sorrow words in his last speech in this scene, stating, Hotspurre-like, 'Front to Front,/Bring thou this Fiend of Scotland, and my selfe' (TLN 2082–3).[77]

Before act four, scene three's various references to Scotland, country, state and nation, there appears Macduffe's previously cited reference to Scotland as 'our downfall Birthdome' – the compound adjective 'downfall' meaning downfallen, which the OED, citing this line from the play, defines as '[t]hat has lost power, prosperity, status, etc.; diminished or defeated' (*adj.* 2). The use of 'Birthdome' – which, surprisingly, has received little critical attention – is remarkable not just because it is the only occurrence of this term in all of Shakespeare's plays but also because it appears to be a word that Shakespeare coined. The OED lists this word's appearance in the play as its sole example, and it offers the following meaning: '[p]ossessions or privileges to which a person is entitled by birth; inheritance, birthright'.[78] This definition of birthdom favours entitlement, possession, privilege and right, which makes sense if we think of 'our downfall Birthdome' as a reference to the Prince of Cumberland's claim to the throne ('[f]rom whom this Tyrant holds the due of Birth') as well as the Thane of Fife's property ('[w]hat had he done, to make him fly the Land?' TLN 1712).[79] But does the invocation of 'Scotland' just three lines after 'our downfall Birthdome', not to mention the scene's refrain-like 'poore Country', invite us to invest this word with other meanings? Whilst some of the play's recent editors stick with the OED's definition of birthdom, others supply alternative ones, ascribing to the word senses associated with a polity.[80] But what form does a polity described as a birthdom take? One possible if not obvious answer is kingdom: the political situation, especially in this scene and throughout the play, allows this meaning; moreover, the presence of the suffix 'dom' establishes a linguistic as well as aural connection. Alternatively, it could be argued that Shakespeare coins the word 'Birthdome' not simply to form a synonym for kingdom but rather to hint at another kind of political representation and communal affiliation. Unlike kingdom, which organises the polity around allegiance and subjection, birthdom evokes a sense of *patria*: that is, it foregrounds one's place of birth, native country or homeland, thereby attributing a sense of belonging less to political subjection and more to a national community. The use of the possessive adjective 'our' reinforces a nation-based concept of community grounded in belonging and bonding. 'Our' never precedes 'kingdom' in *Macbeth*; of the latter word's three uses, two are prefaced by the pronouns 'his' (TLN 203) and the other by 'thy' (TLN 2508). What also distinguishes the word 'birthdom' is that it, unlike kingdom, has maternal connotations, figuring one's place of birth or native land a motherland. Ironically, this word is introduced in the play by the one male character who is not 'of woman borne' (TLN 1621). By no means do I wish to settle on a single meaning for birthdom, for to do so would foreclose investigation into a textual crux that invites and rewards open critical inquiry. Indeed, we could point to Malcolme's '[l]et vs ... Bestride our downfall Birthdome' as another instance, perhaps a prime example, of what A. R. Braunmuller terms the play's notoriously 'unparaphrasable language'.[81]

Macduffe's 'Imperiall charge' (TLN 1836) is, of course, to Malcolme, whom he regards as 'the truest Issue of [Scotland's] Throne' (TLN 1933). His allegiance is also to his country or nation. 'Let vs rather/Hold fast the mortall Sword: and like good men,/Bestride our downfall Birthdome' sets up Malcolme and Macduffe, together, as main players in Scotland's reclamation from the tyrant's grip. Rhetorically, 'Birthdome' works to interpellate Malcolme by appealing both to his monarchical – birthright, inheritance – and his national – native land or country – interests. Shakespeare's neologism, moreover, bears witness to the historical pressures attending the concept of nationhood at the time of the play's production: the less-than-straightforward shift from kingdom/realm to nation/state, James's unprecedented rule of the kingdoms of England, Ireland and Scotland, and the dialogue and debate surrounding the potential union of two of those kingdoms.

'The English powre is neere' (*Macbeth*, TLN 2176)

Where does Macbeth, then, fit into the play's articulation of nationhood? One way of answering this question is to consider whom Macbeth confronts in the play's final scene and, in particular, how he imagines that confrontation. When Menteth states '[t]he English powre is neere', he adds that this army is 'led on by *Malcolme,/ His Vnkle Seyward*, and the good *Macduffe*' (TLN 2176–7), which is why many critics and editors label this army an Anglo-Scottish force. Earlier in the play we learn that the English army consists of ten thousand men, a figure confirmed by Macbeth's servant in act five, scene three. The servant terms this army 'the English Force' (TLN 2235), and it is the English that Macbeth views as his foe. Upon entering Scotland, Seyward's 'ten thousand men' (TLN 2031) are, of course, bolstered by Scottish forces. Cathnes and Menteth, for instance, announce their intention to join forces with Malcolme in support of 'king' and country:

> Well, march we on,
> To giue Obedience, where 'tis truly ow'd:
> Meet we the Med'cine of the sickly Weale,
> And with him poure we in our Countries purge,
> Each drop of vs. (TLN 2205–09)

As supporters of Malcolme's claim to Scotland's throne, the Scottish nobles on stage in this scene also fashion themselves as agents in their country's purgation or cleansing, a metaphor that pervades the final act. In contrast to the reinforcement of Malcome, Seyward and Macduffe's army, Macbeth is victim to desertion and depletion: those he terms 'false Thanes' (TLN 2221) not only abandon him but also join the oncoming Anglo-Scottish force. Macbeth is fully aware that he faces not simply a 'forraine Leuie' (TLN 1181), to borrow a phrase he uses earlier in the play, but an army made up of English and Scottish soldiers. In fact, he acknowledges the presence of Scottish soldiers among the army marching to Dunsinane:

> Were they not forc'd with those that should be ours,
> We might haue met them darefull, beard to beard,
> And beate them backward home. (TLN 2357–7)[82]

'We' here refers to Scots, 'they' and 'them' refers to the English, and 'home' refers to England. Macbeth's 'those that should be ours' posits a desire for battle between ethnically pure armies: us versus them equates to Scots versus English. Just as the Scottish nobles in act five, scene two present themselves as agents in their country's purging or cleansing, so, too, does Macbeth when he solicits the Doctor to 'cast/The Water of my Land, finde her Disease,/And purge it to a sound and pristine Health' (TLN 2273–5). Both Cathnes and Macbeth invoke a diseased Scotland, but what distinguishes their invocations is Cathnes's inclusive 'our Countries' and Macbeth's exclusive 'my Land'. Macbeth continues the rhetoric of purgation or cleansing when he asks '[w]hat Rubard, Cyme, or what Purgatiue drugge/Would scowre these English hence' (TLN 2278–80). Whilst the use of 'scowre' here offers a variety of meanings, the primary one is 'to drive (an enemy, etc.) *out of* the land' (*OED*, *v*.² 11b). Such lines remind us of Orgel's point that the play 'is about the enforced Anglicization of Scotland, which Macbeth is resisting'. Come act five, the spur pricking the sides of Macbeth's intent is 'resistance'; however, valorising Macbeth as a Scottish patriot risks playing down the prejudicial ethnic nationalism underpinning his patriotic pronouncements.

Of his countrymen who have switched allegiance, Macbeth says dismissively '[t]hen fly false Thanes,/And mingle with the English Epicures' (TLN 2221–2). Earlier in the play, Macbeth speaks of mingling with the Scottish lords in attendance at his banquet: '[o]ur selfe will mingle with Society,/And play the humble Host' (TLN 1259–60). The *OED* cites this line for its definition of 'society' as 'a group of people with whom one has companionship or association' (*n*.5e). In this earlier scene Macbeth mingles with people to whom he is connected; in this case on a level of both nationality and, especially, social status: since Macbeth's 'our Countries Honor' is spoken to and refers to Scotland's nobility it marks a shallow, vertical comradeship.[83] When Macbeth commands 'false Thanes' to 'mingle with the English Epicures' he is using the word 'mingle' otherwise, and we can get a fuller appreciation of his caustic use of this verb by considering its presence within the context of Anglo-Scottish union debate.

As discussed in chapter 3, section headed '"[T]he Vnion and commixture of bodies"', Bacon's *Briefe Discovrse* opens with some reflections on natural unions, and amidst his musing on unions in nature he distinguishes between '*Compositio* and *Mistio*; putting together and mingling'.[84] '*Compositio*,' Bacon writes, 'is the ioyning or putting togeather of bodyes, without a new Forme: and *Mistio*, is the ioyning or putting togeather of bodies, vnder a new Forme'.[85] Having established this distinction, and privileged mingling over putting together, he then shifts his discussion of 'putting together and mingling' from the natural world to the realm of politics: 'there hath beene put in practise in gouernment, these two seuerall kindes of pollicie, in vniting & conioyning of states & kingdomes. The one to retaine the auncient formes still seuered, and onely conioyned in Soueraingtie; the other, to superinduce a new forme agreeable and conuenient to the entire estate.'[86] Bacon cites as exemplary the union of the Romans and the Sabines: '[s]oone after the foundation of the Citie of *Rome*, the people of the *Romaines* and the *Sabines* mingled vppon equall termes. Wherin the interchange went so euen, that (as *Liui* noteth) the one nation gaue the name to the place, and the other to the people. For, *Rome* continued the name: but, the people were called *Quirites*, which was the *Sabine* worde deriued of *Cures*, the countrie of *Tacitus*.'[87] Concluding his *Briefe Discovrse* in a cautiously optimistic voice, Bacon writes 'I do wish (and I wish it, not in the nature of an impossibilitie, to my thinking,) that this happye vnion of your Maiesties two Kingdomes of *England* and *Scotland*; may bee in as good an houre; and vnder the like diuine prouidence, as that was, betweene the *Romaines* and the *Sabines*'.[88]

Bacon was not the only author of a union tract to use the word or concept of mingling. An anonymous Scottish tract similarly invokes the Romans and the Sabines, and in its comments on Roman political incorporation it employs a language of mixture and mingling: 'by whois mixture and incorporating with the subdued people, the whole body so mingled became a member of the Roman Empire'. 'No man can deny', the anonymous author adds, 'but the common name of the Quirites, geven to the whole people of both the nations Roman and Sabinien, carried much for the joyning of their hearts in a perfect amitie'. This same tract also speaks in a British context of 'a mingleing of the nobilitie of both the nations by reciproque mariages'.[89] And Hume writes '[h]ow easy it will be for this people to be mingled [the original Latin texts reads 'miscere'] from here on, to look forward to every occurrence of an Anglo-Scot or Scot-Anglo succession. In any event this has perhaps even been achieved by now. For either I am deceived, or he who is nearest in line to the throne in both countries (on that side as well as this) has mixed descent from both peoples.'[90]

There will be no mingling, no superinducing in Macbeth's Scotland. He wants nothing to do with 'English Epicures', an obvious reference to the oncoming English army but possibly a dig at Malcolme and perhaps even those Scots who have marched north from England. In *The Historie of Scotland*, Makduffe's lament for his nation condemns both Makbeth and Malcolme, who has convinced Makduffe that he is the person he feigns to be, and his condemnation of Malcolme is grounded in anti-English sentiment:

> Oh ye vnhappie and miserable Scotishmen, which are thus scourged with so manie and sundrie calamities, ech one aboue other! Ye haue one curssed and wicked tyrant that now reigneth ouer you, without anie right or title, oppressing you with his most bloodie crueltie. This other that hath the right to the crowne, is so replet with the inconstant behauiour and manifest vices of Englishmen, that no trust is to be had vnto anie word he speaketh.[91]

Reworking its source material, the play figures Macbeth as the voice of anti-Englishness. In an essay on Scots in *Macbeth*, Highley notes that the play 'avoids linguistic markers of Scottish identity' except for the 'occasional and unexceptional Scotticism'.[92] One of those occasions is in act five, scene three, when Macbeth, who at this point in the play enacts the prejudicial stereotype of the Scot as 'rough, gruff, and hard to get along with',[93] terms his servant a 'cream-fac'd Loone' (TLN 2226). We should not be surprised that Macbeth offers this Scotticism at this point in the play, where he imagines his resistance to the advancing 'English' force as a defence not of his crown but of his country. As noted, both sides in the play's final scene speak a language of purging, cleansing, Macbeth especially so: 'purge [my Land] to a sound and pristine Health'; '[w]hat Rubard, Cyme, or what Purgatiue drugge/Would scowre these English hence'. Even his 'skirre the Country round', where the primary meaning of 'skirre' involves passing over the country, contains the secondary meaning of scour. As previously noted, Macduffe's 'bloody Sceptred' calls to mind that other prophet's 'sceptred Isle' speech; Macbeth's language in the final act also has much in common with Gaunt's imagining of England, in particular his pronouncement '[t]his Fortresse built by Nature for her selfe,/Against infection' (*R2*, TLN 684–5), the last word denoting 'moral contamination; corruption of character or habits by evil influences' (*OED n*.7). Macbeth, confined to his Dunsinane fortress – '[g]reat Dunsinane he strongly Fortifies' (TLN 2189) – shares Gaunt's desire for national purity in the face of fears of contamination and dilution.

T-shirts and mugs with deictic-rich phrases from Gaunt's 'sceptred Isle' speech populate the business of little England merchandise, a reminder of just how entrenched Shakespeare's Elizabethan history plays are in the English national psyche.[94] I know of no such merchandise sporting Macbeth's 'cast/The Water of my Land, finde her Disease,/And purge it to a sound and pristine Health' or '[w]hat Rubard, Cyme, or what Purgatiue drugge/Would scowre these English hence' or '[t]hen fly false Thanes,/And mingle with the English Epicures'. It is not the case that lines from the play are not marketable; they are, but just not these lines, at least not yet. Although Macbeth's articulations of nationhood have not caught on like select and selective passages from Gaunt's speech, Macbeth's devotion to country has been recognised. Kerrigan speaks of Macbeth's 'self-interested patriotism', adding that Macbeth's appeal to patriotism 'is partly a tactical response to the fact that Malcolme arrives with an English power'.[95] McEachern, too, terms Macbeth 'a Scottish patriot', adding 'we find ourselves cheering on the efforts of Macbeth's defence of Scotland against the English ... Malcolm, with his new-coined earls, and his compliments to the English king, may be a figure of the multicultural political correctness urged by James VI and I; but our heart lies with Macbeth's fierce defence of national integrity'.[96] Does it? Is there nothing disturbing about Macbeth's nationalism? And to whom exactly do the pronouns 'we' and 'our' refer? It is a critical commonplace that Macbeth as tragic hero 'commands the audience's sympathy for much of the play'.[97] But when, if ever, does the audience's sympathy wane? Is it when Macbeth's patriotic sentiments give way to chauvinism? Is it around the moment when many of his soldiers abandon him, signalling the failure of affect or connection? Or is it the case, as McEachern suggests, that Macbeth's nationalism appeals to 'us'? Perhaps Cathnes better captures the possibilities or impossibility of interpreting Macbeth: '[s]ome say hee's mad: Others, that lesser hate him,/Do call it valiant Fury' (TLN 2190–1).

Macduffe's victory over Macbeth is accompanied by the play's other regicide's pronouncement that 'the time is free' (TLN 2507), marking Malcolme's recovery of the realm.[98] The First Folio stage directions read *'Enter Macduffe; with Macbeths head'* (TLN 2503), suggesting perhaps that Macduffe bears Macbeth's head in his hand – an alteration of the source material's '[t]hen cutting his head from his shoulders, he set it vpon a pole, and brought it vnto

Malcolme'.⁹⁹ At the play's opening, we are informed that immediately after slaying Macdonwald Macbeth 'fix'd his Head vpon our Battlements' (TLN 42), which comes close to the source material's 'he caused the head to be cut off, and set vpon a poles end, and so sent it as a present to the king'.¹⁰⁰ At the play's close, and given the revision of the source material, Macduffe's entrance with Macbeth's gory locks may have reminded audience members of Theodore de Bry's widely disseminated image of 'one Picte', which de Bry based on John White's watercolour drawing of 'A Pictish warrior holding a human head'¹⁰¹ (see figure 1). 'These Pictes', according to the Scot James Henrisoun, 'wer a people of Scithia, now called Tartarie'.¹⁰² Highlighting the Picts' Scythian roots is tantamount to proclaiming their incivility. The play's final vision of Macduffe does little to simplify its examination of ways in which characters are shaped by their connection to nation.

The play's final twenty lines include one reference to 'kingdom' – Macduffe's 'I see thee compast with thy Kingdomes Pearle' (TLN 2508) – and three references to Scotland, two of which are repeated in the form of '[h]aile King of Scotland' (TLN 2511, 2512). The other reference to Scotland is Malcolme's

> My Thanes and Kinsmen
> Henceforth be Earles, the first that euer Scotland
> In such an Honor nam'd. (TLN 2515-17)

So much for Macbeth's resistance to the Anglicisation of Scotland. For Robert Crawford, '*Macbeth*'s Scotland can only be saved through English-backed military intervention'; the play, moreover, imposes 'a vision of a broken, treacherous kingdom crying out for English oversight'. 'A theatrical triumph', Crawford says of *Macbeth*, 'it is also the most effective piece of literary propaganda directed against notions of Scottish independence'.¹⁰³ To dismiss Crawford's comments would be unwise, for they call attention to the crucial issue of Scotland's self-determination in the play, which reflects historical pressures of a potential union in place at the time of the play's first performance. *Macbeth*, as has been pointed out, 'includes no explicit acts of either voluntary or forced deference to the English nation'.¹⁰⁴ The English and Scottish sections of Holinshed's *Chronicles* offer different versions of Siward's role in Malcolme's restoration. In the Scottish section, Siward is presented as a supporter of Malcolme: 'old Siward earle of Northumberland

'Our downfall Birthdome'

1 'The trwe picture of one Picte', from Thomas Hariot, *A briefe and true report of the new found land of Virginia* (London, 1590). By permission of The Folger Shakespeare Library.

was appointed with ten thousand men to go with [Malcolme] into Scotland, to support him in this enterprise, for recouerie of his right'.[105] In the English section, Siward is not simply a supporter of Malcolme, he is also granted the role of kingmaker: 'Siward the noble earle of Northumberland with a great power of horssemen went into Scotland, and in battell put to flight Mackbeth that had vsurped the crowne of Scotland, and that doone, placed Malcolme surnamed Camoir, the sonne of Duncane, sometime king of Scotland, in the gouernment of that realme'.[106] When commenting on the play, it is important to recall Shakespeare's indebtedness to and his significant reworking of his chronicle sources. In other words, *Macbeth* owes much but not all of its dramaturgy to a historical narrative, or narratives, that would have been well known to Shakespeare and his contemporaries through Scottish histories, in particular Scottish histories that were written by Scots (in Latin, in Scots), translated (into Scots and into English), and mediated and glossed by biased and Anglocentric English historians. Mason comments astutely on the Scottish section (and other sections) of Holinshed's *Chronicles*, noting that 'the scope and nature of the *Chronicles* ensure that no single or consistent image of the Scots, and no single or consistent understanding of their past, is presented. On the contrary, what is striking is the multivocality of the text and the lack of harmony evident in the various ways in which the Scots are perceived and described.'[107] *Pace* Crawford, I believe that the 'the Scottish play' incorporates the polyphony of voices embedded in the source material upon which the play draws, ideologically wide-ranging Scottish and English perspectives. This is not to say that *Macbeth* is a British play, but in its inscription and interrogation of British history and the cultural identities that have come into being on the island it shares with some contemporary union tracts and treatises a willingness not necessarily to think through, for the theatrical tragedy is not a tract or treatise, but to reflect on the novel political condition of being subject to a single, composite monarch within the space of a doubly sceptred isle. In its evacuation of 'Scottish', 'Scot(s)' and 'Scottishman', *Macbeth*, like *King Lear* and *Cymbeline*, registers a shift from the insular nationhood that marks the Elizabethan history plays to a recognition of the need to redefine nationhood in the wake of James's accession to the English throne.

'[T]his whole Isle' (King James VI and I, 1604 speech to Parliament)

As previously mentioned, the First Folio's post-Elizabethan plays (excluding *Othello* and *The Tempest*) register a diminution in the use of the words 'isle' and 'island'. One reason for this diminution, of course, is that as a member of the King's Men acting company Shakespeare, like his fellow playwrights, was no longer writing the kind of English chronicles that he wrote during the 1590s. Shakespeare's Jacobean plays do not invite imaginings of England as an island-nation or island-realm in the explicit manner that his earlier Elizabethan histories had, but that does not mean that he stopped writing the nation. *King Lear*'s reference in the First Folio to the 'the diuision of the Kingdome' (TLN 7) could easily have used 'division of the island', for both a political as well as a geographical term suffices here – the division is, after all, geopolitical.[108] Shakespeare's single- and co-authored Jacobean plays contain only two instances in which the island of his birth is referred to as an isle. In both instances, whether the reference is to the larger entity of Great Britain or to an imagined geopolitical space within the island is, however, unclear. Of the two instances, one occurs in a play set in ancient Britain, the other in a co-authored play set in Henrician England, which has and has not been considered Shakespeare's final history play. Chronologically – in terms of historical setting as well as time of composition – the first instance occurs in *Cymbeline*, the second in *King Henry the Eight*.

The 'Isle' reference in *Cymbeline* surfaces within the context of the Roman demand in act three, scene one for a tribute to be paid by the Britons, who had been conquered by a Roman army led by Julius Caesar. In defiance of this tribute, Clotten and the Queene spurn the Roman ambassador Lucius in their own unique brand of 'British' patriotism or nationalism. Clotten's puff 'Britaine's a world/By it selfe' (TLN 1390–91) is deflated by the fact that his British boast in the face of Roman authority appropriates a Latin commonplace.[109] Glorying in her son's insularity, the Queene, too, admonishes her husband to defy Rome by invoking memory and geography in a speech reminiscent of Shakespeare's English histories, especially the scene in *Henry the fift* when the high-ranking churchmen and England's nobles incite the king to pursue his claim to the French throne and therefore war with France:

> Remember Sir, my Liege,
> The Kings your Ancestors, together with
> The naturall brauery of your Isle, which stands
> As Neptunes Parke, ribb'd, and pal'd in
> With Oakes vnskaleable, and roaring Waters,
> With Sands that will not beare your Enemies Boates,
> But sucke them vp to' th' Top-mast. A kinde of Conquest
> Caesar made heere, but made not heere his bragge
> Of Came, and Saw, and Ouer-came: with shame
> (The first that euer touch'd him) he was carried
> From off our Coast, twice beaten: and his Shipping
> (Poore ignorant Baubles) on our terrible Seas
> Like Egge-shels mou'd vpon their Surges, crack'd
> As easily 'gainst our Rockes. For ioy whereof,
> The fam'd *Cassibulan*, who was once at point
> (Oh giglet Fortune) to master Caesars Sword,
> Made Luds-Towne with reioycing-Fires bright,
> And Britaines strut with Courage. (TLN 1395–1412)

To what does the Queene's 'your Isle' refer when spoken to a British king who rules in ancient Britain? Is this yet another instance, as in Spenser's Proem to *The Faerie Queene*, of an island-realm pushed beyond its actual bounds? When John Hayward asks his readers 'can wee account the name of *Britaine* either so new or so harsh, which hath continued to bee the name, generally of the whole Iland, but more specially of the parts of *England* and *Wales*, euer since before the inuasion of the Romanes?' he pinpoints the area over which Cymbeline actually ruled: that is, an area roughly equivalent to Roman Britain, which, significantly, did not take in the Scotland of Shakespeare's day.[110] As the Scot Henrisoun reminded his readers in his *Exhortacion* 'Caesar and diuerse other neuer came so farre as Scotla*n*de'.[111] 'When I speak of Britain', writes another Scot, Thomas Craig, 'I refer to the southern part of the island, the Roman Province, below the Roman Wall'.[112] However, the Queene's 'your Isle' – denoting the territory under King Cymbeline's rule – could be using Britain to signify what in Shakespeare's day amounted to England, as it was often used in earlier works. 'The notion of an ancient British heritage had such a powerful hold on the English imagination that "Britain" came to be identified with the kingdom of England itself, in explicit distinction from Wales and Scotland.'[113] Cymbeline's 'Isle' is ancient Britain, but it is not Great Britain. Both

Clotten and the Queene have been received by critics as belated voices of English nationalism that are presented as out of place in a British play indebted to ideas of peace, union and internationalism.[114] The play does offer alternative perspectives on nationhood, especially in lines spoken by Cymbeline's daughter, Imogen. Her later revision of Cloten's allusion to Virgil is a prime example:

> Hath Britaine all the Sunne that shines? Day? Night?
> Are they not but in Britaine? I' th' worlds Volume
> Our Britaine seemes as of it, but not in't:
> In a great Poole, a Swannes-nest, prythee thinke
> There's liuers out of Britaine. (TLN 1823–7)

Although the Queene offers a rousing patriotic speech, her invocation of 'your Isle' exists not only to be critiqued as belated and insular but also to be corrected by passages, such as Imogen's, that go against the grain of such rhetoric. As a member of the King's Men, Shakespeare produced plays more alert to Britain's (and, although less so, Ireland's) geopolitics. Addressing an off-stage Imogen, the Second Lord calls for her to remain resilient: 'that thou maist stand/T' enioy thy banish'd Lord: and this great Land' (TLN 900–01). The presence of a term whose currency was on the rise – namely, Great Britain – reminds us of the play's dual British context. *Cymbeline* invites its viewers and readers to take sides, and the choice between Cloten and Imogen is clear: Cloten's beheading simplifies the choice.[115] This does not necessarily mean that the play is asking its theatre or print audience to choose between two types of political ideology. Anderson argues that national identification is founded 'on an essentially imagined basis'.[116] *Cymbeline* delves to the root by offering and interrogating various imaginings of community.

King Henry the Eight contains the other Jacobean English/British isle reference in the form of the Lord Chamberlain's '[b]ut from this Lady [Anne Bullen], may proceed a Iemme, [Elizabeth I]/To lighten all this Ile' (TLN 1295–6). Once again, we are left to ponder the question to what does 'all this Ile' refer? Does it refer to 'this whole Isle', a phrase used by James in his 1604 speech to Parliament to designate Great Britain?[117] Or, given the reference to Queen Elizabeth, does it mark yet another instance of islanding England? If Shakespeare's post-Elizabethan plays celebrate 'Britain', then would they not imagine Britain rather than England as an island?

Of course, contemporary Britain is never brought to the stage: *Cymbeline* concerns ancient Britain, and *King Henry the Eight*, even as the Shakespearean history play set in a period nearest to the moment of its composition, can only glimpse King James, a moment occurring after a lengthy passage of praise devoted to England's former queen that includes a reference to 'this Land'. The moment in the play (act five, scene four) when James is referenced – in a scene attributed to John Fletcher – includes the play's sole reference to the word nation:

> Where euer the bright Sunne of Heauen shall shine,
> His Honour, and the greatnesse of his Name,
> Shall be, and make new Nations. (TLN 3421–3)

In that other British play, Kent reacts to having been banished by Lear from 'our Dominions' (TLN 191) by speaking of shaping 'his old course, in a Country new' (TLN 201). 'Country new', 'new Nations': these phrases bear witness to a refiguring of place, space and belonging within the context of Jacobean state and identity formation across Britain and Ireland. Drummond's *Forth Feasting* associates James's composite monarchy with 'new Kingdomes'. Poems produced after James's death in March 1625 foreground the monarch's legacy of 'mak[ing] new Nations'. One contemporary manuscript poem states 'thy ioy/Was to plant Nations rather than destroy'.[118] A *c.* 1630 manuscript copy of Jonson's 'On the Union' alters the epigram's final line from '[t]he spoused paire two realmes, the sea the ring' to '[t]he spoused pair two Nations, the sea the ring'.[119]

Returning to *Macbeth*, I want to reflect once more on the play's conclusion, and I wish to do so informed, as Shakespeare no doubt was, by debate on Anglo-Scottish union. A topical reading of this play in relation to union debate is possible. That is, Macbeth could be read as a representative of an anti-union position, and Macduffe and Malcolme could be viewed as the play's pro-union figures. (As noted earlier, Baldo's interpretation of *Macbeth* highlights the play's incorporation of both of these positions.) My argument is that *Macbeth* is distinguished by its profound reflections on nationhood and nationalism. The figure of Macbeth offered early modern theatregoers and readers a representative of a kind of nationalism that underpinned anti-union and anti-naturalisation discourse, one voiced within and outside Parliament in the early seventeenth century. An entry in the *Commons Journals* for 13 February 1607 records Christopher Pigott's 'Invective against the *Scotts* and *Scottish* Nation, using many Words of Scandal and Obloquy, ill beseeming such an Audience, not pertinent to the Matter in hand, and very unseasonable for the Time and Occassion'.[120] James would even use the word '*Piggots*' in his 31 March 1607 speech to Parliament to denote 'seditious and discontented ... persons'.[121] If Macduffe/Malcolme represent a pro-union position, then the position that they represent, given the thanes-to-earls cultural shift, is that of an incorporating union. In his 'Treatise of the Happie and Blissed Unioun', John Russell calls for a union that will 'tend to the gude publict of baith the natiounes'. 'The said unioun' he adds in rejection of an incorporating union, should be 'mutuall and reciproque, not the translatioun of the estait of ane kingdome in ane uther, not of Scotland as subalterne to Ingland, quhilk is not unioun bot ane plaine discord, the ane to be principall, the uther accesor, the ane to command, the uther to obey – thairby ancienne Scotland to loss hir beautie for evir!'[122] Does the play endorse the position of Macduffe/Malcome as an alternative to Macbeth's nationalism? Do Macduffe's and Malcolme's closing speeches provide not only dramatic but also ideological closure? Or is it the case, as I believe, that the play critiques both positions? Produced and performed in 1606, *Macbeth* emerged at a moment when debate on Anglo-Scottish union and the naturalisation of Scots was at its peak but still far from being resolved by Parliament. The play speaks to the political nation, but it offers no easy resolution to the complex issues with which it engages. When in 1607 James said to England's Parliament 'I know there are many *Piggots* amongst them', he used 'them' in reference to the Scottish nation. Pigott was, of course, English, and James's 'as must be in all Common-wealths' seems to be directed to the English members who constituted the majority of his audience.[123] *Macbeth's* critique of its eponymous hero's nationalism is not a critique of Scottish nationalism but of chauvinism itself, including the nationalism that induced Pigott to rail against his monarch's birthdom and fellow countrymen and countrywomen. Superstition, Bacon wrote, 'erecteth an absolute Tyranny in the minde of men'.[124] *Macbeth*, a play rich in superstition, reveals that nationalism, too, produces a tyrannical mindset. From the perspective of *Macbeth*, the Elizabethan history plays seem distant, the product of a different cultural and political moment. Not that

Shakespeare's Jacobean plays are devoid of '*Piggots*'. It is, after all, the villainous, chauvinistic, misogynistic and racist Iago who echoes the insularity and militarism of the Elizabethan history plays when he designates Cyprus 'this Warrelike Isle' (TLN 1169).[125] It is, moreover, the xenophobic Iago who, from the confines of an island, proclaims '[o]h sweet England' (TLN 1200), marking the First Folio's final voicing of the word 'England'.

Notes

1 Onstage maps are acknowledged in *The First Part of Henry the Fourth, with the Life and Death of Henry Sirnamed Hot-spvrre* (act three, scene one), and in *The Tragedie of King Lear* (act one, scene one). Shakespeare's plays, it should be pointed out, never figure Scotland or Wales as islands.
2 Bacon, *Certain Articles*, 222, 223.
3 MacColl observes that select medieval texts, including Bede's *Ecclesiastical History of the English People*, attempt to divide England and Scotland by exaggerating the length of the firths of Clyde and Forth. 'In the middle of the thirteenth century', Bede's geography 'was given visual form in Matthew Paris's maps of Britain, in three of which the firths of Forth and Clyde almost meet, leaving only a narrow isthmus.' 'This construction of British geography', he adds, 'seems to be one of the factors that contributed to the restricted sense of "Britain" as the kingdom of England itself and indeed to the idea of "British" England as an island (or almost an island) physically separate from Scotland': see MacColl, 'The meaning of "Britain"', 260. MacColl's suggestion that Shakespeare believed in a near-geographical separateness is unconvincing. 'Bizarre as its [i.e. 'the Shakespearean image of England as a "sceptred isle"'] later manifestations often are, however, its use in the late sixteenth century may not be merely an example of wishful – and willful – thinking. Something more than a figure of speech, Shakespeare's lines would appear to reflect a commonly held perception of the geographical separation of the territories of England (or England and Wales) and Scotland': *ibid.*, 262.
4 Edmund Spenser, *The Faerie Queene. Disposed into twelue books, fashioning XII. morall vertues* (London, 1590), A2ᵛ.
5 Kate Chedgzoy, 'This Pleasant and Sceptred Isle: insular fantasies of national identity in Anne Dowriche's *The French Historie* and William Shakespeare's *Richard II*', in Philip Schwyzer and Simon Mealor (eds), *Archipelagic Identities: literature and identity in the Atlantic archipelago, 1550–1800* (Aldershot: Ashgate, 2004), 25.

6 William Shakespeare, *The most excellent historie of the merchant of Venice* (London, 1600), B1ᵛ. Nerissa's '[w]hat thinke you of the Scottish Lorde his neighbour?' appears in the First Folio as '[w]hat thinke you of the other Lord his neighbour?' (TLN 267–8), a change that most editors put down to a cultural and, perhaps, censorial sensitivity concerning references to Scots after James's arrival in London. The publication of plays such as *Eastward Hoe* (1605) suggests that not all playwrights and/or printers displayed such sensitivity, or, perhaps, that insensitivity to Scottish characters pleased some early modern theatregoers.
7 Speed's *Theatre of the Empire of Great Britaine* includes Monmouthshire within the second book, which contains the Principality of Wales.
8 Anderson, *Imagined Communities*, 6.
9 [James VI and I], *The Kings Maiesties Speach To the Lords and Commons of this present Parliament at Whitehall, on Wednesday the xxj. of March* (London, 1610) (STC 14396), F4ʳ.
10 Of the four occurrences of 'ilanders'/'islanders', three are Elizabethan (*KJ* and *2H6*) and one is Jacobean (*Oth*). Whereas *The second Part of Henry the Sixt*'s use of 'islanders' alludes to a Mediterranean setting and *Othello*'s is a description of Cyprus's citizens, *The life and death of King Iohn*'s 'ilanders' and 'islanders' designate subjects of England: '[a]nd coopes from other lands her Ilanders' (TLN 318); '[h]aue I not heard these Islanders shout out/Uiue le Roy' (TLN 2356–7).
11 *The Historie of Scotland*, in *The first and second volumes of Chronicles*, 172. As recorded in Holinshed's *Chronicles*, Fleance's son, Walter Stewart, returned to Scotland, and his son, Robert, inherited the Scottish throne as Robert II. Upon mention of Banquho, the *Chronicles* add, 'of whom the house of the Stewards is descended': Holinshed, *The Historie of Scotland*, in *The first and second volumes of Chronicles*, 168. In the 1603 London publication of his 1598 Edinburgh-published work, Monipennie labels Robert II 'the first of the *Stewards*': John Monipennie, *Certayne Matters Concerning the Realme of Scotland* (London, 1603), D1ʳ.
12 'Denmark-Norway-Sweden had not relinquished possession of the far north of Scotland until the late fifteenth century, and the status of Orkney and Shetland was still disputed in 1605–06 (the islands were not fully incorporated into Scotland until 1612).' Moreover, the 'independent Lordship of the Isles was forfeited to the Scottish crown in 1493': Kerrigan, *Archipelagic English*, 101, 99.
13 Daniel, *The first part of the historie of England*, 62. In Holinshed, Edward the Confessor is represented as having suppressed Welsh rebellion and as having 'granted the rule of Wales' to Gruffudd ap Lwywelyn's two half-brothers in return for 'homage': see Holinshed,

The historie of England, in *The first and second volumes of Chronicles*, 193.
14 R. R. Davies, *The First English Empire: power and identities in the British Isles 1093–1343* (Oxford: Oxford University Press, 2000), 37.
15 For readings attentive to the ways in which *The Life of Henry the Fift* anticipates James's accession to the English throne (or may have been revised after James's accession), see Ivic, 'Making and remaking' and Rhodes, 'Wrapped in the strong arms of the union'.
16 Kerrigan, *Archipelagic English*, 14. Shakespeare, Rhodes argues, 'wrote his English plays in Elizabeth's reign and his British plays after 1603': Rhodes, 'Wrapped in the strong arms of the union', 37.
17 Rhodes, 'Wrapped in the strong arms of the union', 50.
18 The Lord Chamberlain's Men became the King's Men on 19 May 1603 when King James became the company's patron.
19 Hugh Craig, 'Shakespeare's style, Shakespeare's England', in Rachel Orgis and Matthias Heim (eds), *Fashioning England and the English* (Switzerland: Palgrave Macmillan, 2018), 83–4. Craig's focus on 'the sole author plays' means that *Macbeth*, which includes eight instances of 'England' and six of 'English', is absent from his calculations – a significant and surprising omission although understandable given his focus.
20 Christopher Wortham, 'Shakespeare, James I and the matter of Britain', *English*, 45 (1996), 97.
21 The following passage, which follows the line '[a] shew of eight Kings, and Banquo last, with a glasse in his hand' (TLN 1657), is generally read as both referring to and complimenting King James VI and I's royal lineage and rule of multiple of kingdoms:

> And yet the eight appeares, who beares a glasse,
> Which shewes me many more: and some I see,
> That two-fold Balles, and treble Scepters carry. (TLN 1666–8)

'None of these [eight] kings', Sally Mapstone notes, 'was of course King James VI and I's ancestor': Sally Mapstone, 'Shakespeare and Scottish kingship: a case history', in Sally Mapstone and Juliette Wood (eds), *The Rose and the Thistle: essays on the culture of late medieval and Renaissance Scotland* (East Linton: Tuckwell Press, 1998), 181. For an in-depth discussion of these lines and James's title(s), see E. B. Lyle, '"Twofold balls and treble scepters" in *Macbeth*', *Shakespeare Quarterly*, 28 (1977), 516–19. For a reading of *Macbeth* as royalist propaganda, see Alvin Kernan, *Shakespeare, the King's Playwright: theater in the Stuart court, 1603–1613* (New Haven, CT and London: Yale University Press, 1995), 71–88. When the Witches hail Banquo as '[l]esser then *Macbeth*, and greater' (TLN

165) the play's Banquo–James genealogy as well as James's 1604 assumption of the title King of Great Britain makes it difficult not to invest the word 'greater' with political significance.
22 Cedric Watts, 'Macbeth as royalist propaganda', in Linda Cookson and Bryan Loughrey (eds), *Critical Essays on Macbeth* (Essex: Longman, 1988), 102.
23 David Norbrook, '*Macbeth* and the politics of historiography', in Kevin Sharpe and Steven Zwicker (eds), *Politics of Discourse: the literature and history of seventeenth-century England* (Berkeley: University of California Press, 1987), 95, 94. Shakespeare, according to the editors of the Arden *Macbeth*, inherits the negative representation of Scotland from his historiographical sources: '[i]n Holinshed Shakespeare found a medieval Scotland which was war-torn and primitive, desperately in need of the civilizing hand of England': Sandra Clark and Pamela Mason (eds), *Macbeth* (London: Bloomsbury, 2015), 83. Such a pronouncement renders this key source text too monologic.
24 Jonathan Baldo, '"A rooted sorrow": Scotland's unsuable past', in Nick Moschovakis (ed.), *Macbeth: new critical essays* (New York and London: Routledge, 2008), 91, 94.
25 *Ibid.*, 93–4.
26 Helgerson, *Forms of Nationhood*, 245.
27 See, for example, Jean Howard and Phyllis Rackin, *Engendering a Nation: a feminist account of Shakespeare's English histories* (London: Routledge, 1997), Ralf Hertel, *Staging England in the Elizabethan History Play: performing national identity* (Farnham: Ashgate, 2014) and Christopher Ivic, *Shakespeare and National Identity: a dictionary* (London: Bloomsbury, 2017).
28 For a reading of *Coriolanus* within the context of Anglo-Scottish union, see Alex Garganigo, '*Coriolanus*, the union controversy, and access to the royal person', *Studies in English Literature*, 42 (2002), 335–59.
29 Holinshed, *The Historie of Scotland*, in *The first and second volumes of Chronicles*, 168–76.
30 William Warner, *A Continvance of Albions England* (London, 1606), 376, 378. In his *Scotorum Historia*, Boece invented the myth that Banquo was the founder of the Stewart dynasty (Hector Boece, *Scotorum historiae a prima gentis origine libri xvii* (Paris, 1527)): see Mapstone, 'Shakespeare and Scottish kingship', 181.
31 Kerrigan, *Archipelagic English*, 92.
32 Pocock, *The Discovery of Islands*, 29.
33 The phrase 'gracious England' appears again at TLN 2030. Most editors gloss 'gracious England' not as a reference to the country but rather as referring to King Edward.

34 Cornwallis, *The Miracvlovs and Happie Union of England and Scotland*, D4ᵛ–E1ʳ.
35 Kerrigan, *Archipelagic English*, 102.
36 Holinshed, *The Historie of Scotland*, in *The first and second volumes of Chronicles*, 175. In both the play and its source the line is spoken by Macduffe/Makduffe.
37 Frank Kermode, *Shakespeare's Language* (London: Penguin, 2000), 203.
38 Ian McKellen, '[On the 1976 Trevor Nunn *Macbeth*]', in Robert S. Miola (ed.), *Macbeth*, 2nd ed. (New York: W. W. Norton, 2014), 117.
39 Willy Maley, '"A Thing Most Brutish": depicting Shakespeare's multi-nation state', *Shakespeare*, 3 (2007), 86.
40 Kerrigan, *Archipelagic English*, 114. It has been suggested that *Macbeth* 'emerged in a transformative moment in the establishment of a communal identity, containing and negotiating various positions related to the Union': see Sharon Alker and Holly Faith Nelson, '*Macbeth*, the Jacobean Scot, and the politics of union', *Studies in English Literature 1500–1900*, 47 (2007), 390. I share Kerrigan's belief that reading this play in relation to 'the establishment of a communal [British] identity' is anachronistic.
41 Jean E. Howard, 'Shakespeare, geography, and the work of genre on the early modern stage', *Modern Language Quarterly*, 64 (2003), 299.
42 Ibid., 305–06.
43 Howard's remarks are complicated by the fact that England is not always the setting in the English histories (at times France is, at times Wales is), and the imaginings of England as an isle or island render Howard's use of 'actual geography', with its hint of accuracy, problematic. Moreover, if 'England is embodied and personified in its monarch', then what nationality does King Henry V, who says to Fluellen 'I am Welch you know good Countriman' (TLN 2635) and whom the French Queene hails as 'brother Ireland' (TLN 2999), embody and personify?
44 The *OED* definition of skirr (*v.*3) directs readers to 'scour' (*v.*¹2), meaning 'to pass rapidly over or along (a tract of land or water); esp. to traverse in quest of something, or in order to capture or drive away a foe'.
45 On the uneasy shift from tanistry to primogeniture in Scotland, Roger Mason writes: '[i]t was not a change that was instituted without a struggle – the internecine conflict that saw the murder of Duncan, the tyranny of Macbeth, and his overthrow by Malcolm III (Canmore) was its immediate result – but its longer-term consequences were of immense dynastic significance': see Roger Mason, 'Scotland', in Paulina Kewes, Ian W. Archer and Felicity Heal (eds), *The Oxford*

Handbook of Holinshed's 'Chronicles' (Oxford: Oxford University Press, 2013), 653.

46 'Certainly Macbeth was the last actual "Celtic" king of Scotland', Andrew Power writes, 'traceable to the line of the *mormaers* of Moray whose origins go back to the original *Scotti* from Ireland who settled in Argyll under Fergus Mor mac Ere in the fifth century': Andrew J. Power, '"Why should I play the Roman fool, and die/On mine own sword?": the Senecan tradition in *Macbeth*', in Willy Maley and Rory Loughnane (eds), *Celtic Shakespeare: the bard and the borderers* (Farnham: Ashgate, 2013), 139. For Mary Floyd-Wilson, '*Macbeth* represents an already-degenerate Scotland desperately in need of anglicized civility and government. Scotland suffers, instead, under the barbaric rule of the Macbeths, whose home in Inverness establishes them as the play's only Highlanders': Mary Floyd-Wilson, 'English epicures and Scottish witches', *Shakespeare Quarterly*, 57 (2006), 135. If residence decides identity, then are Banquo, Thane of Lochaber, Rosse, Cathnes, Angus also Highlanders? Speed's division of Scotland – '[t]his Kingdome is principally divided into two parts; North and Sovth, of the Riuer Taye' – situates Loquabrea, Anguish, Rosse, Cathens 'in the north' and Lennox, Fife and Menteith 'in the south': Speed, *Theatre of the Empire of Great Britaine*, 129. A. R. Braunmuller labels 'most of the cast of *Macbeth*' 'Highland males': A. R. Braunmuller (ed.), *Macbeth* (Cambridge: Cambridge University Press, 2008), 259.

47 Claire McEachern, 'The Englishness of the Scottish play: *Macbeth* and the poetics of Jacobean union', in Allan I. Macinnes and Jane Ohlmeyer (eds), *The Stuart Kingdoms in the Seventeenth Century* (Dublin: Four Courts Press, 2002), 103.

48 Braunmuller labels *Macbeth* 'arguably Shakespeare's most history-play-like tragedy': Braunmuller, ed., *Macbeth*, 28.

49 'The place to turn for this prehistory of Anglo-Scottish relations', writes David Baker on the subject of Shakespeare's pre-*Macbeth* engagements with Scotland, 'is first of all the *Henriad*, where the tensions between a centralizing English monarchy and a disruptive Anglo-Scottish frontier are played out in advance of *Macbeth*': see David J. Baker, '"Stands Scotland where it did?" Shakespeare on the march', in Maley and Murphy (eds), *Shakespeare and Scotland*, 23. Baker's essay highlights the permeable borders that sought to demarcate England, Scotland and Wales in the Elizabethan period.

50 William Shakespeare, *The tragedy of King Richard the third Containing, his treacherous plots against his brother Clarence: the pittiefull murther of his iunocent [sic] nephewes: his tyrannicall vsurpation: with the whole course of his detested life, and most deserued death* (London, 1597), L2^r. Had a quarto version of *Macbeth* been

published, this 1597 title, especially 'his tyrannicall vsurpation', could easily have been appropriated with minor revisions.
51 In *The life and death of King Richard the Second*, Northumberland's 'Port le Blan/A Bay in *Britaine*' (TLN 927–8) is an obvious instance of the use of 'Britaine' to refer to Brittany.
52 'A native or inhabitant of Wales' (*OED n.* and *adj.* 1b).
53 Philip Schwyzer, 'A scum of Britons?: *Richard III* and the Celtic reconquest', in Maley and Loughnane (eds), *Celtic Shakespeare*, 25.
54 Holinshed, *The Description of Scotland*, in *The first and second volumes of Chronicles*, 22.
55 Baldo, '"A rooted sorrow"', 91. The play offers very little of this 'English army', introducing us to only Seyward and his son. Edward, King of England, never graces the stage. Of Danish descent, the historical Siward, or Sigvarthr, earl of Northumbria, was more Anglo-Danish than English. Stating that Malcolm III 'was backed by a powerful Northumbrian army', the *ODNB* posits regional rather than national support for Malcolm, who was Siward's nephew: William M. Aird, 'Siward, earl of Northumbria', *ODNB*, https://doi.org/10.1093/ref:odnb/25652. Accessed 25 April 2019. Holinshed describes Duncane's wife as 'the daughter of Siward earle of Northumberland': Holinshed, *The Historie of Scotland*, in *The first and second volumes of Chronicles*, 171.
56 Powell, *A Welch Bayte to spare Prouender*, D4^r.
57 Christopher Highley, 'The place of Scots in the Scottish play: *Macbeth* and the politics of language', in Maley and Murphy (eds), *Shakespeare and Scotland*, 61.
58 Stephen Orgel, '*Macbeth* and the antic round', in Miola (ed.), *Macbeth*, 261.
59 George Buchanan, *The History of Scotland*, trans. T. Page (London, 1690), 214. Boece's *Scotorum historiae*, which was translated from Latin into Scots by John Bellenden in the 1530s, formed the basis of the English language version of *The Historie of Scotland* found in Holinshed's *Chronicles*. On 'Boece's history, Bellenden's translation, Holinshed's use of Boece, Bellenden and other Scottish sources', see Mapstone, 'Shakespeare and Scottish kingship', 161.
60 Holinshed, *The Historie of Scotland*, in *The first and second volumes of Chronicles*, 169.
61 Monipennie, *Certayne Matters Concerning the Realme of Scotland*, C2^v.
62 Highley, 'The place of Scots', 61.
63 Paul Innes notes that Macduffe's 'lands, crucially, lie in anglicized Fife'. Innes terms Malcolme a 'semi-anglicized lowlander': see Paul Innes, 'Harming *Macbeth*: a British translation', in Liz Oakley-Brown

(ed.), *Shakespeare and the Translation of Identity in Early Modern England* (London: Continuum, 2011), 114, 109. Alker and Nelson term Malcolme 'an embryonic Scot': Alker and Nelson, 'Macbeth, the Jacobean Scot', 389.
64 Vimala C. Pasupathi, 'The quality of mercenaries: contextualizing Shakespeare's Scots in *1 Henry IV* and *Henry V*', in Maley and Loughnane (eds), *Celtic Shakespeare*, 38, 41.
65 Buchanan, *The History of Scotland*, 207. Buchanan returns to these Gaelic soldiers after Mackbeth's defeat of Macduald: '[t]he *Islanders* and the *Irish*, their Flight being stopp'd, were driven into great Despair, and in a fierce fight were every one of them slain'; and he has this to say of Mackbeth's capture of Macduald's Highland soldiers: '[t]hose of the Red-shanks, which he took, he caused to be slain': *The History of Scotland*, 208.
66 Pont, 'Of the Union', 22.
67 In his earlier histories, Shakespeare always associates kerns with Ireland. *The second Part of Henry the Sixt* mentions '[t]h' vnciuill Kernes of Ireland' (TLN 1615). The Dauphin's reference in *Henry the fift* to kerns displays a knowledge of Irish soldiery, in particular the practice of riding bareback: 'O then belike she was old and gentle, and you rode like a Kerne of Ireland, your French Hose off, and in your strait Strossers' (TLN 1678–80). *The second Part of Henry the Sixt* offers an alternative perspective on the wild, rude Irish soldier, as a messenger announces:

> The Duke of Yorke is newly come from Ireland,
> And with a puissant and a mighty power,
> Of Gallow-glasses and stout Kernes,
> Is marching hitherward in proud array. (TLN 2277–80)

The *OED* notes that kern was '[s]ometimes applied to Scottish Highlanders' (*n*.1a), so Irish kern or kerns of Ireland is not necessarily pleonastic. Jonson's 'Ode ἀλληγορική' speaks of Charles Blount, Lord Mountjoy's defeat of 'the *Kerne*, and wildest *Irishry*': Holland, *Pancharis*, A8ᵛ. As Speed's section on Ulster reveals, a hybrid Irish-Scottish identity was assumed in the period: '[t]his Prouince and furthest part of *Ireland*, affortteh the *Scotish* Islands which are called the *Hebrides*, and are scattered in the Seas betweene both kingdomes; whose inhabitants at this day is the *Irish-Scot*, successor of the old *Scythian*': Speed, *Theatre of the Empire of Great Britaine*, 145.
68 Peter Holland, '"Stands Scotland Where It Did?": the location of *Macbeth* on film', in Miola (ed.), *Macbeth*, 273.
69 A few lines later, Duncan says '[w]e will establish our Estate vpon/ Our eldest, *Malcolme*' (TLN 324–5). Like Macbeth's use of 'State',

Duncan's use of 'Estate' carries more than one meaning: 'our Estate' could refer to Duncan's status as king; it could also refer to the body politic, in this case, the kingdom.

70 This same scene also includes a reference to 'the gentle Weale' (TLN 1348), which seems to refer to a universal rather than specific state or community.

71 Although Scotland is not explicitly mentioned, Macbeth's 'this Kingdome' clearly refers to Scotland. But if the play was performed at court in King James's presence – no record of a court performance exists – then the deictic could also point to the Kingdom of England (or even Britain), for the kingdom within which the actor would have delivered these lines would have been England (or Great Britain). For an intriguing hypothesis on court performances of the play, one that reads the play's 'this great King' (TLN 1678) as a reference to King James rather than Macbeth, see Orgel, '*Macbeth* and the antic round'. Barroll suggests that *Macbeth*'s initial performance may have been at court some time between December 1606 and February 1607: see Leeds Barroll, *Politics, Plague, and Shakespeare's Theater: the Stuart years* (Ithaca, NY and London: Cornell University Press, 1991), 153.

72 Shakespeare's earlier uses of 'fiend' include Talbot terming Pucelle '[f]oule Fiend of France' (*1H6*, TLN 1487) and Posthumus labelling Iachimo 'Italian fiend' (*Cym*, TLN 3492).

73 Holland, 'The location of *Macbeth*', 273.

74 Malcolme's failure to recognise Rosse may have to do with the actor playing Rosse wearing a blue cap, or what a near-contemporary anti-Scot manuscript poem terms a 'bonny blew bonnet': see Folger Library, MS V.a.345, fols 287–8. Unfortunately we know little to nothing about how Scottishness in *Macbeth* was (or if it was) sartorially marked on the stage.

75 Holinshed, *The Historie of Scotland*, in *The first and second volumes of Chronicles*, 174–5.

76 Adrian Poole, 'Laughter, forgetting and Shakespeare', in Michael Cordner, Peter Holland and John Kerrigan (eds), *English Comedy* (Cambridge: Cambridge University Press, 1994), 96.

77 I have in mind Hotspurre's 'Harry to Harry, shall [h]ot Horse to Horse/Meete, and ne're part, till one drop downe a Coarse' (TLN 2354–5). Of Macbeth, Innes writes '[t]he over-mighty war leader on the periphery of the kingdom is a very well known personage on London's stages – Hotspur from *1 Henry IV* (*c.* 1596–97) being an obvious example': see Innes, 'Harming *Macbeth*', 113.

78 Samuel Johnson rejected previous editors of Shakespeare who replaced the First Folio's 'Birthdome' with 'birthdoom', which Johnson deemed

'unintelligible'. Concerning the denotation of 'birthdom', Johnson favoured 'privilege of birth': see Anne McDermott, 'The defining language: Johnson's *Dictionary* and *Macbeth*', *The Review of English Studies*, 44 (1993), 533.

79 Of Malcolme's 'Prince of Cumberland' title Kerrigan writes '[t]hat the title also lays claim to what was for Jacobean audiences a piece of northern England continues, from the opening scenes, the idea of Duncan's Scotland as provisionally bounded, intermeshed with other polities, and, in a word, archipelagic': see Kerrigan, *Archipelagic English*, 107.

80 Nicholas Brooke's Oxford edition of *Macbeth* settles on the *OED*'s 'birthright', but other editions provide alternative definitions. Here are a few examples: the Norton Critical Edition (Robert S. Miola, ed.) gives 'our fallen native land'; *The Norton Shakespeare* (Stephen Greenblatt et al., eds) supplies 'our downfallen native land'; the Arden edition (Sandra Clark and Pamela Mason, eds) lists 'our downfallen country'; the New Folger Library edition (Barbara Mowat and Paul Werstine, eds) gives 'our prostrated country'; the New Cambridge edition (A. R. Braunmuller, ed.) offers 'inheritance, birthright; perhaps "native kingdom"'.

81 Braunmuller (ed.), *Macbeth*, 44.

82 Perhaps there is an echo here of Richard III's 'whom our Fathers/Haue in their owne Land beaten, bobb'd, and thump'd' (TLN 3803–04).

83 I have in mind here Anderson's 'the nation is always conceived as a deep, horizontal comradeship': Anderson, *Imagined Communities*, 7.

84 [Bacon], *A Briefe Discovrse*, B2^v.

85 *Ibid.*, B4^r.

86 *Ibid.*, B4^v.

87 *Ibid.*, B5^v–B6^r.

88 *Ibid.*, C3^v. Pont looks forward to a time when 'their shal be a commixtion of the commonwealth and blood of both nations, that a Scot in time will not be knowen from an Englishman': Pont, 'Of the Union', 28.

89 [Anon.], 'A treatise about the Union of England and Scotland', in Galloway and Levack (eds), *The Jacobean Union*, 43, 62, 61.

90 McGinnis and Williamson (eds and trans.), *The British Union*, 117.

91 Holinshed, *The Historie of Scotland*, in *The first and second volumes of Chronicles*, 175.

92 Highley, 'The place of Scots', 57. As Alker and Nelson suggest, 'of the few Scotticisms used in the play, Macbeth utters most of them, suggesting that the most vicious Scot in the play is also the most "Scottish"': Alker and Nelson, '*Macbeth*, the Jacobean Scot', 385. The editors of the Arden *Macbeth* note that 'Shakespeare avoids linguistic

indications of Scottish identity, such as the risible Scottish accents and expressions that were deliberately used in comedies like *James IV* and *Eastward Ho*': Sandra Clark and Pamela Mason (eds), *Macbeth*, 29.

93 Hume, *The British Union*, 81. Hume is at once citing and contesting English stereotypes of the Scots.

94 See Sarah Grandage, 'Imagining England: contemporary encodings of "this sceptred isle"', in Willy Maley and Margaret Tudeau-Clayton (eds), *This England, That Shakespeare: New Angles on Englishness and the Bard* (Farnham: Ashgate, 2010), 127–46.

95 Kerrigan, *Archipelagic English*, 102. Power terms Macbeth's 'choice of death in battle over death by suicide' as perhaps highlighting 'the traditionally Scottish (perhaps Celtic) valour of his character … for choice in nationalism': Power, '"Why should I play the Roman fool"', 155.

96 McEachern, 'The Englishness of the Scottish play', 105.

97 Clark and Mason (eds), *Macbeth*, 86.

98 The language comes from the source material: 'MAlcolme Cammore thus recouering the relme … by support of King Edward, in the 16 yeere of the same Edwards reigne, he was crowned at Scone': Holinshed, *The Historie of Scotland*, in *The first and second volumes of Chronicles*, 176.

99 Holinshed, *The Historie of Scotland*, in *The first and second volumes of Chronicles*, 176. Because of Macduffe's '[b]ehold where stands/ Th' Vsurpers cursed head' (TLN 2506–07) editors of the play tend to argue that 'stands' necessarily infers 'on a pole' or 'on his sword', etc. Macduffe's use of 'stands' does not preclude the possibility that Macduffe holds up Macbeth's head in his hand whilst delivering these lines to Malcolme.

100 Holinshed, *The Historie of Scotland*, in *The first and second volumes of Chronicles*, 169.

101 Theodore de Bry's engraving of a 'trwe picture of one Picte' is included in a supplementary section titled 'Som Pictvre, of the Pictes which in the olde tyme dyd habite one part of the great Bretainne' at the end of Thomas Hariot's *A briefe and true report of the new found land of Virginia* (London, 1590).

102 Harrison (Henrisoun), *An exhortacion*, c.ii.^{r}.

103 Robert Crawford, *Bannockburns: Scottish independence and literary imagination, 1314–2014* (Edinburgh: University of Edinburgh Press, 2014), 45.

104 Alker and Nelson, '*Macbeth*, the Jacobean Scot', 390.

105 Holinshed, *The Historie of Scotland*, in *The first and second volumes of Chronicles*, 175.

106 Holinshed, *The Historie of England*, in *The first and second volumes of Chronicles*, 192.
107 Mason, 'Scotland', 647. Mason then details 'the three most obvious and discordant views of the northern kingdom to be found in Holinshed': 1) 'how Scotland is represented in the *Scottish Chronicle* itself, derived essentially from Scottish sources, and presenting an image of the Scottish kingdom as ancient and autonomous, using its glorious past to legitimize its present independence'; 2) 'in the marginalia to this self-congratulatory narrative a degree of editorial scepticism, if not outright hostility, is introduced; and this second much less flattering representation of Scotland and the Scots is equally evident in the chronicle of England where the Scottish crown's feudal dependence on its English counterpart is built into the narrative from the very outset'; 3) 'If there are hints too of underlying assumptions of cultural superiority, contrasting Scottish barbarism with English civility, such ethnic stereotyping, and the Anglocentric master narrative that it informs, surfaces with a vengeance in Harrison's *Description of Britain*': Mason, 'Scotland', 647.
108 The quarto, of course, uses the plural 'the diuision of the kingdomes': William Shakespeare, *M. William Shak-speare: his true chronicle historie of the life and death of King Lear and his three daughters With the vnfortunate life of Edgar, sonne and heire to the Earle of Gloster, and his sullen and assumed humor of Tom of Bedlam: as it was played before the Kings Maiestie at Whitehall vpon S. Stephans night in Christmas hollidayes* (London, 1608), A2[r].
109 Virgil's '*Et penitus toto divisus orbe Britannos*' would have been well-known to English readers through Harrison's *Description of Britain*, wherein the Virgilian citation is prefaced by '[a]nd whereas by Virgil (speaking of our Iland) saith': Harrison, *The Description of Britain*, in *The first and second volumes of Chronicles*, 2. To whom Harrison's 'our' refers is unclear. Camden, too, cites and translates Virgil: '*Et penitus toto divisos orbe Britannos*: And Britans people quite disjoin'd from all the world besides': Camden, *Britain*, 1.
110 Hayward, *A Treatise of Vnion of the two Realmes of England and Scotland*, 54.
111 Harrison (Henrisoun), *An exhortacion*, c.ii.[v].
112 Craig, *De Unione*, 216.
113 MacColl, 'The meaning of "Britain"', 249.
114 'The political plot of *Cymbeline*, in marked contrast to the prevailing spirit of nationalism in Shakespeare's earlier history plays, culminates in a vision of harmonious internationalism and accommodation that mirror's James's own policy. The British and Roman ensigns wave "Friendly together," the fragmented kingdom of Britain is reunited,

and the nation embarks on a new and fertile era of peace': Leah Marcus, *Puzzling Shakespeare: local reading and its discontents* (Berkeley: University of California Press, 1988), 122. For a reading of *Cymbeline* alert to James's investment in Britain's military power, see Stewart Mottram, 'Warriors and ruins: *Cymbeline*, heroism and the union of the crowns', in Maley and Loughnane (eds), *Celtic Shakespeare*, 169–83.

115 On Cloten's beheading, see Kerrigan, 'Prologue *Díonbrollach*: how Celtic was Shakespeare?', in Maley and Loughnane (eds), *Celtic Shakespeare*, xv–xli, xxxiii–xxxvi.
116 Anderson, *Imagined Communities*, 77.
117 [James VI and I], *The Kings Maiesties Speech*, C2^v.
118 Trinity College Library, Dublin, MS 877, fol. 479.
119 'In Vnionem Angliæ & Scotiæ', British Library, Add. MS 15227, fol. 8^v.
120 *Journal of the House of Commons*, I, 333. Craig refers to Pigott numerous times: for example, 'Scotland, according to Pigott, is the barrenest land in existence': Craig, *De Unione*, 415.
121 [James VI and I], *His Maiesties Speech to Both the Houses of Parliament*, F2^v.
122 Russell, 'A Treatise of the Happie and Blissed Unioun', 84.
123 [James VI and I], *His Maiesties Speech to Both the Houses of Parliament*, F2^v.
124 Bacon, *The Essaies of Sr Francis Bacon Knight*, 94.
125 I have in mind Yorke's reference in *The second Part of Henry the Sixt* to England as 'this Warlike Isle' (TLN 132), but I also realise that this is a stock phrase. *Othello* contains another description (Cassio's) of Cyprus as 'the warlike Isle' (TLN 801).

Conclusion:
the Jacobean writing of Britain

'As far as possible', writes Thomas Craig in 1605 regarding histories of England and Scotland, 'the public annals of the two countries should be revised. Errors and irritating expressions must be expunged (though in this matter our own histories are not so provocative as those of our neighbours), and a new history of Britain should be written.'[1] Craig's call for a rewriting of Britain's history was echoed south of the border. In a letter to Thomas Egerton, England's lord chancellor, Bacon comments on 'the unworthiness of the history of England ... and the partiality and obliquity of that of Scotland'; 'it would be an honour', he continues, 'for his Majesty, and a work very memorable, if this island of Great Britain, as it is now joined in Monarchy for the ages to come, so were joined in History, for the times past; and that one just and complete History were compiled of both nations'.[2] Bacon never wrote such a history. His *The Beginning of the History of Great Britain* (*c.* 1610)[3] is brief (less than 2,000 words) and never really pushes before or beyond 1603. Many of James's subjects committed themselves to writing 'this island of Great Britain'. Ironically, given its title, Helgerson's *Forms of Nationhood: the Elizabethan writing of England* offered one of the first in-depth studies of two such texts: Drayton's *Poly-Olbion* and Speed's *Theatre of the Empire of Great Britaine*, although Helgerson's focus on English nationhood obscures the rich British dimensions of these two key Jacobean texts. Other histories that contributed to the Jacobean writing of Britain include Speed's *History of Great Britaine* (1611), Edward Ayscu's *A Historie Contayning the Warres, Treaties, Marriages, and Other Occurrents betweene England and Scotland, from King William the Conqueror, Untill the Happy Vnion of Them Both in Our Gratious King James* (1607), Daniel's *The First*

Part of the Historie of England (1612), Camden's *Remaines of a Greater Worke, Concerning Britaine* (1605) as well as the 1610 English edition of *Britannia*, John Clapham's *The Historie of Great Britainne* (1606) – a revision and extension of his *The Historie of England* (1602) – William Warner's 1606 and 1612 editions of *Albion's England* – the list goes on. Even Verstegan's pro-English/ Saxon *Restitvtion of Decayed Intellengence*, which includes a commendatory poem that begins '[n]o large discourse of ancient *Britaines* fame/And gloryes greatnes, heers to be expected', stakes a place among this heterogeneous Jacobean writing of Britain, despite, or precisely because of, its writing against Britain and Britishness.[4]

Ayscu's *A Historie Contayning the Warres, Treaties, Marriages, and Other Occurrents betweene England and Scotland*, D. R. Woolf suggests, 'actually fulfilled Bacon's wish that the two kingdoms be united in history'.[5] Ayscu's *Historie* seemingly promises its readers a union-inspired history: it traces 'the many leagues and happy marriages betweene the two kingdomes of this Iland'; moreover, it hails the Stewarts as embodying 'the common bloud of both nations'.[6] The paratextual 'To the Reader' sets out the scope of Ayscu's history: 'I Haue here ... vndertaken to set downe in a continued discourse, whatsoever hath passed betweene *England & Scotland* from the last Conquest, vntill the decease of our late Soveraigne (neuer to be forgotten) the renowned Elizabeth'.[7] Ayscu's desire to write an Anglo-Scottish history manifests itself not just in content but also in form. The reader finds atop the verso page the name of Scotland's monarch and atop the recto that of England's, so in the final section one finds on facing pages the names of 'James the sixt King of Scotland' and 'Elizabeth Queene of England'. Ayscu asserts that his Jacobean history marks a break from a long tradition of biased national histories:

> wheras the Chronicles of both Nations contain matter of reproach and disgrace one against the other: I haue had an especiall care to carry my selfe so indifferently betweene them as I hope neither of both shall have iust cause to take offence therat ... Since wee al now happily become Subiects unto one most gratious Soueraigne [Ayscu continues] let us value one the others vertues at one and the same price, and setting apart all partialitie, detraction, and vaine glorie, let vs deuide the true honour and glorie attayned on both sides indifferently betweene us. Are we not all (for the most part) the broode and

off-spring of the same parents, the auntient *English Saxons*? what preheminence shall we give to the one Nation aboue the other?[8]

Ayscu's invocation of '*English Saxons*' reveals an investment in Anglo-Saxonism at odds with a British history – British in the Galfridian sense – as is evident when he mocks 'the Fables of *Dioclesian* his Daughters, and of their successors the *Troyans*, vnder the conduct of (I know not what) *Brute*, coyned in some Munkish mint about foure hundred yeares agone'.[9] If Ayscu's history is committed to Anglo-Scottish union, then the kind of union it favours is an incorporating one, as the incorporation of Lowland Scots, but not Highlanders (descendants, Ayscu reminds his readers, of the Irish), into a shared and politically charged Anglo-Saxon ethnicity attests, as does the text's many references to Scotland's kings paying 'homage' to England's. The final page's reference to James being proclaimed 'the onely lawfull, lineall, and rightfull King of *England, France* and *Ireland*' is an accurate reflection of the royal proclamation that announced Elizabeth's successor, but James's preferred title – King of 'Great Britain' – is conspicuous by its absence.[10]

One might expect the majority of these works to be dedicated to the king (as Verstegan's was); the reality is that another subject of Britain, Prince Henry, was emerging as a major patron and therefore dedicatee.[11] Ayscu's book was dedicated not to James but to Henry. In his dedicatory epistle 'To the Prince', Ayscu celebrates Henry's '[p]rincely and powerfull aspect', although he is quick to add 'without deminution of his super-eminent Majestie, whence you derive it'.[12] After describing the mixed feelings of James's Scottish subjects at the time of his departure from Scotland in 1603, the Presbyterian and republican-leaning Hume adds '[t]his was especially the case as they realized that Prince Henry, the light of their lives (as it were), their great expectation, was being taken away from them'.[13] The conventional narrative of Prince Henry would have us believe that in England a knowledge community emerged around the Scottish Prince of Wales that was antagonistic to Henry's father, especially in its commitment to the kind of militant Protestantism that the prince embodied and that the pacifist king sought to curb. This narrative is not inaccurate, but it obscures the ideological heterogeneity of the body of work, print and scribal, that emerged around Henry, including that of such self-proclaimed 'Scoto-Brittaines' as David Murray.[14] For all his antipathy to the

King, Daniel, who benefitted from Henry's patronage, advised the prince on more than one occasion to pursue a pacific path. In June of 1610, Prince Henry was installed as Prince of Wales in a ceremony that amounted to a coronation. Among the year's court festivities celebrating Henry's investiture were Daniel's and Inigo Jones's *Tethys Festival* and Jonson and Jones's *Barriers* entertainment (in which Henry tilted) as well as the *Oberon* masque (in which the prince performed). That both Daniel and Jonson contributed to the celebration of Henry's investiture hints at the ideological diversity of writings produced throughout the prince's *annus mirabilis*. 'The Britain promoted at the king's court', critics agree, 'differed considerably from the one imagined at Prince Henry's'.[15]

The year 1612 saw a number of texts dedicated to Prince Henry published, including Drayton's *Poly-Olbion*. It was, of course, the year in which Prince Henry died, at the age of 18. Bacon intended to dedicate his 1612 *Essaies* to the Prince; indeed, a manuscript copy of the second edition of the *Essaies* is dedicated to 'the most high and excellent Prince Henry, Prince of Wales, Duke of Cornwall and Earl of Chester'.[16] The same year also saw the publication of Daniel's *The First Part of the Historie of England* and Speed's *Theatre* – Speed's *History of Great Britaine* appeared in the previous year. How do these texts represent Britain? One would be hard pressed to locate explicit material on Britain in Bacon's 1612 *Essaies*; however, 'Of Empire' and 'Of greatnes of Kingdomes' suggest that Bacon's writing on state formation was shifting from an Anglo-Scottish framework to a more imperial one. As its title suggests, and as discussed in chapter 2, section headed '[A] new Bodie of people', Daniel's *Historie of England*, dedicated to Robert Carr [Kerr], a countryman and favourite of the king's and recently created viscount Rochester, was restricted temporally to the medieval period and spatially to England. It was also a successful publication, attracting many buyers. The dedicatory epistle to Carr reads like an ethnically specific history lesson, produced by an English author for a Scottish courtier who requires instruction in order to perceive the world around him from an English perspective: 'this I addresse to you ... in respect you being now a publicke person, and thereby ingaged in the State of *England*, as well as incorporated into the Body thereof, may here learne, by the obseruance of affaires past (for that, Reason is strengthened by the successe of exa*m*ple) to iudge the righter of things present'.[17] Once again Daniel insists on terming the English polity a 'State' with an upper case 'S'. Not only is this a conscious refusal of Great Britain, it resists the name and concept of 'Kingdom'. When Daniel's dedicatory epistle to Carr does invoke King James, the author's politics are transparent: 'yet will it bee much to the glory of his Reigne, that in his daies was a true History written: a liberty proper onely to Common-wealthes, and neuer permitted to Kingdoms, but vnder good Princes'.[18] Daniel's historical prose contributes to the Jacobean writing of Britain by writing against the grain of British histories, thereby revealing the range of ideas and ideologies produced by subjects of a self-proclaimed British monarch.

Dedicated to 'the High and Mightie, *Henrie, Prince of Wales*', Drayton's *Poly-Olbion* announces itself in opposition to Daniel's England-centred, anti-James history. Drayton describes Henry as 'the hopefull Heyre of the kingdoms of this Great *Britaine*: whose Delicacies, Chorographicall Description, and Historie, be my subiect'. 'May I breath' he adds, 'to arriue at the *Orcades* (whither in this kind I intend my course, if the Muse faile me not) I shall leaue your whole British Empire, as this first and southerne part, delineated'.[19] Mention of Great Britain and plans to expand his Anglo-Cambrian text to include Scotland suggests a British text, which *Poly-Olbion* is, but not in the sense that it slavishly serves the monarch's political agenda. That it is dedicated to Henry speaks volumes, as does the fact that 'your whole British Empire' is addressed not to the reigning monarch but rather his eldest son. Drayton's early modern readers would, no doubt, have noticed that 'this Great *Britaine*' italicises 'Britaine' but not 'Great'.[20] In other words, the text devotes itself to a Britain (meaning England and Wales) that is great but not the Great Britain that was being promoted at James's court. Who, we might ask, does Drayton imagine as his readers? Since *Poly-Olbion* restricts itself temporally and spatially to England and Wales, Drayton's reference to 'the Rarities & Historie of their owne Country deliuered by a true natiue Muse' in his 'To the Generall Reader' appears to be addressing an exclusively English and Welsh readership.[21]

Another 1612 text that appears to be in line with James's British vision is Speed's *Theatre*, an atlas that made visible to early modern readers for the first time the islands of Great Britain and Ireland (and adjoining isles) in one impressive folio. Speed's cartographic and chorographic atlas – the maps are backed by geographical and historiographical prose descriptions – is dedicated to 'IAMES, of Great Britaine, France, and Ireland King ... Inlarger and Vniter of the British Empire; Restorer of the British Name; Establisher of Perpetvall Peace, in Chvrch, and Commonwealth'.[22] The first map encountered by readers is that of '[t]he Kingdome of Great Britaine and Ireland', or what the accompanying prose material terms '[t]he British Ilands', and includes panoramas of England's and Scotland's capital cities. Two coins on the map depict the figures of 'Britannia', or Britain (sometimes the British Isles) personified in female form, and 'Cvnobelin', or Cunobelinus (Cymbeline), an ancient king of (southern) Britain who maintained peace with Rome and therefore probably compliments James's pacificist policies. Among the national maps that follow are those of England, Wales, Scotland and Ireland, although Scotland is the only nation that is presented 'in one Generall': that is, whereas England, Wales and Ireland are rendered in detail in the form of maps of English (forty-three) and Welsh counties (thirteen) and Irish provinces (four),[23] a less-than-fully mapped Scotland appears in the form of one national map only. To put it another way, the chapter (or description) of the Kingdom of Scotland covers two pages, similar to the description of the Kingdom of Ireland, but then Munster, Leinster, Connaught and Ulster are afforded their own chapters. By no means is this an instance of ideological resistance on Speed's part; rather, Speed lacked detailed cartographic knowledge or source material to present a more accurate image of England's northern neighbour. Acknowledging 'this third, though short booke' on Scotland, Speed states 'as *England*, I entended to describe it, had I not beene happily preuented by a learned Gentleman of that Nation', which is accompanied by a gloss naming the contemporary Scottish surveyor 'M. Timothy Pont'.[24] The *Theatre* offers its viewers in uneven detail Britain's and Ireland's national and, excepting Scotland, local 'finite, if elastic' borders, an imaging of space hitherto unseen in the period.[25]

Traditional readings of the *Theatre* view it as a celebration of James's British Empire, but Helgerson was the first to challenge such readings. Although he describes Speed as 'rabidly ... loyal to the crown', Helgerson's brilliant analysis of early modern chorography's and, especially, cartography's presentation of the land, the nation at the expense of royal authority, leads him to declare that what 'we see when we open *The Theater* ... is not the king but the country'.²⁶ Perhaps because Helgerson is less interested in the wider British-Irish framework of the *Theatre*, he neglects to mention that Speed's map of Scotland includes in its margins, what Speed terms the maps' '*Emblematicall compartments*', members of the royal family: King James, Queen Anne, Prince Henry and Prince Charles. And it is an archipelagic royal family that we see: written below the images of the four figures is 'James King of Great Britain, Fraunce & Ireland', 'Queen Anna of Great Britain, Fraunce & Ireland', 'Henry Prince of Wales & Ireland' and 'Charles Duke of York and Albany'.²⁷ We do, therefore, see the king, but Helgerson's point is well taken, especially since James, his queen and his male heirs are connected to their birthdom (well, the male figures are; Anne was born in Denmark), reminding the *Theatre*'s readers of James's foreignness. The *Theatre* is by no means an anti-British or anti-James text. Nor is it simply and straightforwardly a celebration of Englishness. Speed's material on Scotland acknowledges Anglo-Scottish proximity: 'their more Southern people', he writes, 'are from the same Original with vs the *English*, being both alike the *Saxon* branches'.²⁸ The title page, which depicts a Norman, a Dane, a Saxon, a Roman and, in pride of place at the top, a 'Britaine', reminds its readers that 'Englishness is self-evidently the product of the complex interactions of peoples and cultures (Britons, Romans, Saxons, Norsemen, Normans)' (see figure 2).²⁹ Speed's *Theatre* has in common with some pro-union tracts and treatises a desire to erode notions of pure, original identities by highlighting the common ancestry, the cultural hybridity of Britain's, though not necessarily Ireland's, inhabitants.

Before early modern readers of Speed's *Theatre* access the maps and descriptions, they are greeted with three pages of commendatory material: poems and prose by the antiquarian and historian John Barkham,³⁰ the antiquarian, MP and author of the anti-union 'Of the Union' Henry Spelman, the antiquarian and herald Richard St George, as well as Alexander Gil, John Davies and John Sanderson. Some of these figures were, like Speed, members of the Society of Antiquaries, so we can get a sense of the knowledge community to which Speed belonged – not that association with this ideologically diverse community determines one's political views. What does this material commend? 'The glory of our nation', St George writes, 'being almost buried in the pit of obscurity, is herein reuiued, the contiuance of Christianity traced from age to

2 John Speed, title page, *Theatrum imperii Magnæ Britanniæ*
[*The Theatre of the Empire of Great Britaine*] (London, 1616).
By permission of The Folger Shakespeare Library.

age, the antiquity and situation of our Townes, Castles, Religions, Houses, Nobilty, and all other memorable matters so liuely portraied'. St George's use of 'our nation' must refer to England or England and Wales, for his reference to 'our Townes, Castles ... Houses' cannot refer to underrepresented Scotland. He adds 'the glory of *Great Britaine* [is] made more famous to the world as well in the Geographicall demension of the Lands situation as in the historicall relations of her most famous monarchs and glorious actions; no Kingdome hitherto so particularly described, nor Nations history by true record more faithfully penned'.[31] Is the 'Kingdome' Britain, the 'Nations history' Britain's, or does the initial invocation of Great Britain give way to England? No less confusing is Alexander Gil's poem, with its many references to Speed's 'country': of 'thy dear country', 'thy Countries sake', 'thy country dedicate'. Which country does Gil have in mind? The following lines suggest the answer is Great Britain:

> Now may shee see her beauty, and her riches store,
> What erst shee was in eu'rie age, and change of state,
> And present greatnes such as neuer heretofore,
> Since this great Monarch rul'd from North to Southerne shore.[32]

Not unlike Drayton's address to his readers, Speed's 'To the well-affected and favorable Reader' assumes a British readership, but British here signifies, as it does for Drayton, Anglo-Welsh. The 'zeale of my countries glory so transported my senses', Speed proclaims, adding in an address to his readers 'thy loue with mine being alike obliged vnto this our natiue land. Whose beauties and benefits ... but by mine traules through eury prouince of *England* and *Wales* mine eyes haue beheld.'[33] Given the cartographer's perambulations through England and Wales, it is hard to see where Scotland stands. Speed goes on to write 'safely may it be affirmed that there is not any one kingdome in the world so exactly described, as is this our *Iland* of *Great Brittaine*'. Speed's 'our *Iland* of *Great Brittaine*' pushes beyond Anglocentric insularity; indeed, designating the '*Iland*' 'one kingdome' acknowledges James's British rule. But because Scotland is not 'described' in any detail and since Ireland is a separate island, cartographically and chorographically 'our *Iland* of *Great Brittaine*' amounts to England and Wales only. Significantly, of the four national maps, the map of Wales is the only one not to include national subjects in its '*Emblematicall compartments*', suggesting, perhaps, that Speed, like many of his fellow English subjects, viewed the Welsh as culturally incorporated by the English.

The address to the reader concludes with Speed lauding 'my country' as 'my most beautifull *Nurse*, whose *wombe* was my conception, whose *breasts* were my nourishment, whose *bosome* my cradle, and lap (I doubt not) shall be my bed of sweete rest'.[34] Speed's 'mother country', his 'birthdome' is England.[35] To paraphrase Bacon, Speed presents himself not as a man born in Britain, but as a man born and who will die in England. *The Theatre of the Empire of Great Britaine*, perhaps more than any other Jacobean work, owes its existence to the novel geopolitics of James's composite monarchy. But it is also a belated cultural artefact, residually Elizabethan, conditioned by the patriotism and nationalism that firmly and forcefully took hold of so many of England's subjects during the years of Elizabeth's reign and which continued to take hold of English men and women throughout James's English rule.

Notes

1 Craig, *De Unione*, 468.
2 Francis Bacon, 'A letter to the Lord Chancellor, touching the history of Britain', in Spedding (ed.), *Letters and Life*, III, 250. An almost verbatim version of this sentence appeared in print: see Bacon, *Aduancement of Learning*, Cc4^v.
3 Bacon, *The Beginning of the History of Great Britain*, 405–10.
4 Verstegan, *Restitvtion of Decayed Intellengence*, †††1^v.
5 D. R. Woolf, *The Idea of History in Early Stuart England: erudition, ideology, and 'The Light of Truth' from the accession of James I to the Civil War* (Toronto: University of Toronto Press, 1990), 59.
6 Edward Ayscu, *A Historie Contayning the Warres, Treaties, Marriages, and Other Occurrents betweene England and Scotland* (London, 1607), A3^{r-v}, A3^v.
7 *Ibid.*, A5^r.
8 *Ibid.*, sig. A6, A6^{r-v}.
9 *Ibid.*, 1.
10 *Ibid.*, 396.
11 Verstegan's dedicatory epistle reads '[t]o the Kings Most Excellent Maiestie, James by the grace of God, King of Great Britain, France, and Ireland', although he describes James as 'descended of the chiefest blood royall of our ancient *English-Saxon* kings': Verstegan, *Restitvtion of Decayed Intellengence*, †2^{r-v}, †2^r.

12 Ayscu, *A Historie Contayning*, A4ʳ, A4ʳ⁻ᵛ.
13 McGinnis and Williamson (eds and trans.), *The British Union*, 122–3.
14 See David Murray, *The Tragicall Death of Sophonisba. Written by David Mvrray. Scoto-Brittainne* (London, 1611).
15 McGinnis and Williamson (eds and trans.), *The British Union*, 53. 'The establishment of the Prince's household provided something that had never existed in the reign of Elizabeth,' McCabe writes, 'a royal alternative to crown patronage as a potential centre for oppositional politics': McCabe, *'Ungainefull Arte'*, 302.
16 British Library, Birch MS 4259, fol. 155. See also Vickers, *Francis Bacon: The Major Works*, 677.
17 Daniel, *The Historie of England*, A3ᵛ–A4ʳ.
18 *Ibid.*, A4ʳ.
19 Drayton, *Poly-Olbion*, π2ʳ.
20 In a dedicatory poem titled 'To My Friends, the Cambro-Britains', Drayton writes 'this my intended progresse, through these vnited kingdomes of great *Britaine*'. In this instance, given the mention of 'these vnited kingdomes', 'great *Britaine*' appears to signify England and Scotland, but 'great' remains unitalicised as well as free of the upper case 'G': Drayton, *Poly-Olbion*, A1ᵛ.
21 *Ibid.*, A1ʳ. We know, however, that William Drummond owned a copy of *Poly-Olbion*.
22 Speed, *Theatre of the Empire of Great Britaine*, ¶1ʳ.
23 For a reading of Speed's section on Ireland, especially his map and description of Ulster, in relation to Ulster plantation literature, see Christopher Ivic, 'Mapping British identities: John Speed's *Theatre of the Empire of Great Britaine*', in David J. Baker and Willy Maley (eds), *British Identities and English Renaissance Literature* (Cambridge: Cambridge University Press, 2002), 135–55.
24 Speed, *Theatre of the Empire of Great Britaine*, 131.
25 Anderson, *Imagined Communities*, 19.
26 Helgerson, *Forms of Nationhood*, 128, 145.
27 Speed, *Theatre of the Empire of Great Britaine*, 4. The *Theatre*'s maps are not paginated; the map of Scotland appears between pages 131 and 132.
28 *Ibid.*, 131.
29 Morrill, 'The British problem', 2. In his *Historie*, Speed describes the Britons as 'our poore and rude *Progenitours*': Speed, *History of Great Britaine*, 179.
30 Speed, according to Woolf, 'acknowledged Barkham's assistance in providing material for *The History of Great Britaine* (1611). Barkham contributed the life of King John in that work, and was probably also the

author of the life of Henry II': D. R. Woolf, 'Barkham, John', *ODNB*, https://doi.org/10.1093/ref:odnb/1421. Accessed 11 May 2019.
31 Speed, *Theatre of the Empire of Great Britaine*, ¶2ʳ.
32 *Ibid.*
33 *Ibid.*, ¶3ʳ.
34 *Ibid.*, ¶3ᵛ, ¶4ʳ.
35 *Cf.* Craig: '[n]ow, Britain is the common mother of her indwellers; at any rate she is the nurse whose breast has reared those born upon her soil. All Britons are ... brothers, sprung from the womb of the same mother, Britain': Craig, *De Unione*, 232.

Bibliography

Primary Sources

Abbot, George. *A briefe description of the whole worlde wherein are particularly described all the Monarchies, Empires, and kingdomes of the same, with their seuerall titles and situations thereunto adioyning.* London, 1599.

Adamson, John. *Ta tōn Mousōn eisodia: The Muses welcome to the high and mighty prince Iames by the grace of God King of Great Britaine France and Ireland, defender of the faith &c. At His Majesties happie returne to his olde and natiue kingdome of Scotland, after 14 yeeres absence in anno 1617. Digested according to the order of his Majesties progresse, by I. A.* Edinburgh, 1618.

Allott, Robert. *Englands Parnassus.* London, 1600.

[Anon.]. 'A briefe Replicacion to the Aunswers of the Obiections against the Vnion'. British Library, Stowe 158.

[Anon.]. 'The Diuine Providence in the misticall and reall union of England and Scotland both by nature and oth[er] coherences wth motives for reconcilinge such differences as may now seeme to hinder the same'. British Library, Additional MS 38139.

[Anon.]. 'Notes on Doctor Haywards Book of the Union. Imperfect', British Library, Harleian MS 292.

[Anon.]. *Englands Wedding Garment. Or A preparation to King Iames his Royall Coronation.* London, 1603.

[Anon.]. *An excellent new Ballad, shewing the Petigree of our Royall King Iames, the first of that name in England. To the tune of, Gallants all come mourne with mee.* London, 1603.

[Anon.]. *A mournefull dittie, entituled Elizabeths losse together with a welcome for King Iames. To a pleasant new tune.* London, 1603.

[Anon.]. *A new song to the great comfort and reioycing of all true English harts, at our most Gracious King Iames his Proclamation, vpon the 24. of March last past in the Cittie of London. To the tune of Englands pride is gone.* Edinburgh, 1603.

[Anon.]. *Sorrowes Ioy. Or, a Lamentation for our late deceased Souereigne Elizabeth, with a triumph for the prosperous succession of our gracious King, Iames, &c.* Cambridge, 1603.

[Anon.]. 'Concerning the alteration of the name of England', Bodleian Library, Tanner MS 75.

Ayscu, Edward. *A Historie Contayning the Warres, Treaties, Marriages, and Other Occurrents betweene England and Scotland, from King William the Conqueror, Untill the Happy Vnion of Them Both in Our Gratious King James. With a brief declaration of the first Inhabitants of this Island: And what seuerall Nations haue sithence settled them-selves one after an other.* London, 1607.

[Bacon, Francis]. *A Briefe Discovrse, Touching the Happie Vnion of the Kingdomes of England, and Scotland Dedicated in priuate to his Maiestie.* London, 1603.

Bacon, Francis. 'Sir Fra: Bacons Answer to Mr Fullers Speach against Union Anno 4th Iacobi'. British Library, Harleian MS 6842.

Bacon, Francis. *The Twoo Bookes of Francis Bacon. Of the proficience and aduancement of Learning, diuine and humane. To the King.* London, 1605.

Bacon, Francis. *The Essaies of Sr Francis Bacon.* London, 1612.

Bacon, Francis. *The Essayes of Couvnsels, Civill and Morall, of Francis Lo. Vervlam, Viscovnt St Alban.* London, 1625.

Bodin, Jean. *The Six Bookes of a Commonweale.* Trans. Richard Knolles. London, 1606.

Boece, Hector. *Scotorum historiae a prima gentis origine libri xvii.* Paris, 1527.

Buchanan, George. *The History of Scotland.* Trans. T. Page. London, 1690.

Calendar of the Manuscripts of the Most Hon. the Marquess of Salisbury, preserved at Hatfield House, Hertfordshire. 23 vols. London: HMSO, 1883–1976.

Calendar of State Papers and Manuscripts Relating to English Affairs, Existing in the Archives and Collections of Venice and in other Libraries of Northern Italy. Horatio F. Brown, Rawdon Brown, A. B. Hinds, George Bentinck Lord (eds). 38 vols. London: Longman, Green, Longman, Roberts and Green, 1864–1947.

Camden, William. *Remaines of a Greater Worke, Concerning Britaine, the inhabitants thereof, their Languages, Names, Surnames, Empreses, Wise speeches, Poësies, and Epitaphes.* London, 1605.

Camden, William. *Britain, or a Chorographicall description of the most flourishing Kingdomes, England, Scotland, and Ireland, and the Ilands adioyning, out of the depth of Antiquitie beautified with mappes of the severall shires of England: written first in Latine by William Camden*

Clarenceux K. of A. *Translated newly into English by Philémon Holland Doctour in Physick: finally, revised, amended, and enlarged with sundry additions by the said author.* Trans. Philemon Holland. London, 1610.

Chapman, George, Ben Jonson, John Marston. *Eastward Hoe. As it was playd in the Black-friers. By the Children of her Maiesties Reuels. Made by Geo: Chapman. Ben: Ionson. Ioh: Marston.* London, 1605. STC 4970.

Charron, Pierre, *Of Wisdome Three Bookes Written in French by Peter Charron.* Trans. Samson Lennard. London 1608.

Chettle, Henry. *Englandes Mourning Garment: Worne here by plaine Shepheards; in memorie of their sacred Mistresse, Elizabeth, Queene of Vertue while shee liued, and Theame of Sorrow being dead. To the which is added the true manner of her Emperiall Funerall. After which foloweth the Shepheards Spring-Song, for entertainment of King Iames our most potent Soueraigne. Dedicated to all that loued the deceased Queene, and honor the liuing King.* London, 1603. STC 5121.

Chettle, Henry. *Englands Mourning Garment: Worne heere by plaine Shepheards, in memorie of their sacred Mistresse, Elizabeth; Queene of Vertue while she liued, and Theame of Sorrow being dead. To the which is added the true manner of her Emperiall Funerall. With many new additions, being now againe the second time reprinted, which was omitted in the first Impression. After which followeth the Shepheards Spring-Song, for entertainment of King Iames our most potent Soueraigne. Dedicated to all that loued the deceased Queene, and honor the liuing King.* London, 1603. STC 5122.

Clerk, William. 'Ancillans Synopsis. Such an additional to that awnswere of the Reverand B. to certaine obieccions against the happie and desired union of the two famous kingdomes England and Scotland. Conteining matter of example, and of lawe'. Trinity College Library, Dublin, MS 635.

Coke, Edward. *The Fourth Part of the Institutes of the Laws of England.* London, 1648.

Cornwallis, William. *The Miracvlovs and Happie Union of England and Scotland; by how admirable meanes it is effected; how profitable to both Nations, and how free of any inconuenience either past, present, or to be discerned.* London, 1604. STC 5782.

Craig, Alexander. *The Poeticall Essayes of Alexander Craige, Scotobritane.* London, 1604.

Craig, Alexander. *The Amorose Songes, Sonets, and Elegies: of M. Alexander Craige, Scoto-Britane.* London, 1606.

Craig, Thomas. *Serenissimi, & invictissimi Principis, Iacobi Britanniarvm et Galliarvm Regis, Stephanophoria.* Edinburgh, 1603.

Craig, Thomas. *Ad Serenissimvm Britanniarum Principem Henricum, è Scotia discendentem propempticon.* Edinburgh, 1603.

Craig, Thomas. *De Unione Regnorum Britanniæ Tractatus.* Ed. C. S. Terry. Scottish History Society, first series, number 60. Edinburgh: T. and A. Constable, 1909.
Daniel, Samuel. *Delia. Contayning certayne sonnets: with the complaint of Rosamond.* London, 1592.
Daniel, Samuel. *The works of Samuel Daniel newly augmented.* London, 1602.
Daniel, Samuel. 'A Panegyrick congratulatorie To the Kinges most Sacred Maiestie By Samuel Danyel'. British Library, Royal MS A 18. LXXII.
Daniel, Samuel. *A Panegyrike Congratvlatorie to The Kings Maiestie. Also certaine Epistles.* London, 1603. STC 6258.
Daniel, Samuel. *A Panegyrike Congratvlatory. Deliuered to the Kings most excellent maiesty at Burleigh Harrington in Rutlandshire. By Samvel Daniel. Also Certaine Epistles. With a Defence of Ryme, heeretofore written, and now published by the Author.* London, 1603. STC 6259.
Daniel, Samuel. *A Panegyrike Congratvlatorie deliuered to the Kings most excellent Maiestie at Bvrleigh Harrington in Rvtlandshire. By Samuel Daniel. Also certaine Epistles, with a Defence of Ryme heretofore written, and now pvblished by the Avthor.* London, 1603. STC 6260.
Daniel, Samuel. *The Vision of the 12. Goddesses, presented in a Maske the 8. of Ianuary, at Hampton Court: By the Queenes most excellent Maiestie, and her Ladies.* London, 1604.
Daniel, Samuel. *A Funerall Poem Vppon the Death of the Late noble Earle of Deuonshyre.* London, 1606.
Daniel, Samuel. *The Civile Wares betweene the Howses of Lancaster and Yorke corrected and continued by Samuel Daniel one of the groomes of hir Maiesties most honorable Priuie Chamber.* London, 1609.
Daniel, Samuel. *Tethys Festival: Or the Qveenes Wake.* London, 1610.
Daniel, Samuel. *The First Part of the Historie of England.* London, 1612.
Daniel, Samuel. *Hymens Triumph. A Pastorall Tragicomædie.* London, 1615.
Davies, John. *A Discoverie of the trve cavses why Ireland was neuer entirely Subdued, nor brought vnder Obedience of the Crowne of England, vntill the Beginning of his Maiesties happie raigne.* London, 1612.
Dekker, Thomas. *1603. The Wonderfull yeare. Wherein is shewed the picture of London, lying sicke of the plague. At the ende of all (like a mery Epilogue to a dull Play) certaine Tales are cut out in sundry fashions, of purpose to shorten the liues of long winters nights, that lye watching in the darke for vs.* London, 1603.
Dekker, Thomas. *The Magnificent Entertainment: Giuen to King Iames, Queene Anne his wife, and Henry Frederick the Prince, vppon the day of his Maiesties Tryumphant passage (from the Tower) through his honourable Cittie (and Chamber) of London, being the 15. of March. 1603.* London, 1604.

Bibliography 219

Drayton, Michael. *The tragicall legend of Robert, Duke of Normandy, surnamed Short-thigh, eldest sonne to William Conqueror. With the legend of Matilda the chast, daughter to the Lord Robert Fitzwater, poysoned by King Iohn. And the legend of Piers Gaueston, the great Earle of Cornwall: and mighty fauorite of king Edward the second. By Michaell Drayton. The latter two, by him newly corrected and augmented.* London, 1596.

Drayton, Michael. *Englands Heroicall Epistles.* London, 1597.

Drayton, Michael. *To the Maiestie of King James: A Gratulatorie Poem.* London, 1603. STC 7231.

Drayton, Michael. *The Owle.* London, 1604.

Drayton, Michael. *A pæan trivmphall Composed for the Societie of the Goldsmiths of London: congratulating his Highnes magnificent entring the Citie. To the Maiestie of the King.* London, 1604.

Drayton, Michael. *Poems: by Michaell Draiton Esquire.* London, 1605.

Drayton, Michael. *Poemes Lyrick and Pastorall: Odes, Eglogs, the Man in the Moone.* London, 1606.

Drayton, Michael. *Poly-Olbion.* London, 1612.

Drayton, Michael. *Poems: by Michael Drayton Esquire. Viz. The barons warres, Englands heroicall epistles, Idea, Odes, The legends of Robert, Duke of Normandie, Matilda, Pierce Gaveston, and, Great Cromwell, The Owle, Pastorals, contayning Eglogues, with the Man in the moone.* London, 1619.

Drayton, Michael. *The battaile of Agincourt Fought by Henry the fift of that name, King of England, against the whole power of the French: vnder the raigne of their Charles the sixt, anno Dom. 1415. The miseries of Queene Margarite, the infortunate wife, of that most infortunate King Henry the sixt. Nimphidia, the court of Fayrie. The quest of Cinthia. The shepheards Sirena. The moone-calfe. Elegies vpon sundry occasions.* London, 1627.

Drummond, William. *Forth Feasting. A Panegyricke to the Kings most excellent Maiestie.* Edinburgh, 1617.

Echlin, John. *De regno Angliae, Franciæ, Hiberniæ ad serenissimum et inuictiss. Iacobum 6. Scotorum Regem vltrò delato. Panegyricon.* Edinburgh, 1603.

Egerton, Thomas. *The Speech of the Lord Chancellor of England, in the Eschequer Chamber, touching the post-nati.* London, 1609.

England and Wales. Privy Council. *Forasmuch as it hath pleased Almighty God to call to his mercy out of this transitory life our soueraigne lady, the high and mighty prince, Elizabeth late Queene of England, France, and Ireland.* London, 1603.

England and Wales. Privy Council. *By the King forasmuch as the Kings Maiestie, in his princely disposition to iustice hauing euer a speciall care* and regard to haue repressed the slaughters, spoyles, robberies and other enormities which were so frequent and common vpon the borders of these realmes. London, 1603.

England and Wales. Privy Council. *By the King. As often as we call to minde the most ioyfull and iust recognition made by the whole body of our realme.* London, 1604.

England and Wales. Sovereign. *A Booke of Proclamations, published since the beginning of his Maiesties most happy reigne ouer England, &c. Vntill this present Moneth of Febr. 3. anno Dom. 1609.* London, 1610.

Fenton, John. *King Iames His Welcome to London With Elizaes tombe and epitaph, and our Kings triumph and epitimie. Lamenting the ones decease, and reioycing at the others accesse.* London, 1603.

Fletcher, Robert. *A Briefe and Familiar Epistle shewing His Maiesties most lawfull, honourable and iust title to all his Kingdomes. With an Epitaph or briefe lamentation for the late Maiestie Royall of most famous, godly, and honourable memory: With a reioycing after sorrow for the same. And lastly a prayer for his Maiesties most happy succession, and for the Queene and their children.* London, 1603.

Gainsford, Thomas. *The Glory of England, Or A True Description of Many Excellent Prerogatives and Remarkeable Blessing, whereby She Triumpheth over all the Nations of the World.* London, 1618.

Geffe, Nicholas. *The perfect vse of silk-wormes, and their benefit.* London, 1607.

Gordon, John. *A Panegyrique of Congratulation for the Concord of the Realmes of Great Britaine in Vnitie of Religion, and vnder one King. To the most high, most puissant and magnanimous, Iames King of England, Scotland, France and Ireland. Written in French by Iohn Gordon Scottishman, Lord of Long-Orme, and one of the Gentlemen of the French Kings Chamber. Translated into English by E. Grimston.* London, 1603.

Hall, Joseph. *The Kings Prophecie: or Weeping Ioy. Expressed in a Poeme, to the Honor of Englands too great Solemnities.* London, 1603.

Hariot, Thomas. *A briefe and true report of the new found land of Virginia.* London, 1590.

Harrison, James. *An exhortacion to the Scottes, to conforme them selfes to the honorable, expedie[n]t, and godly vnion, betwene the twoo realmes of Englande and Scotlande.* London, 1547.

Harrison, Stephen. *The Arch's of Trivmph Erected in Honor of the High and Mightie Prince. James. the First of that name King, of England. and the sixt of Scotland. at his Maiesties entrance and passage through his honorable citty & chamber of London. vpon the 15th. day of march 1603.* London, 1604.

Harry, George Owen. *The Genealogy of the High and Mighty Monarch, Iames, by the grace of God, King of Great Brittayne, &c. with his lineall* descent from Noah, by diuers direct lynes to Brutus, first inhabiter of this ile of Brittayne. London, 1604.

Hay, John. *A Speach, Deliuered to the Kings most excellent Maiestie, At his Entrie into his Good-Towne of Edinbvrgh.* Edinburgh, 1617.

Hayward, John. *An Answer to the First Part of a Certain Conference Concerning Succession.* London, 1603.

Hayward, John. *A Treatise of Vnion of the two Realmes of England and Scotland.* London, 1604.

Holinshed, Raphael. *The first and second volumes of Chronicles, comprising 1 The description and historie of England, 2 The description and historie of Ireland, 3 The description and historie of Scotland: first collected and published by Raphaell Holinshed, William Harrison, and others: now newlie augmented and continued.* London, 1587.

Holland, Hugh. *Pancharis: the first booke. Containing the preparation of the loue betweene Owen Tudyr, and the Queene, long since intended to her maiden Maiestie: and now dedicated to the inuincible Iames, second and greater Monarch of great Britaine, King of England, Scotland, France, and Ireland, with the islands adiacent.* London, 1603.

Hume, David of Godscroft. *De Vnione Insulæ Britannicæ Tractatus. 1. Per Dauidem Humium Theagrium.* London, 1605.

Hume, David of Godscroft. 'Vincvla Vnionis Sive Scita Britannicæ id est De Unione Insvlæ Britannicæ Tractatvs Secvndvs. Per Davidem Hvmivm Theagrivm', Edinburgh University Library, MS Laing III, 249.

Hume, David of Godscroft. *The British Union: A Critical Edition and Translation of David Hume of Godscroft's De Unione Insulae Britannicae.* Paul J. McGinnis and Arthur H. Williamson (eds and trans.). Aldershot: Ashgate, 2002.

Hume, David of Godscroft. *Regi suo, post bis septennium in patriam ex Angliâ redeunti, Scotiæ gratulatio.* Edinburgh, 1617.

[James VI]. *Basilikon dōron. Devided into three bookes.* Edinburgh, 1599.

James VI and I, *Basilikon Doron. Or His Maiesties instructions to his dearest sonne, Henry the prince.* London, 1603 (STC 14350).

James VI and I. *The Trve Lawe of Free Monarchies. Or the Reciprock and mutuall dutie betwixt a free King, and his naturall Subiects.* London, 1603.

[James VI and I]. *The Kings Maiesties Speech, as it was deliuered by him in the vpper house of the Parliament to the Lords Spirituall and Temporall, and to the Knights, Citizens and Burgesses there assembled, On Munday the 19. day of March 1603. being the first day of this present Parliament, and the first Parliament of His Maiesties Raigne.* London, 1604 (STC 14390).

[James VI and I]. *His Maiesties speech to both the houses of Parliament, in his Highnesse great chamber at Whitehall, the day of the adiournement of the last session, which was the last day of March 1607.* London, 1607.

[James VI and I]. *The Kings Maiesties Speach To the Lords and Commons of this present Parliament at Whitehall, on Wednesday the xxj. of March.* London, 1610. STC 14396.

Jonson, Ben. *B. Ion: His Part of King Iames his Royall and Magnificent Entertainement through his Honorable Cittie of London, Thursday the 15. of March. 1603. So much as was presented in the first and last of their Triumphall Arch's. With his speech made to the last Presentation, in the Strand, erected by the inhabitants of the Dutchy, and Westminster. Also, a briefe Panegyre of his Maiesties first and well auspicated entrance to his high Court of Parliament, on Monday, the 19. of the same Moneth. With other Additions.* London, 1604.

Jonson, Ben. *The Characters of Two royall Masques. The one of Blacknesse, the other of Beautie. personated By the most magnificent of Queenes Anne Queene of great Britaine, &c. With her honorable Ladyes, 1605. and 1608. at White-hall: and Inuented by Ben: Ionson.* London, 1608.

Jonson, Ben. *The Workes of Beniamin Jonson.* London, 1616.

Journal of the House of Commons: Volume 1, *1547–1629*. London, 1802.

Lanyer, Aemilia. *Salve Devs Rex Ivdæorvm.* London, 1611.

Martin, Richard. *A Speach Delivered, to the Kings most excellent Maiestie in the Name of the Sheriffes of London and Middlesex.* London, 1603.

Meres, Francis. *Palladis tamia Wits treasury being the second part of Wits common wealth.* London, 1598.

M[illington], T[homas]. *The True Narration of the Entertainment of his Royall Maiestie, from the time of his departure from Edenbrough; till his receiuing at London: with all or the most speciall Occurrences. Together with the names of those Gentlemen whom his Maiestie honoured with Knighthood.* London, 1603.

Monipennie, John. *Certaine matters composed together.* Edinburgh, 1594.

Monipennie, John. *Certayne Matters Concerning the Realme of Scotland.* London, 1603.

Monnipennie, Iohn. *The abridgement or Summarie of the Scots Chronicles, with a short description of their originall, from the comming of Gathelvs their first Progenitor out of Græcia into Egypt.* London, 1612.

Munday, Anthony. *The Triumphes of re-vnited Britania. Performed at the cost and charges of the Right Worship: Company of the Merchant-Taylors, in honor of Sir Leonard Holliday kni: to solemnize his entrance as Lorde Mayor of the Citty of London, on Tuesday the 29. of October. 1605.* London, 1605.

Murray, David. *The Tragicall Death of Sophonisba. Written by David Mvrray. Scoto-Brittainne.* London, 1611.

Nixon, Anthony. *Elizaes memoriall. King Iames his arriuall. And Romes downefall.* London, 1603.

Bibliography 223

Petowe, Henry. *Elizabetha quasi viuens Eliza's Funerall. A fewe Aprill drops, showred on the hearse of dead Eliza. Or The Funerall teares af [sic] a true hearted Subiect.* London, 1603.

Powell, Thomas. *A Welch Bayte to spare Prouender. Or, A looking backe vpon the times past. Written dialogue wise. This booke is diuided into three parts, the first, a briefe discourse of Englands securitie, while her late Maiestie was liuing, with the maner of her proceeding in gouernment, especially towards the papists and puritanes of England, whereof a letter written late before her death, specifics, as followeth in this first part. The second, a description of the distractions during her Maiesties sickenesse with the composing of them. The third, of the aptnesse of the English and the Scotte to incorporate and become one entire monarchie: with the meanes of preseruing their vnion euerlastingly, added therevnto.* London, 1603.

Pricket, Robert. *A Souldiers Wish vnto His Soveraigne Lord King Iames.* London, 1603.

Pricket, Robert. *Vnto the Most High and Mightie Prince, his Soueraigne Lord King Iames. A poore Subiect sendeth, a Souldiors Resolution; humbly to waite vpon his Maiestie.* London, 1603.

Rogers, Thomas. *Anglorum Lacrimæ: In a sad passion complayning the death of our late Soueraigne Lady Queene Elizabeth: Yet comforted againe by the vertuous hopes of our most Royall and Renowned King Iames: whose Maiestie God long continue.* London, 1603.

Rowlands, Samuel. *Aue Cæsar. God saue the King. The ioyfull Ecchoes of loyall English hartes, entertayning his Maiesties late ariuall in England. With an Epitaph vpon the death of her Maiestie our late Queene.* London, 1603.

Savile, John. *King Iames his entertainment at Theobalds: With his welcome to London, together with a salutatorie Poeme.* London, 1603.

[Shakespeare, William]. *The tragedy of King Richard the third Containing, his treacherous plots against his brother Clarence: the pittiefull murther of his iunocent [sic] nephewes: his tyrannicall vsurpation: with the whole course of his detested life, and most deserued death. As it hath beene lately acted by the Right honourable the Lord Chamberlaine his seruants.* London, 1597.

[Shakespeare, William]. *The cronicle history of Henry the fift with his battell fought at Agin Court in France. Togither with Auntient Pistoll. As it hath bene sundry times playd by the Right honorable the Lord Chamberlaine his seruants.* London, 1600.

Shakespeare, William. *The most excellent historie of the merchant of Venice. With the extreame crueltie of Shylocke the Iewe towards the sayd merchant, in cutting a iust pound of his flesh: and the obtayning of Portia by the choyse of three chests. As it hath beene diuers times acted* by the Lord Chamberlaine his Seruants. Written by William Shakespeare. London, 1600.

Shakespeare, William. *M. William Shak-speare: his true chronicle historie of the life and death of King Lear and his three daughters With the vnfortunate life of Edgar, sonne and heire to the Earle of Gloster, and his sullen and assumed humor of Tom of Bedlam: as it was played before the Kings Maiestie at Whitehall vpon S. Stephans night in Christmas hollidayes.* London, 1608.

Speed, John. *The History of Great Britaine under the conquests of ye Romans, Saxons, Danes and Normans. Their originals, manners, warres, coines & seales: with ye successions, lives, acts & issues of the English monarchs from Iulius Cæsar, to our most gracious soueraigne King Iames. by Iohn Speed.* London, 1611.

Speed, John. *The Theatre of the Empire of Great Britaine: presenting an exact geography of the kingdomes of England, Scotland, Ireland, and the iles adioyning: with the shires, hundreds, cities and shire-townes, within ye kingdome of England, divided and described by Iohn Speed.* London, 1612.

Spelman, Henry. 'Of the Union'. British Library, Sloane MS 3521.

Spenser, Edmund. *The Faerie Queene. Disposed into twelue books, fashioning XII. morall vertues.* London, 1590.

Spenser, Edmund. *A View of the Present State of Ireland.* W. L. Renwick (ed.). Oxford: Clarendon Press, 1970.

Thornborough, John. *A Discovrse Plainely Prouing the euident vtilitie and vrgent necessitie of the desired happie Vnion of the two famous Kingdomes of England and Scotland: by way of answer to certaine obiections against the same.* London, 1604.

Verstegan, Richard. *A Restitvtion of Decayed Intellengence: In Antiquities. Concerning the most noble and renowmed English nation.* Antwerp, 1605.

Warner, William. *Albions England. Or historicall map of the same island: prosecuted from the liues, actes, and labors of Saturne, Iupiter, Hercules, and Æneas: originalles of the Brutons, and English-men, and occasion of the Brutons their first aryuall in Albion. Continuing the same historie vnto the tribute to the Romaines, entrie of the Saxones, inuasion by the Danes, and conquest by the Normaines. With historicall intermixtures, inuention, and varietie: proffitably, briefly, and pleasantly, performed in verse and prose by William Warner.* London, 1586.

Warner, William. *A Continvance of Albions England.* London, 1606.

Secondary Sources

Albanese, Denise. 'The New Atlantis and the uses of Utopia'. *English Literary History*, 57 (1990), 503–28.
Alker, Sharon and Holly Faith Nelson. '*Macbeth*, the Jacobean Scot, and the politics of union'. *Studies in English Literature 1500–1900*, 47 (2007), 379–401.
Anderson, Benedict. *Imagined Communities: reflections on the origin and spread of nationalism*. Rev. ed. London: Verso, 1991.
Arber, Edward (ed.). *A Transcript of the Registers of the Company of Stationers of London: 1554–1640 AD*, 5 vols. London: Privately printed, 1876.
Baker, David J. *Between Nations: Shakespeare, Spenser, Marvell, and the question of Britain* (Stanford, CA: Stanford University Press, 1997).
Baker, David J. '"Stands Scotland where it did?" Shakespeare on the march'. In Willy Maley and Andrew Murphy (eds), *Shakespeare and Scotland*. Manchester: Manchester University Press, 2004, 20–36.
Baldo, Jonathan. '"A rooted sorrow": Scotland's unsuable past'. In Nick Moschovakis (ed.), *Macbeth: new critical essays*. New York and London: Routledge, 2008, 88–103.
Barroll, Leeds. *Politics, Plague, and Shakespeare's Theater: the Stuart years*. Ithaca, NY and London: Cornell University Press, 1991.
Barroll, Leeds. *Anna of Denmark, Queen of England: a cultural biography*. Philadelphia: University of Pennsylvania Press, 2001.
Beal, Peter. *Index of English Literary Manuscripts*, Volume 1: *1450–1625*. London: Mansell, 1980.
Bell, Sandra. '"No Scot, No English Now": literary and cultural responses to James VI and I's policies on union', *Renaissance Forum: An Electronic Journal of Early-Modern Literary and Historical Studies*, 7 (2004). www.hull.ac.uk/renforum/v7/bell.htm. Accessed 12 May 2014.
Bevington, David, Martin Butler and Ian Donaldson (eds). *The Cambridge Edition of the Works of Ben Jonson*. 7 vols. Cambridge: Cambridge University Press, 2012.
Bindoff, S. T. 'The Stuarts and their style'. *The English Historical Review*, 60 (1945), 192–216.
Braunmuller, A. R. (ed.). *Macbeth*. Cambridge: Cambridge University Press, 2008.
Brink, Jean R. *Michael Drayton Revisited*. Boston, MA: Twayne, 1990.
Brown, Keith M. 'The vanishing emperor: British kingship and its decline, 1603–1707'. In Keith M. Brown and Roger A. Mason (eds), *Scots and Britons: Scottish political thought and the union of 1603*. Cambridge: Cambridge University Press, 1987, 58–90.

Burgess, Glenn, Rowland Wymer and Jason Lawrence (eds). *The Accession of James I: historical and cultural consequences*. Basingstoke: Palgrave, 2006.

Butler, Martin. '"Servant, but not slave": Ben Jonson at the Jacobean court'. *Proceedings of the British Academy*, 90 (1996), 65–94.

Butler, Martin. *The Stuart Court Masque and Political Culture*. Cambridge: Cambridge University Press, 2008.

Cadman, Daniel, '"Th'accession of these mighty States": Daniel's *Philotas* and the union of the crowns'. *Renaissance Studies*, 26 (2011), 365.

Cain, Thomas. *Praise in 'The Faerie Queene'*. Lincoln: University of Nebraska Press, 1978.

Canny, Nicholas and Andrew Carpenter. 'The early planters: Spenser and his contemporaries'. In Seamus Deane (ed.), *The Field Day Anthology of Irish Writing*. Vol. 1. Derry: Field Day Publications, 1991, 171–4.

Chedgzoy, Kate. 'This Pleasant and Sceptred Isle: insular fantasies of national identity in Anne Dowriche's *The French Historie* and William Shakespeare's *Richard II*'. In Philip Schwyzer and Simon Mealor (eds) *Archipelagic Identities: literature and identity in the Atlantic archipelago, 1550–1800*. Aldershot: Ashgate, 2004, 25–42.

Clark, Sandra and Pamela Mason (eds). *Macbeth*. London: Bloomsbury, 2015.

Colley, Linda. *Britons: forging the nation 1707–1837*. New Haven, CT: Yale University Press, 1992.

Colley, Linda. 'Britishness and otherness: an argument'. *Journal of British Studies*, 31 (1992), 309–29.

Collinson, Patrick. 'The monarchical republic of Queen Elizabeth I'. *Bulletin of the John Rylands Library*, 69 (1987), 394–424.

Corns, Thomas. *A History of Seventeenth-Century English Literature*. Oxford: Blackwell, 2007.

Craig, Hugh. 'Shakespeare's style, Shakespeare's England'. In Rachel Orgis and Matthias Heim (eds), *Fashioning England and the English*. Switzerland: Palgrave Macmillan, 2018, 71–95.

Crawford, Robert. *Bannockburns: Scottish independence and literary imagination, 1314–2014*. Edinburgh: University of Edinburgh Press, 2014.

Croft, Pauline. *King James*. Basingstoke: Palgrave, 2003.

Curran, Kevin. *Marriage, Performance, and Politics at the Jacobean Court*. London: Routledge, 2009.

Davies, Sir John. *The Works in Verse and Prose of Sir John Davies*. Alexander Grossart (ed.). 3 vols. Lancashire, 1869–76.

Davies, Sir John. *The Poems of Sir John Davies*. Robert Krueger and Ruby Nemser (eds). Oxford: Oxford University Press, 1975.

Davies, R. R. *The First English Empire: power and identities in the British Isles 1093–1343*. Oxford: Oxford University Press, 2000.

Doelman, James. '"A King of Thine Own Heart": the English reception of King James VI and I's *Basilikon Doron*'. *The Seventeenth Century*, 9 (1994), 1–9.

Doelman, James. 'The accession of James I and English religious poetry'. *Studies in English Literature*, 34 (1994), 19–40.

Donaldson, Ian. *Ben Jonson: a life*. Oxford: Oxford University Press, 2011.

Doran, Susan and Paulina Kewes (eds). *Doubtful and Dangerous: the question of succession in late Elizabethan England*. Manchester: Manchester University Press, 2014.

Dutton, Richard. *Jacobean Civic Pageants*. Edinburgh: Edinburgh University Press, 1996.

Epstein, Joel J. 'Francis Bacon and the issue of union, 1603–1608'. *Huntington Library Quarterly*, 33 (1970), 121–32.

Evans, Robert. *Ben Jonson and the Poetics of Patronage*. Lewisburg, PA: Bucknell University Press, 1989.

Floyd-Wilson, Mary. 'English epicures and Scottish witches'. *Shakespeare Quarterly*, 57 (2006), 131–61.

Galbraith, David. *Architectonics of Imitation in Spenser, Daniel and Drayton*. Toronto: University of Toronto Press, 2000.

Galloway, Bruce. *The Union of England and Scotland, 1603–1608*. Edinburgh: John Donald, 1986.

Galloway, Bruce R. and Brian P. Levack (eds). *The Jacobean Union: six tracts of 1604*. Scottish History Society, fourth series, number 21. Edinburgh and London: Clark Constable, 1985.

Garganigo, Alex. '*Coriolanus*, the union controversy, and access to the royal person'. *Studies in English Literature*, 42 (2002), 335–59.

Garrison, James D. *Dryden and the Tradition of Panegyric*. Berkeley: University of California Press, 1975.

Goldberg, Jonathan. *James I and the Politics of Literature: Jonson, Shakespeare, Donne and their contemporaries*. Stanford, CA: Stanford University Press, 1989.

Grandage, Sarah. 'Imagining England: contemporary encodings of "this sceptred isle"'. In Willy Maley and Margaret Tudeau-Clayton (eds), *This England, That Shakespeare: new angles on Englishness and the Bard*. Farnham: Ashgate, 2010, 127–46.

Greenfeld, Liah. *Nationalism: five roads to modernity*. Cambridge: Cambridge University Press, 1992.

Hadfield, Andrew. 'Michael Drayton's brilliant career'. *Proceedings of the British Academy*, 125 (2004), 119–47.

Hardin, Richard F. *Michael Drayton and the Passing of Elizabethan England*. Lawrence: The University of Kansas Press, 1973.

Hechter, Michael. *Internal Colonialism: the Celtic fringe in British national development, 1536–1966*. Berkeley: University of California Press, 1975.
Helgerson, Richard. *Forms of Nationhood: the Elizabethan writing of England*. Chicago: University of Chicago Press, 1992.
Hertel, Ralf. *Staging England in the Elizabethan History Play: performing national identity*. Farnham: Ashgate, 2014.
Highley, Christopher. 'The place of Scots in the Scottish play: *Macbeth* and the politics of language'. In Willy Maley and Andrew Murphy (eds), *Shakespeare and Scotland*. Manchester: Manchester University Press, 2004, 53–66.
Highley, Christopher. *Catholics Writing the Nation in Early Modern Britain and Ireland*. Oxford: Oxford University Press, 2008.
Hill, J. Michael. 'The origins of the Scottish plantations in Ulster to 1625: a reinterpretation'. *Journal of British Studies*, 32 (1993), 24–43.
Hill Burton, John and David Masson (eds). *The Register of the Privy Council of Scotland*. 14 vols. Edinburgh, 1877–98.
Hinman, Charlton (ed.). *The Norton Facsimile: the First Folio of Shakespeare*. New York: W. W. Norton, 1968.
Holland, Peter. '"Stands Scotland Where It Did?": the location of *Macbeth* on film'. In Robert S. Miola (ed.), *Macbeth*, 2nd ed. New York: W. W. Norton, 2014, 270–94.
Howard, Jean E. 'Shakespeare, geography, and the work of genre on the early modern stage'. *Modern Language Quarterly*, 64 (2003), 299–322.
Howard, Jean and Phyllis Rackin. *Engendering a Nation: a feminist account of Shakespeare's English histories*. London: Routledge, 1997.
Innes, Paul. 'Harming *Macbeth*: a British translation'. In Liz Oakley-Brown (ed.), *Shakespeare and the Translation of Identity in Early Modern England*. London: Continuum, 2011, 103–30.
Ivic, Christopher. 'Mapping British identities: John Speed's *Theatre of the Empire of Great Britaine*'. In David J. Baker and Willy Maley (eds), *British Identities and English Renaissance Literature*. Cambridge: Cambridge University Press, 2002, 135–55.
Ivic, Christopher. '"Our British Land": Anne Bradstreet's Atlantic perspective'. In Simon Mealor and Philip Schwyzer (eds), *Archipelagic Identities: literature and identity in the Atlantic archipelago, 1550–1800*. Farnham: Ashgate, 2004, 195–204.
Ivic, Christopher. *Shakespeare and National Identity: a dictionary*. London: Bloomsbury, 2017.
Ivic, Christopher. 'Making and remaking the British kingdoms – *Henry V*, then and now'. In Karen Britland and Line Cottegnies (eds), *King Henry V: A Critical Reader*. London: Bloomsbury, 2018, 156–79.
Jardine, Lisa and Alan Stewart. *Hostage to Fortune: the troubled life of Francis Bacon*. London: Gollancz, 1998.

Kermode, Frank. *Shakespeare's Language*. London: Penguin, 2000.
Kernan, Alvin. *Shakespeare, the King's Playwright: theater in the Stuart court, 1603–1613*. New Haven, CT and London: Yale University Press, 1995.
Kerrigan, John. *Archipelagic English: literature, history, and politics 1603–1707*. Oxford: Oxford University Press, 2008.
Kewes, Paulina, and Andrew McRae (eds), *Stuart Succession Literature: moments and transformations*. Oxford: Oxford University Press, 2019.
Larkin, James F. and Paul L. Hughes (eds), *Stuart Royal Proclamations*. Volume I: *Royal Proclamations of King James I, 1603–1625*. Oxford: Oxford University Press, 1973.
Levack, Brian P. *The Formation of the British State: England, Scotland, and the union 1603–1707*. Oxford: Oxford University Press, 1987.
Loomis, Catherine. '"Withered Plants Do Bud and Blossome Yeelds": naturalizing James I's succession'. In Robert S. Sturges (ed.), *Law and Sovereignty in the Middle Ages and the Renaissance*. Turnhout, Belgium: Brepols, 2011, 133–50.
Loxley, James, Anna Groundwater and Julie Sanders (eds), *Ben Jonson's Walk to Scotland: An Annotated Edition of the 'Foot Voyage'*. Cambridge: Cambridge University Press, 2015.
Lyle, E. B. '"Twofold balls and treble scepters" in *Macbeth*'. *Shakespeare Quarterly*, 28 (1977), 516–19.
MacColl, Alan. 'The meaning of "Britain" in medieval and early modern England'. *Journal of British Studies*, 45 (2006), 248–69.
MacDougall, Hugh A. *Racial Myth in English History: Trojans, Teutons, and Anglo-Saxons*. Hanover, NH and London: University Press of New England: 1982.
Maley, Willy. *Nation, State and Empire in English Renaissance Literature*. Basingstoke: Palgrave Macmillan, 2003.
Maley, Willy. '"A Thing Most Brutish": depicting Shakespeare's multination state'. *Shakespeare*, 3 (2007), 79–101.
Mapstone, Sally. 'Shakespeare and Scottish kingship: a case history'. In Sally Mapstone and Juliette Wood (eds), *The Rose and the Thistle: essays on the culture of late medieval and Renaissance Scotland*. East Linton: Tuckwell Press, 1998, 158–89.
Marcus, Leah. *Puzzling Shakespeare: local reading and its discontents*. Berkeley: University of California Press, 1988.
Marshall, Tristan. *Theatre and Empire: Great Britain on the London stages under James VI and I*. Manchester: Manchester University Press, 2005.
Mason, Roger A. 'Scotching the Brut: politics, history and national myth in sixteenth-century Britain'. In Roger A. Mason (ed.), *Scotland and England, 1286–1815*. Edinburgh: Edinburgh University Press, 1987, 60–84.

Mason, Roger. 'Scotland'. In Paulina Kewes, Ian W. Archer and Felicity Heal (eds), *The Oxford Handbook of Holinshed's 'Chronicles'*. Oxford: Oxford University Press, 2013, 647–62.

Mayer, Jean-Christophe (ed.). *The Struggle for the Succession in Late Elizabethan England: politics, polemics and cultural representations*. Montpellier: Astraea Collection, 2004.

McCabe, Richard A. 'The poetics of succession, 1587–1605: the Stuart claim'. In Susan Doran and Paulina Kewes (eds), *Doubtful and Dangerous: the question of succession in late Elizabethan England*. Manchester: Manchester University Press, 2014, 192–211.

McCabe, Richard A. *'Ungainefull Arte': poetry, patronage, and print in the early modern era*. Oxford: Oxford University Press, 2016.

McCabe, Richard A. 'Panegyric and its discontents: the first Stuart succession'. In Paulina Kewes and Andrew McRae (eds), *Stuart Succession Literature: moments and transformations*. Oxford: Oxford University Press, 2019, 19–46.

McDermott, Anne. 'The defining language: Johnson's *Dictionary* and *Macbeth*'. *The Review of English Studies*, 44 (1993), 521–38.

McEachern, Claire. *The Poetics of English Nationhood, 1590–1612*. Cambridge: Cambridge University Press, 1996.

McEachern, Claire. 'The Englishness of the Scottish play: *Macbeth* and the poetics of Jacobean union'. In Allan I. Macinnes and Jane Ohlmeyer (eds), *The Stuart Kingdoms in the Seventeenth Century*. Dublin: Four Courts Press, 2002, 94–112.

McRae, Andrew and John West (eds), *Literature of the Stuart Successions: an anthology*. Manchester: Manchester University Press, 2017.

Miola, Robert S. *Early Modern Catholicism: an anthology of primary sources*. Oxford: Oxford University Press, 2007.

Miola, Robert S. (ed.). *Macbeth*, 2nd ed. New York: W. W. Norton, 2014.

Morrill, John. 'The fashioning of Britain'. In Steven G. Ellis and Sarah Barber (eds), *Conquest & Union: fashioning a British state, 1485–1725*. London and New York: Longman, 1995, 8–39.

Morrill, John. 'The British problem, c. 1534–1707'. In Brendan Bradshaw and John Morrill (eds), *The British Problem, c. 1534–1707: state formation in the Atlantic archipelago*. Basingstoke: Palgrave Macmillan, 1996, 1–38.

Mottram, Stewart. 'Warriors and ruins: *Cymbeline*, heroism and the union of the crowns', In Willy Maley and Rory Loughnane (eds), *Celtic Shakespeare: the bard and the borderers*. Farnham: Ashgate, 2013, 169–83.

Mowat, Barbara and Paul Werstine (eds). *Henry V*. New York: Washington Square-Pocket, 1995.

Murphy, Andrew. *But the Irish Sea Betwixt Us: Ireland, colonialism, and Renaissance literature*. Lexington: The University of Kentucky Press, 1999.

Netzloff, Mark. '"Counterfeit Egyptians" and imagined borders: Jonson's *The Gypsies Metamorphosed*'. *English Literary History*, 68 (2001), 763–93.

Newdigate, Bernard H. *Michael Drayton and His Circle*. Oxford: Basil Blackwell & Mott, 1961.

Norbrook, David. 'Panegyric of the monarch and its social context under Elizabeth I and James I'. D. Phil. University of Oxford, 1978.

Norbrook, David. '*Macbeth* and the politics of historiography'. In Kevin Sharpe and Steven Zwicker (eds), *Politics of Discourse: the literature and history of seventeenth-century England*. Berkeley: University of California Press, 1987, 78–116.

Norbrook, David. *Writing the English Republic: poetry, rhetoric, and politics, 1627–1660*. Cambridge: Cambridge University Press, 1999.

Norbrook, David. *Poetry and Politics in the English Renaissance*. Rev. ed. Oxford: Oxford University Press, 2002.

Ó Buachalla, Brendán. 'James our true king: the ideology of Irish royalism in the seventeenth century'. In D. G. Boyce, Robert Eccleshall and Vincent Geoghegan (eds), *Political Thought in Ireland since the Seventeenth Century*. London: Routledge, 1993, 7–35.

Ong, Walter. *Interfaces of the Word: studies in the evolution of consciousness and culture*. Ithaca, NY: Cornell University Press, 1977.

Orgel, Stephen. '*Macbeth* and the antic round'. In Robert S. Miola (ed.), *Macbeth*, 2nd ed. New York: W. W. Norton, 2014, 255–70.

Parry, Graham. *The Golden Age Restor'd: the culture of the Stuart court, 1603–42*. New York: St. Martin's Press, 1981.

Pasupathi, Vimala C. 'The quality of mercenaries: contextualizing Shakespeare's Scots in *1 Henry IV* and *Henry V*'. In Willy Maley and Rory Loughnane (eds), *Celtic Shakespeare: the bard and the borderers*. Farnham: Ashgate, 2013, 35–59.

Peltonen, Markku. *Classical Humanism and Republicanism in English Political Thought, 1570–1640*. Cambridge: Cambridge University Press, 1995.

Perry, Curtis. *The Making of Jacobean Culture: James I and the renegotiation of Elizabethan literary practice*. Cambridge: Cambridge University Press, 1997.

Phillippy, Patricia. 'London's mourning garment: maternity, mourning and royal succession'. In Naomi J. Miller and Naomi Yavneh (eds), *Maternal Measures: figuring caregiving in the early modern period*. Aldershot: Ashgate, 2000, 319–32.

Pitcher, John. *Samuel Daniel: The Brotherton Manuscript, a study in attribution*. Leeds: Leeds Texts and Monographs, 1981.

Pitcher, John. 'Samuel Daniel's letter to Sir Thomas Egerton'. *Huntington Library Quarterly*, 47 (1984), 55–61.
Pitcher, John. 'Samuel Daniel, the Hertfords, and a question of love'. *The Review of English Studies*, 35 (1984), 449–62.
Pitcher, John. 'Editing Daniel'. In W. Speed Hill (ed.), *New Ways of Looking at Old Texts: papers of the Renaissance English Text Society, 1985–1991*. Binghamton, NY: Medieval & Renaissance Texts & Studies, 1993, 57–73.
Pitcher, John. 'Essays, works and small poems: divulging, publishing and augmenting the Elizabethan poet, Samuel Daniel'. In Andrew Murphy (ed.), *The Renaissance Text: theory, editing, textuality*. Manchester: Manchester University Press, 2000, 8–29.
Pitcher, John. 'Samuel Daniel's gifts of books to Lord Chancellor Egerton'. *Medieval and Renaissance Drama in England*, 17 (2005), 216–38.
Pocock, J. G. A. 'Conclusion: contingency, identity, sovereignty'. In Alexander Grant and Keith J. Stringer (eds), *Uniting the Kingdom?: the making of British history*. London and New York: Routledge, 1995, 292–302.
Pocock, J. G. A. *The Discovery of Islands: essays in British history*. Cambridge: Cambridge University Press, 2005.
Poole, Adrian. 'Laughter, forgetting and Shakespeare'. In Michael Cordner, Peter Holland and John Kerrigan (eds), *English Comedy*. Cambridge: Cambridge University Press, 1994, 85–99.
Power, Andrew J. '"Why should I play the Roman fool, and die / On mine own sword?": the Senecan tradition in *Macbeth*'. In Willy Maley and Rory Loughnane (eds), *Celtic Shakespeare: the bard and the borderers*. Farnham: Ashgate, 2013, 139–56.
Quint, David. *Epic and Empire: politics and generic form from Virgil to Milton*. Princeton, NJ: Princeton University Press, 1993.
Rees, Graham. 'Bacon's speculative philosophy'. In Markku Peltonen (ed.), *The Cambridge Companion to Bacon*. Cambridge: Cambridge University Press, 2006, 121–45.
Richards, Judith M. 'The English accession of James VI: "national" identity, gender and the personal monarchy of England'. *The English Historical Review*, 117 (2002), 513–35.
Rickard, Jane. *Writing the Monarch in Jacobean England: Jonson, Donne, Shakespeare and the writings of King James*. Cambridge: Cambridge University Press, 2015.
Riggs, David. *Ben Jonson: a life*. Cambridge, MA: Harvard University Press, 1989.
Rhodes, Neil. 'Wrapped in the strong arms of the union: Shakespeare and King James'. In Willy Maley and Andrew Murphy (eds), *Shakespeare and Scotland*. Manchester: Manchester University Press, 2004, 37–52.
Robinson, Philip S. *British Settlement in an Irish Landscape, 1600–1670*. Dublin: Gill and Macmillan; New York: St. Martin's Press, 1984.

Bibliography 233

Russell, Conrad. '1603: The end of English national sovereignty'. In Glenn Burgess, Rowland Wymer and Jason Lawrence (eds), *The Accession of James I: historical and cultural consequences*. Basingstoke: Palgrave, 2006, 1–14.

Schwyzer, Philip. *Literature, Nationalism, and Memory in Early Modern England and Wales*. Cambridge: Cambridge University Press, 2004.

Schwyzer, Philip. 'A scum of Britons?: *Richard III* and the Celtic reconquest'. In Willy Maley and Rory Loughnane (eds), *Celtic Shakespeare: the bard and the borderers*. Farnham: Ashgate, 2013, 25–34.

Sharpe, Kevin. *Remapping Early Modern England: the culture of seventeenth-century politics*. Cambridge: Cambridge University Press, 2000.

Smuts, R. Malcolm. 'Occasional events, literary texts and historical interpretation'. In Robin Headlam Wells, Glenn Burgess and Rowland Wymer (eds), *Neo-historicism, Studies in Renaissance Literature, History, and Politics*. London: D. S. Brewer, 2000, 179–98.

Smuts, R. Malcom, 'States, monarchs and dynastic transitions: the political thought of John Hayward'. In Susan Doran and Paulina Kewes (eds), *Doubtful and Dangerous: the question of succession in late Elizabethan England*. Manchester: Manchester University Press, 2014, 276–94.

Sommerville, Johann P. (ed.). *King James VI and I: political writings*. Cambridge: Cambridge University Press, 1994.

Spedding, James (ed.). *The Letters and the Life of Francis Bacon*. 7 vols. London, 1861–72.

Spedding, James, R. L. Ellis and D. D. Heath (eds). *The Works of Francis Bacon*. 14 vols. London, 1857–74.

Tabor, Stephen. 'The Bridgewater Library'. In William Baker and Kenneth Womack (eds), *Pre-Nineteenth-Century British Book Collectors and Bibliographers. Dictionary of Literary Biography*. Vol. 213. Detroit: The Gale Group, 1999.

Vickers, Brian (ed.). *Francis Bacon: the major works*. Oxford: Oxford University Press, 2002.

Watkins, John. *Representing Elizabeth in Stuart England: literature, history, sovereignty*. Cambridge: Cambridge University Press, 2002.

Watts, Cedric. '*Macbeth* as royalist propaganda'. In Linda Cookson and Bryan Loughrey (eds), *Critical Essays on Macbeth*. Essex: Longman, 1988, 102–09.

Williamson, Arthur H. *Scottish National Consciousness in the Age of James VI: The Apocalypse, the union and the shaping of Scotland's public culture*. Edinburgh: John Donald, 2003.

Williamson, Arthur. 'Radical Britain: David Hume of Godscroft and the challenge to the Jacobean British vision'. In Glenn Burgess, Rowland Wymer and Jason Lawrence (eds), *The Accession of James I: historical and cultural consequences*. Basingstoke: Palgrave Macmillan, 2006, 48–68.

Woolf, D. R. 'Two Elizabeths? James I and the late Queen's famous memory'. *Canadian Journal of History*, 20 (1985), 167–91.

Woolf, D. R. 'Community, law and state: Samuel Daniel's historical thought revisited'. *Journal of the History of Ideas*, 49 (1988), 61–83.

Woolf, D. R. *The Idea of History in Early Stuart England: erudition, ideology, and 'The Light of Truth' from the accession of James I to the Civil War*. Toronto: University of Toronto Press, 1990.

Wormald, Jenny. 'James VI and I, *Basilikon Doron* and *The Trew Law of Free Monarchies*: the Scottish context and the English translation'. In Linda Levy Peck (ed.), *The Mental World of the Jacobean Court*. Cambridge: Cambridge University Press, 1991, 36–54.

Wormald, Jenny. 'The creation of Britain: multiple kingdoms or core and colonies?' *Transactions of the Royal Historical Society*, sixth series, 2 (1992), 175–94.

Wortham, Christopher, 'Shakespeare, James I and the matter of Britain'. *English*, 45 (1996), 97–122.

Wright, Gillian. 'What Daniel really did with the *Pharsalia*: *The Civil Wars*, Lucan, and King James'. *The Review of English Studies*, 55 (2004), 210–32.

Index

Note: 'n.' after a page reference indicates the number of a note on that page; page numbers in *italic* refer to illustrations.

Abbot, George
  Briefe description of the whole worlde 29
Act in Restraint of Appeals 16
Adamson, John
  Muses Welcome 38, 43n.29
Albion 29, 48n.91, 67, 71–2, 81, 102n.89, 121, 138, 149
Alexander, William 67
Alker, Sharon 182, 194n.40, 197n.63, 199n.92
Alleyn, Edward 92
Allott, Robert
  Englands Parnassus 48n.91, 102n.89
Anderson, Benedict 2, 25, 150, 187, 199n.83, 208
Anglo-Saxons 4, 17, 29, 60, 62–3, 78, 82, 92, 113–14, 167, 204–5, 209, *210*, 212n.11
Anne of Denmark 19, 76, 80–1, 84, 87, 209
Arthur 60, 112
Ayscu, Edward
  Historie Contayning the Warres, Treaties, Marriages, and Other Occurrents between England and Scotland 203–5

Bacon, Francis 4, 7–8, 11–12, 22, 60, 117–19, 125–40, 189, 212
  Aduancement of Learning 133, 212n.2
  Beginning of the History of Great Britain 11–12, 42n.14, 60, 83, 203
  Briefe Discovrse 7–8, 28, 30–1, 84, 122, 126–7, 129–31, 133–4, 178–9
  Certain Articles 126, 128–31, 135, 142n.24, 149
  Certain Considerations 135–6
  New Atlantis 8, 133–4
  'Of Counsel' 129–30
  'Of Praise' 68
Baker, David J. 2, 195n.46
Baldo, Jonathan 155–6, 162, 167, 188
Barkham, John 209
Barroll, Leeds 198n.71
Beal, Peter 93–4
Bell, Sandra 54
Berwick 150–1
Bindoff, S. T. 49n.92, 71
Blount, Charles 23, 197n.67
Bodin, Jean
  Six Bookes of a Commonweale 69–70
Boece, Hector 166, 193n.30
Borders 34, 55, 64, 97n.10, 114
Braunmuller, A. R. 176, 195n.46, n.48

Index

Brink, Jean 65
Britain
  ancient Britons 27–31, 59–60, 62–3, 78, 92, 136–7, 204, 210, 213n.29
  Britishness 3–4, 7, 36, 66, 71, 85, 122–40, 154, 159, 204
  geography 31–2, 149–51
  histories of 35, 203–7
  maps of 40n.5, 149, 190n.1, n.3, 207–9, 211
  name 26, 28, 39, 48n.87, 64, 66, 72, 81–2, 92–3, 110n.200, n.202, 112, 116–18, 120–2, 146n.111, 149, 159, 186–7, 208
  Trojan origins 28, 63, 82, 205
Brown, Keith M. 41n.10
Brutus 28, 35, 60, 62–4, 82, 88, 140n.1, 159, 205
Bry, Theodore de 182, *183*, 200n.101
Buchanan, George 120
  Rerum Scoticarum historia 168–9, 197n.65
Burgess, Glenn 14, 83, 109n.190, 118–19
Burrow, Colin 95
Butler, Martin 88–90, 94–5, 105n.139, 106n.154, 107n.176, 110n.200, 139

Camden, William 31, 62, 75–6, 82, 86, 92, 204
  Britainnia 1, 27–9, 49n.99, 62, 86, 92, 99n.47, 110n.202, 201n.109, 204
  Remaines of a Greater Worke 31, 76, 92, 204
Campion, Thomas 123
Canny, Nicholas 144n.59
Carpenter, Andrew 144n.59
Carr, Robert 138, 206–7
Cecil, Robert 16, 20, 116, 137
Charles, Prince of Wales 67, 209
Charron, Pierre
  Of Wisdome 101n.79

Chedgzoy, Kate 2, 149
Chettle, Henry 18, 27
  Englandes Mourning Garment 17–19, 21–3, 31, 63, 67
Clapham, John 204
Clark, Sandra 181, 193n.23, 199n.92
Claudian 86
Clerk, William 44n.37, 119
Clifford, Anne 74
Clifford, Margaret 74
Coke, Edward 78
Colley, Linda 9n.6, 140
Commons Journals 116, 127, 189
Conestaggio, Gerolamo Franchi di 16
Corns, Thomas 96n.3
Cornwall 23, 61, 99n.41
Cornwallis, William 119
  Miracvlovs and Happie Union of England and Scotland 114, 160
Cotton, Robert 90, 135
Craig, Alexander 38, 108n.185
Craig, Hugh 154, 192n.19
Craig, Thomas 37, 119, 132
  De Unione 10, 22, 42n.25, 88, 107n.175, 111n.206, 186, 202n.120, 203, 214n.35
Crawford, Robert 182, 184
Croft, Pauline 37
Cunobelinus (Cymbeline) 208

Danes 17, 38, 63, 78, 92, 209, 210
Daniel, Samuel 6–7, 12, 17–18, 52–4, 58, 68–85, 89–93, 96, 152, 203–4, 206–7
  Civile Wares betweene the Howses of Lancaster and Yorke 71, 75–7
  Defence of Ryme 75
  Delia 71
  First Part of the Historie of England 8, 82–3, 101n.82, 152, 191n.13, 203–4, 206–7

Index

'Panegyrick congratulatorie
  To the Kinges most Sacred
  Maiestie' 17–18, 72–3, 77
*Panegyrike Congratvlatorie to
  The Kings Maiestie* 6, 68–80,
  96
Tethys Festival 81, 106n.150,
  206
Tragedy of Philotas 79
Vision of the 12. Goddesses
  80–1
Davies, Sir John 23, 46n.58, 139,
  209
  *Discoverie of the trve cavses why
    Ireland was neuer entirely
    Subdued* 137, 139
  'Kinges Welcome' 23, 46n.58
Davies, R. R. 153
Dekker, Thomas 52
  1603. The Wonderfull year 13,
    19, 23, 25–6, 108n.183
  Magnificent Entertainment
    47n.72, 87–8
Devereux, Robert 26, 79, 130,
  136
Devereux, Walter 136
Doelman, James 11, 13–14
Donaldson, Ian 91, 108n.179,
  110n.206
Doran, Susan 16, 43n.26, 98n.20,
  104n.114
Dover 162
Drayton, Michael 6–7, 12, 38, 52,
  54, 57–68, 70, 76, 80, 83–5,
  89–91, 93, 203, 206–7, 211
  Englands Heroicall Epistles 62
  Mortimeriados 58
  'Owen Tudor to Queen
    Katherine' 62–3
  Owle 65
  Pæan trivmphall 64–5
  Poems (1605) 62
  Poly-Olbion 1, 8, 38, 44n.38,
    64, 67–8, 93, 100n.65, 203,
    206–7, 213n.20
  'To my frinds the Camber-
    britans and theyr harp' 66

To the Maiestie of King James
  57–65, 68, 70, 97n.17
'To the Virginian voyage' 66
*Tragicall legend of Robert, Duke
  of Normandy* 62
Drummond, William, of
  Hawthornden 50n.126, 67,
  213n.21
Forth Feasting 38–9
Dutton, Richard 65

Edward VI 32
Edward the Confessor 152–3
Egerton, Thomas 70, 74, 78,
  144n.62, 146n.113, 203
Elizabeth I 11, 13, 16–20, 31,
  57–9, 76, 80, 83–4, 88, 115,
  130, 140, 149, 151, 158, 187
England
  island-nation/-realm 149–51,
    185–90
  national sovereignty 13, 75–7,
    117
  nationhood 2, 15–16, 19–20, 27,
    82–3, 86, 153–90, 212
  Englands Wedding Garment
    14–15, 21, 23, 26–8, 34–6
Epstein, Joel 127–8

Fenton, John
  *King Iames His Welcome to
    London* 24
Fergus I 60, 195n.46
Fletcher, John 188
Fletcher, Robert
  Briefe and Familiar Epistle 21–2,
    29, 31–3
Floyd-Wilson, Mary 195n.46
France 13, 42n.22, 115, 121,
  142n.24, 185
Fuller, Thomas 135

Gainsford, Thomas
  The Glory of England 108n.177
Galbraith, David 105n.141
Galloway, Bruce 6, 116, 118
Garrison, James 68, 73

Index

Geffe, Nicholas 66
   Perfect vse of silk–wormes 66
Gentili, Alberico 119
Gil, Alexander 209, 211
Godwineson, Harold 152
Goldberg, Jonathan 109n.187
Gordon, John
   Panegyrique of Congratulation 30–1, 34, 55
Greenfeld, Liah 2, 155
Guy, John 155

Hadfield, Andrew 2, 67, 98n.21, 104n.114
Hall, Joseph
   Kings prophecie 22, 29–31
Hardin, Richard F. 57
Hariot, Thomas
   Briefe and true report of the new found land of Virginia 183
Harington, Lucy 73–4, 80
Harrison, Stephen
   The Arch's of Trivmph 88, 107n.169
Harrison, William 27
   Description of Britaine 27, 48n.87, 201n.107, n.109
Harry, George Owen
   Genealogy of the High and Mighty Monarch 49n.100, 61
Hay, John 38
Hayward, John 119, 121–2, 131–2
   Treatise of Vnion of the two Realmes of England and Scotland 5, 121, 186
Hechter, Michael 140
Helgerson, Richard 1–2, 93, 100n.67, 156, 162, 203, 208–9
Henrisoun, James
   Exhortacion to the Scottes 32–3, 182, 186
Henry Frederick, Prince of Wales 23, 30, 37, 56, 66–7, 76, 81–2, 84, 87, 112, 205–7, 209
Henry V 66
Henry VI 151
Henry VII 12, 21, 31, 33, 59, 77, 82, 113
Henry VIII 2, 15–16, 20–1, 59, 91
Highley, Christopher 167, 169, 180
Holinshed, Raphael
   Description of Scotland 166
   First and second volumes of Chronicles 157–8, 183
   Historie of England 184, 191n.13
   Historie of Scotland 152, 158, 161, 168, 173, 180–4, 191n.11, 196n.55, 200n.98
Holland, Hugh 85–6, 153
   Pancharis 85
   'Vpon the Lines and Life of the Famous Scenicke Poet, Master William Shakespeare' 153
Holland, Peter 170, 172
Howard, Frances 138
Howard, Henry 74
Howard, Jean 161–2, 194n.43
Hume, David, of Godscroft 4, 7–8
   British Union (McGinnis and Williamson, eds) 14, 120–6, 131–2, 134–6, 179–80, 200n.93, 205
   De Vnione Insulæ Britannicæ Tractatus. 1 50n.126, 119, 122
   'De Unione Insvlæ Britannicæ Tractatvs Secvndvs' 119

Innes, Paul 196–7n.63, 198n.77
Ireland
   kerns and gallowglasses 168–9, 170, 197n.67
   Nine Years' War 23–4, 61, 130, 156
   subjects 35, 124–5, 130, 135–40, 209
   Tudor incorporation of 2, 156

James IV 21, 34
James VI and I 1, 6–7, 9, 11–39, 52–96, 112–19, 123, 124–5,

Index 239

140, 151, 153–7, 159, 188–9, 205–9
accession (1603) 3, 6, 11–37, 52–3, 58, 61–3, 67–71, 83–5, 90–1, 112, 154
Basilikon Doron 11, 56–7, 63, 68–9, 77, 112, 115, 123, 134, 140–1n.1, 141n.13
desire for Anglo–Scottish union 4, 54–7, 112–19, 127–9, 159
lineage 20–2, 58–61, 68, 91
return to Scotland (1617) 14, 37–9
royal entry (1604) 25, 52, 84–7
speeches to Parliament 4, 11, 89, 107n.177, 109n.192, 113–15, 118, 151, 187, 189
Trve Lawe of Free Monarchies 58, 60, 69, 134
Jardine, Lisa 129
Johnson, Samuel 198n.78
Jones, Inigo 206
Jonson, Ben 6–7, 24–5, 52, 68, 76, 81, 83–96, 113, 123, 138–9, 155, 188, 206
Eastward Hoe 110n.206, 191n.6
Hymenaei 85
Irish Masque at Court 8, 85, 138–9
Masque of Beauty 85
Masque of Blacknesse 81, 85, 88
Oberon 206
'Ode ἀλληγορική [Allegorical]' 85–6, 91, 197n.67
'On the Vnion' 7, 89–96, 188
manuscript copies of 93–6
Panegyre 84, 89, 91, 113, 123
Particvlar Entertainment of the Qveene and Prince their Highnesse to Althorpe 83
Prince Henry's Barriers 206
Royall and Magnificent Entertainement 83–4, 86, 92, 94

'To the memory of my beloued, The Avthor Mr. William Shakespeare' 92–3
Workes of Beniamin Jonson 89

Kermode, Frank 161
Kerrigan, John 2–3, 38, 106n.159, 109n.193, 153, 159–61, 181, 194n.40, 199n.79
Kewes, Paulina 16, 40n.4, 43n.26, 98n.20, 104n.114

Lanyer, Aemilia
Salve Devs Rex Ivdæorvm 76
Lawrence, Jason 14, 83, 109n.190, 118–19
Leech, John 38
Levack, Brian 3, 34, 97n.10, 118
Loomis, Catherine 22

McCabe, Richard 78, 103n.104, 213n.15
MacColl, Alan 186, 190n.3
McDermott, Anne 198n.78
MacDougall, Hugh A. 60
McEachern, Claire 13, 164, 181
McGinnis, Paul 120, 131, 134, 206
McKellen, Ian 161
McRea, Andrew 7, 37, 40n.4, 99n.31
Mair [Major], John
Historia majoris Britanniae tam Angliae quam Scotiae 29
Maley, Willy 2, 161
Mapstone, Sally 192n.21, 196n.59
Marcus, Leah 201n.114
Margaret [Tudor] 21, 34, 59–60
Mary, queen of Scots 19–20, 27, 32–3, 59
Martin, Richard
Speach Delivered, to the Kings most excellent Maiestie 24–5
Mason, Pamela 181, 193n.23, 199n.92
Mason, Roger 35, 50n.116, 60, 184, 194n.45, 201n.107
Melville, Andrew 120

Meres, Francis
  Palladis Tamia 67, 103n.108
Middleton, Thomas 52, 87
Milford Haven 81, 150, 162
Millington, Thomas
  True Narration 14–15, 20, 24, 102n.97
Miola, Robert 109n.190
Monipennie, John
  Certaine Matters Composed Together 99n.34
  Certayne Matters Concerning the Realme of Scotland 48n.86, 168, 191n.11
Monmouth, Geoffrey of 27, 30, 99n.47, 205
Morrill, John 3, 5, 35, 49n.101, 95–6, 118, 209
Munday, Anthony 88
  Triumphes of Re-united Britania 48n.91, 107n.173
Murray, David 67, 205
Murphy, Andrew 107n.160

Nelson, Holly Faith 182, 194n.40, 197n.63, 199n.92
Newdigate, Bernard 97n.17
Nixon, Anthony
  Elizaes memoriall 21, 28–9, 45n.44, 51
Norbrook, David 81, 93, 102n.91, 103n.109, 155
Normans 17, 38, 60, 62, 78, 92, 153, 209, *210*

'Obiections agaynst the Chaunge of the name or Stile' 117, 119–20, 126, 128, 142n.19
O'Neill, Hugh 23
Ong, Walter 94–5, 111n.209
Orgel, Stephen 167, 178, 198n.71

panegyric 52–3, 68–74, 83–7
Parker, Richard 18
Parker, William 92
Parry, Graham 84
Pasupathi, Vimala 169

Peltonen, Markku 104n.114, 133–4
Percy, Henry 129
Perry, Curtis 60, 72, 81, 89–90, 100n.54
Persons, Robert 16
Petowe, Henry
  Elizabetha quasi viuens Eliza's Funerall 20, 23, 44
Picts 38, 60, 63, 167, 182–3
Pigott, Christopher 189–90, 202n.120
Pitcher, John 69, 73–5, 79, 102n.95, 105n.131, 105n.141
Pocock, J. G. A. 139–40, 159
Pont, Robert 8, 119
  'Of the Union of Britayne' 46n.59, 77, 115, 137–8, 169, 199n.88
Pont, Timothy 208
Poole, Adrian 174
Powell, Thomas
  Welch Bayte to spare Prouender 54, 167
Power, Andrew J. 195n.46, 200n.95
Prickett, Robert
  Souldiers Wish 26, 76
  Vnto the Most High and Mightie Prince 26

Quint, David 76

Rees, Graham 131–2
Reynolds, Henry 67
Rhodes, Neil 153–4, 192n.16
Richard II 88, 168
Richard III 33
Rickard, Jane 108n.184
Riggs, David 89
Rogers, Thomas
  Anglorum Lacrimæ 19
Romans 34, 62, 78, 92, 132, 167, 179, 185–6, 209, *210*
Rowlands, Samuel
  Aue Cæsar 13, 24
Russell, Conrad 117

Russell, John
    'Treatise of the Happie and
        Blissed Unioun' 34, 53, 189

Sabines 132, 179
St George, Richard 209, 211
Salusbury, John 85
Sanderson, John 209
Sandys, George 65
Savile, Henry 132
    'Historicall Collections' 121
Savile, John
    *King Iames his entertainment at
        Theobalds* 23, 28–9
Scaramelli, Giovanni Carlo 112
Schwyzer, Philip 2–3, 6, 71, 166
Scotland
    English claim to suzerainty over
        2, 33, 150
    geography 162–3
    Highlands 8, 123–4, 140, 164,
        195n.46, 197n.65, n.67, 205
    Islands 8, 86, 123–4, 137–8,
        152, 162–3, 164, 169,
        197n.65, n.67
    Lowlands 123–4, 137,
        147n.121, 169, 196n.63,
        205
    Scottishness 21–2, 27, 37–9,
        158–9
Scythians 54, 182, 197n.67
Selden, John 100n.47
Seton, Alexander 16, 117
Seymour, Edward 32
Shakespeare, William 1–2, 5–6, 13,
    29, 58, 77, 93, 149–90
    1 Henry IV 150, 156
    1 Henry VI 150, 165, 198n.72
    2 Henry VI 48n.91, 168,
        197n.67, 202n.125
    3 Henry VI 48n.91, 77, 150–1
    Coriolanus 157
    Cymbeline 8, 150, 153, 159,
        172, 184–8, 198n.72
    Henry V 48n.91, 115, 150, 153,
        156, 158, 165, 185, 194n.43,
        197n.67

    Henry VIII 45n.44, 150, 154,
        185, 187–8
    King John 158
    King Lear 3, 6, 8, 48n.91, 153,
        159, 184–5, 188, 201n.108
    Macbeth 8, 150–84, 188–9,
        192n.21
    Merchant of Venice 150,
        191n.6
    Othello 151, 171, 185, 190,
        202n.125
    Richard II 26, 62, 168, 174, 180
    Richard III 25, 33–4, 150,
        165–6, 171–2, 199n.82
    Tempest 151, 185
Sharpe, Kevin 20, 103n.103
Siward, earl of Northumbria 152
Smith, Sir Thomas 136
Smuts, R. Malcolm 17, 73
Sommerville, Johann 80
Speed, John 67, 203
    Historie of Great Britaine 203,
        206, 213n.29
    *Theatre of the Empire of Great
        Britaine* 1, 8, 67, 191n.7,
        195n.46, 197n.67, 203,
        206–9, 210, 211–12
Spelman, Henry
    'Of the Union' 72, 125, 209
Spenser, Edmund 103n.106
    Faerie Queene 2, 27, 149, 186
    *View of the Present State of
        Ireland* 28, 47n.81, 124–5, 130
Stewart, Alan 129
Stuart, Esmé 85
succession literature (1603) 11–37

Thornborough, John 119–20,
    131–2, 134
    Discovrse Plainely Proving 5,
        120, 128, 142n.19

Ulster 8, 124, 135–40, 157, 208
union
    Anglo-Scottish Union
        Commission 37, 111n.206,
        116–17, 126, 130

union (*cont.*)
  early concepts of 31–6, 53–7
  Parliamentary debate on 7, 72, 116–17, 135
  Rough Wooing as precedent for 31–2
  tracts and treatises 4–5, 7–8, 53–4, 72, 113–38, 160, 178–9, 184
  union of the crowns 4, 24, 55–6, 112

Verstegan, Richard
  Restitvtion of Decayed Intelligence 4, 29, 82, 204–5, 212n.11
Vickers, Brain 127, 133
Virgil 86, 115, 187, 201n.109

Waldegrave, Robert 24, 56
Wales 62, 150–2
  site of Britishness 31, 62–3, 85
  Tudor incorporation of 2, 35, 70, 113–14, 134, 156, 160, 211–12
Warner, William
  Albions England 29, 204
  Continvance of Albions England 159
Wars of the Roses 22, 33, 58, 69, 76, 79
Watkins, John 20
Watts, Cedric 154
West, John 7, 37, 99n.31
White, John 182
William the Conqueror 62
Williamson, Arthur 120, 124–5, 131, 134, 206
Woolf, D. R. 12, 69–70, 77, 204, 213n.30
Wormald, Jenny 24, 43n.30, 57, 98n.22
Wortham, Christopher 154
Wright, Gillian 103n.110
Wriothesley, Henry 74
Wymer, Rowland 14, 83, 109n.190, 118–19

EU authorised representative for GPSR:
Easy Access System Europe, Mustamäe tee 50,
10621 Tallinn, Estonia
gpsr.requests@easproject.com

www.ingramcontent.com/pod-product-compliance
Lightning Source LLC
Chambersburg PA
CBHW071204240426
43668CB00032B/2050